TRUSTED DATA

TRUSTED DATA

A New Framework for Identity
and Data Sharing

revised and expanded edition

edited by Thomas Hardjono, David L. Shrier,
and Alex Pentland

MIT Connection Science & Engineering
connection.mit.edu

The MIT Press
Cambridge, Massachusetts
London, England

This book was set in Stone Serif and Pangram by Westchester Publishing Services.

Library of Congress Cataloging-in-Publication Data
Names: Hardjono, Thomas editor. | Shrier, David L., editor. |
    Pentland, Alex, 1952- editor.
Title: Trusted data : a new framework for identity and data sharing /
    edited by Thomas Hardjono, David L. Shrier, and Alex Pentland.
Description: Revised and expanded edition. | Cambridge, MA : The MIT
    Press, [2019] | Includes bibliographical references and index.
Identifiers: LCCN 2019006325 | ISBN 9780262043212 (pbk. : alk.
    paper)
Subjects: LCSH: Electronic data interchange--Security measures. |
    Data transmission systems. | Trust--Economic aspects.
Classification: LCC HF5548.37 .T79 2019 | DDC 005.8/3--dc23
    LC record available at https://lccn.loc.gov/2019006325

CONTENTS

CURRENT

ARCHITECTURE

1 TRUST IN DIGITAL SOCIETIES

Alex Pentland

This book is about gaining truth through the ability to share data safely. Obviously, I do not mean "The Truth," but rather truth in the scientific sense of unbiased, complete, and continuous assessment of all available data. This is not a book about philosophy; instead, it is a about a very practical software architecture and legal framework that has already been prototyped, deployed, and tested in countries around the world. This architecture is called Open Algorithms (OPAL) and it has a big sister named ENIGMA.

The reaction to our invention of OPAL and ENIGMA software and legal architecture has been gratifying. The head of big data initiatives at the United Nations said: "This will change everything." The CTO of the United States Health and Human Services Department said: "Holy ***! The implications for healthcare are enormous." The reason they said these things was perhaps best explained by famous Harvard Law School Professor Larry Lessig: "This makes it possible to use and maintain data without holding it." In other words, you can obtain insights from data held by many different people, companies, or governments without doing anything that legally counts as sharing data and without risk of revealing the underlying data—and that indeed changes everything.

To give the reader a better sense of the critical issues involved in data in our developing digital society, I will begin with a review data privacy, security, ownership, and trust, and how these issues are coming together to produce a data revolution.

BUILDING TRUST

The world depends on having civic systems that we can all trust. The science of building civic systems that can sustain a healthy, safe, and efficient society is a challenge dating back to the 1800s when the Industrial Revolution spurred rapid urban growth and created huge social and environmental problems. Then, the remedy was to engineer centralized networks that delivered clean water and safe food, removed waste, provided energy, facilitated transportation, and offered access to centralized healthcare, police, and educational services.

These nineteenth-century solutions are still with us today and are increasingly obsolete. Integrated digital systems have the potential to deliver a far better world than is possible with today's civic systems. Without these integrated systems, our current civic structures cannot take advantage of new digital feedback technologies that would allow them to be dynamic and responsive, more inclusive and fair, and more safe and efficient.

There is real concern, however, that such systems would place too much power in too few hands. And what about privacy? Security? To address these concerns, in 2007 I proposed the New Deal on Data—putting citizens in control of data that are about them—and I also helped create a data commons to improve both government and private industry. This led to my co-leading a World Economic Forum (WEF) discussion group that was able to productively explore the risks, rewards, and cures for these big data problems. The research and experiments I conducted in support of this discussion helped shape both the US Consumer Privacy Bill of Rights and the EU Data Protection laws, and is now helping China determine its data protection policies. While privacy and concentration of power will always be a concern, as we will see there are good solutions available through a combination of technology standards (e.g., "Open Algorithms" described below) and policy (e.g., open data, including aggregated, low-granularity data from private data stores).

The New Deal on Data
The first step toward creating an information market is to define ownership rights, just as with financial and commodity markets. This is the reason why the subtitle of the World Economic Forum (WEF) report refers to data as "a new asset class." The simplest approach to defining what it means to "own your own data" is to draw an analogy with the English common law tenets of possession, use, and disposal:

- *You have the right to possess data about you.* Regardless of what entity collects the data, the data belong to you, and you can access your data at any time. Data collectors would play a role akin to a bank, managing the data on behalf of their "customers."

- *You have the right to full control over the use of your data.* The terms of use must be opt-in and clearly explained in plain language. If you are not happy with the way a company uses your data, you can remove the data—just as you would close your account with a bank that is not providing satisfactory service.

- *You have the right to dispose of or distribute your data.* You have the option to destroy data about you or redeploy it elsewhere.

We will expand on these concepts in later chapters, but briefly: Ownership rights over data must be balanced with the need of collaborators, services, and governments to use certain data—account activity, billing information, and so on—to run their day-to-day operations. The proposed New Deal on Data therefore gives individuals the right to possess, control, and dispose of copies of these data as well as all the other incidental data collected about them—for instance, location and similar context—that other participants in the ecology must not retain.

Enforcing personal data ownership rights goes beyond simply authenticating an individual's identity; rather, it involves validating whole series of "claims" and "privileges" of an individual, institution, or even device to access and use such data. As more business, financial, and government services collect and use personal data, the integrity and interoperability of a global authentication and "claims" infrastructure will become paramount. Because no single authority can micromanage all transactions, failures, and attacks, such a global infrastructure—like the Internet itself—must be highly distributed and user-centric to assure rapid innovation, containment, and self-correction.

TRUSTED DATA ARCHITECTURE

Key to realizing trusted "next generation" data architectures is the evolution of not only data acquisition architectures, but also significant issues in building practical systems such as privacy, data ownership, data sharing, and security. To address these issues, we have developed the Open Algorithms (OPAL) architecture, along with the high-security ENIGMA architecture, which builds on OPAL.

The concept of OPAL is that instead of copying or sharing data, algorithms are sent to existing databases, executed behind existing firewalls, and only the encrypted results are shared. This minimizes opportunities to attack databases or divert data for unapproved use. OPAL may be combined with anonymization identifying elements to reduce risk, and we believe that in the long run it will evolve toward a fully encrypted, computation friendly model we have named ENIGMA.

The Open Algorithms (OPAL) paradigm seeks to address the increasing need for individuals and organizations to share data in a secure, privacy-preserving manner. Today there are a number of open challenges with regards to the information sharing ecosystem:

- *Data is siloed.* This makes data unavailable to support good decision-making.
- *Privacy is inadequately addressed.* European regulations and other forces are beginning to address this problem, but it is still far from solved.
- *Security is failing.* The current "firewall" architecture is fundamentally inadequate, as the almost daily reports of hacking events and lost customer data demonstrate.

To address these problems, the concept of OPAL evolved from several research projects over the past decade within my Human Dynamics Lab at the MIT Media Lab, particularly the thesis work of my students Yves-Alexandre de Montjoye (now at Imperial College) and Guy Zyskind (now CEO and founder of Enigma.co).

The OPAL principles for secure, privacy-preserving sharing of insights are simple and relatively easy to implement. Through our MIT Trust Data Consortium (trust.mit.edu), we have created an alliance of countries and multinational and multilateral organizations that are supporting the OPAL paradigm as a promising foundation for the future of the Internet. The various aspects of the OPAL principles are discussed in-depth in several chapters in this book, but briefly they are:

- *Move the algorithm to the data.* Instead of pooling data into a centralized location for processing, it is the algorithm that should be sent to the data repositories for processing there. The goal here is to share insights instead of sharing raw data.
- *Data must never leave its repository.* Data must never be exported from (or copied from) its repository, except as required for specific legally required reasons.

- *Vetted algorithms.* Algorithms should be studied, reviewed, and vetted by experts to address concerns over safety, fairness, accuracy, and the like.

The goal here is to provide all entities in the ecosystem with a better understanding and assessment of the quality of algorithms from the perspective of bias, unfairness, and other possible unintended/unforeseen side effects.

Building on OPAL, ENIGMA is a decentralized platform that at its core uses a blockchain protocol to enable secure data sharing such that it removes the need for a trusted third party and enables the autonomous control of personal data. Given the properties of blockchain, ENIGMA users are able to share and sell their personal data with cryptographic guarantees regarding their privacy.

ENIGMA itself is comprised of a network of computers that store and execute queries. Using secure multi-party computation (sMPC or MPC), each computer only sees random pieces of the data, a fact that prevents information leaks. Furthermore, queries carry a micropayment for the computing resources, as well as a micropayment to those users whose data is queried, thus providing the foundation for the rise of a data market.

The ENIGMA system offers owners not only full control of the personal data but also transparency as to which services are accessing their data and for what purposes. Service providers would be able to monetize the personal data available in the system without ever having access to the raw data. Finally, thanks to ENIGMA's blockchain technology, all transactions would take place while preserving privacy and data integrity.

THE DATA REVOLUTION

It is not only citizens, corporations, and governments in wealthy nations that need trusted data. Since the beginning of time, humans have lived in a world where distance clouded perception and where the experience and the thoughts of people who were just a few miles away were unknown, let alone those of people who were on the other side of the world. The spread of literacy and later the access to rich media content—such as photographs, recordings, and video—enabled us to share experiences with a broader set of people, but provided only a small window into reality, without much context. In fact, as recently as a few decades ago, it was possible to have a large-scale genocide (remember the Tutsi genocide in Rwanda), mass starvation (the 1983–1985 famine in Ethiopia), ecological disasters, or pandemics without the rest of the world knowing. For this reason, there is an urgent need to mobilize the data revolution for all people and the entire planet to help prevent such disasters and/or to hold governments accountable.

In 2014 a group of big data scientists (including myself), representatives of big data companies, and the heads of National Statistical Offices from nations in both the north and south, met within the United Nations headquarters and plotted a revolution. We proposed that all the nations of the world measure poverty, inequality, injustice, and sustainability in a scientific, transparent, accountable, and comparable manner. Surprisingly, the UN General Assembly approved this proposal in 2015, as part of the 2030 Sustainable Development Goals.

This agreement describes what is known as the *Data Revolution* within the UN, because for the first time there is an international commitment to discover and tell the truth about the state of the human family as a whole. Throughout history most people have been isolated, invisible to government, and without information about, or input to, government health, justice, education, or development policies. But in the last decade this has changed. As our UN Data Revolution report, titled "A World That Counts," put it:

Data are the lifeblood of decision-making and the raw material for accountability. Without high-quality data providing the right information on the right things at the right time, designing, monitoring and evaluating effective policies becomes almost impossible. New technologies are leading to an exponential increase in the volume and types of data available, creating unprecedented possibilities for informing and transforming society and protecting the environment. Governments, companies, researchers and citizen groups are in a ferment of experimentation, innovation and adaptation to the new world of data, a world in which data are bigger, faster and more detailed than ever before. This is the data revolution.

More concretely, the vast majority of humanity now has a two-way digital connection that can send voice, text, and most recently, images and digital sensor data, because cell phone networks have spread nearly everywhere. Information is suddenly something that is potentially available to everyone. The data revolution combines this enormous new stream of data about human life and behavior with traditional data sources, enabling a new science of "social physics" that can let us detect and monitor changes in the human condition, and to provide precise, nontraditional interventions to aid human development.

Some people may ask why anyone would believe that something will actually come from a UN General Assembly promise that the National Statistical Offices of the member nations will measure human development openly, uniformly, and scientifically? It is not because anyone hopes that the UN will manage or fund the measurement process. Instead we believe that uniform, scientific measurement of human development will happen because international development donors are finally demanding scientifically sound data to guide aid dollars and trade relationships.

Moreover, once reliable data about development starts becoming familiar to business people, we can expect that supply chains and private investment will start paying attention. A nation with poor measures of justice or inequality normally also has higher levels of corruption, and a nation with a poor record in poverty or sustainability normally also has a poor record in economic stability. As a consequence, nations with low measures of development are less attractive to business than nations with similar costs but better human development numbers.

Building a Data Revolution

How are we going to enable this data revolution and bring transparency and accountability to governments worldwide? The key is safe, reliable, uniform data about the human condition. To this end, we have been able to carry out country-scale experiments that have demonstrated that this is a practical goal that is achievable using an OPAL-style data architecture. For instance, the Data for Developments (D4D) experiments I helped organize for Cote d'Ivoire and Senegal, each of which had the participation of hundreds of research groups from around the world, have shown that satellite data, cell phone data, financial transaction data, and human mobility data can be used within an OPAL architecture in order to measure progress on the sustainable development goals reliably and cheaply. These new data sources won't replace existing survey-based census data, but rather will allow this rather expensive data to be quickly extended in breadth, granularity, and frequency.*

The Open Algorithms (OPAL) project, originally developed as an open source project by my research group at MIT (see trust.mit.edu), is now being deployed as a multi-partner socio-technological platform led by Data-Pop Alliance, Imperial College London, the MIT Media Lab, Orange S.A., and the World

---

* It is worth mentioning that this buries the classic arguments against utilitarianism: the nations of the world have agreed that you can in fact measure the quality of human life.

Economic Forum, that aims to open and leverage private sector data for public good purposes (see htttp://opalproject.org). The project came out of the recognition that accessing data held by private companies (e.g., call detail records collected by telecom operators, credit card transaction data collected by banks, etc.) for research and policy purposes requires an approach that goes beyond ad-hoc data challenges or non-disclosure agreements (NDAs). These types of engagements have offered ample evidence of the promise, but they do not scale or address some of the critical challenges, such as privacy, accountability, etc.

More diverse, timely, and trustworthy information can lead to better decision-making, and, in turn, it can enable individuals, public and private institutions, and companies to make choices that are good for them and for the world they live in. This is what the United Nations refers to as the data revolution, which has resulted in international standardized monitoring requirements being built into the UN's Sustainable Development Goals (SDGs), as originally envisioned in a white paper "A World That Counts," commissioned by the UN Secretary General (and which appears here as Appendix B).

Moreover, the recently created Global Partnership on Sustainable Development Data (see http://www.data4sdgs.org/, where I am a founding member of the Board of Directors) aims to respond to these needs: it consists of a global network of governments, non-governmental organizations (NGOs), and businesses working together to strengthen and develop innovation efforts in the way that data is used to address the world's sustainable development goals. Specifically, the role of this network is to work to bring the resources of national governments, independent nonprofit organizations, and private companies to develop a framework of indicators to monitor the progress towards the achievement of the SDGs at the local, national, regional, and global levels. A sound framework of indicators will turn the SDGs into a management tool to help countries and the global community in developing implementation strategies and allocating resources accordingly.

THE PROMISE OF TRUSTED DATA

Historically, we have been blind to the living conditions of the rest of humanity; violence or disease could spread to pandemic proportions before the news would make it to the ears of central authorities. We are now beginning to be able to see the condition of all of humanity with unprecedented clarity because we live in a historic moment: the availability of vast amounts of human behavioral data, combined with advances in machine learning, are enabling us to tackle complex problems through algorithmic decision-making. The opportunities to have positive social impact through more fair and transparent decisions are astonishing. Of course, there are great challenges that we need to tackle before such opportunities can become a reality and that is the goal of the software and legal architectures discussed in this book.

Today it is hard to even imagine a world where we have reliable, up-to-the-minute data about how government policies are working and about problems as they begin to develop. Imagine, for instance, that we have deployed systems like Open Algorithms (OPAL), which allow statisticians in government statistics departments around the world to publish a more accurate, real-time census and more timely and accurate social surveys. Better public data can allow both the government and private sectors to function better, and with these sorts of improvements in transparency and accountability we can hope to build a world where our government and social institutions work correctly.

A New Social Contract
The architectures of OPAL and ENIGMA are also designed to bring together stakeholders to determine what data—both

private and public—should be made accessible and used, and for what purposes and by whom. Therefore, they add a new dimension and new method to the notion of "social contract," namely that people must agree among themselves to form a civic system that shares some types of data but not others. This provides a forum and mechanism for deciding what levels of transparency and accountability are best for society as a whole. It also provides a natural mechanism for developing evidence-based policies and a continuous monitoring of the various dimensions of societal wellbeing, thus offering the possibility of building a much deeper and more effective science of public policy.

In this book, we will describe a data architecture that places humans and their societal values at the center of our discussions, as humans are ultimately both the actors and the subjects of the decisions made via algorithmic and/or human means. By involving people and ensuring that their values are met, we should be able to realize the positive potential of data-driven algorithmic decision-making, while minimizing the risks and possible negative unintended consequences.

In my view, OPAL is a key contribution to the UN Data Revolution—it is developing and testing a practical system that insures that every person counts, that their voices are heard, their needs are met, their potentials are realized, and their rights are respected. Never again should it be possible to say, "we didn't know."

2 TOWARDS AN INTERNET OF TRUSTED DATA

Alex Pentland, David L. Shrier,
Thomas Hardjono, and
Irving Wladawsky-Berger

Summary of recommendations from a July 2016 meeting at MIT with senior executives from AT&T, IBM, MasterCard, Qualcomm, and the US Departments of Treasury and Commerce.

EXECUTIVE SUMMARY

As the economy and society move from a world where interactions were physical and based on paper documents, toward a world that is primarily governed by digital data and digital transactions, our existing methods of managing identity and data security are proving inadequate. Large-scale fraud, identity theft, and data breaches are becoming common, and a large fraction of the population have only the most limited digital credentials. Even so, our digital infrastructure is recognized as a strategic national asset that must be resilient to threat. If we can create an Internet of Trusted Data that provides safe, secure access for everyone, then huge societal benefits can be unlocked, including better health, greater financial inclusion, and a population that is more engaged with and better supported by its government.

The future of National Cyber Security should be supported by an Internet of Trusted Data in order to enable both auditable provenance of identity and the credibility of data, with an end to enhancing economic viability of new technology solutions, policies, and best practices. Simultaneously, an Internet of Trusted Data must protect the privacy of people, ensure public safety, economic and national security, and foster public, individual, and business partnerships.

In order to accomplish these goals, thought leaders in federal, state, and local governments should join with academia and carrier-scale private industry to work toward an Internet of Trusted Data.

An Internet of Trusted Data includes:

- *Robust digital identity*. Identity, whether personal or organizational, is the key that unlocks all other data and data sharing functions. Digital identity includes not only having unique and unforgeable credentials that work everywhere, but also the ability to access all the data linked to your identity and the ability to control the "persona" that you present in different situations. These pseudonym identities, or personas, include the "work you," the "health system you," the "government you," and many other permutations specific to particular aspects of your individual relationship with another party. Each of these pseudonym identities will have different data access associated with them, and be owned and controlled only by the core "biological you." To accomplish this there needs to be a global strategy for Identity and Access Management that genuinely enables trusted, auditable sharing relationships, and functions without compromising personal anonymity or security. This is technically straightforward: the basics were established by the NIST's National Strategy for Trusted Identity in Cyberspace program and now are widely available from, for instance, mobile operators and similar regulated services. The nation now needs to begin requiring such robust digital identity in order to achieve our goals in cybersecurity and universal access.

- *Distributed Internet trust authorities*. We have repeatedly seen that centralized system administration is the weakest link in cybersecurity, enabling both insiders and opponents to destroy our system security with a single exploit. The most practical solution to this problem is to have authority distributed among many trusted actors, so that compromise of one or even a few authorities does not destroy the system security consensus. This already standard practice for the highest security systems: no one single actor can launch nuclear missiles, for instance. Now we need to implement this sort of consensus security widely. Examples such as the blockchain that underlies most digital cryptocurrencies show that distributed ledgers can provide worldwide security, even in very hostile environments. Today there is a huge amount of investment by private companies to deploy software defined network technology that can transparently expose efficient, convenient versions of this consensus ledger technology, and the US should set policies that take advantage of these new capabilities in collaboration with the private and education sectors, in such a way that digital identities can be originated by individuals and issued with verification from multiple access providers.

- *Distributed safe computation.* Our critical systems will suffer increasing rates of damage and compromise unless we move decisively toward pervasive use of data minimization, more encryption, and distributed computation. Current firewall, event sharing, and attack detection approaches are simply not feasible as long-run solutions for cybersecurity, and we need to adopt an inherently more robust approach. The "optimal" technology for such an inherently safe data ecosystem is currently being built and tested; for reference see MIT's ENIGMA project. Because of the importance of acting quickly, the EU data protection authorities are supporting a simplified, easy-to-deploy version called OPAL (Open Algorithms, which originated at MIT with French support) for pilot testing within certain countries. The concept of OPAL is that instead of copying or sharing data, algorithms are sent to existing databases, executed behind existing firewalls, and only the encrypted results are shared. This minimizes opportunities to attack databases or divert data for unapproved use, but places restrictions on the ability of an ecosystem to collaborate on data when it is in an encrypted state. Note that OPAL may be combined with anonymization identifying elements in order to reduce risk, and in the long run will evolve toward a fully encrypted, computation friendly model. Approaches such as homomorphic encryption and secure multi-party computation can enable encrypted data to be used in an approved, auditable manner by parties that can't decrypt it or read it. In particular, the ability to permissibly ask questions of data in the form of "attributes" will be a key pattern to maintaining digital privacy while enabling innovation ecosystems. The US Government should create a roadmap for progressing from the current situation, through transition technologies such as OPAL, to complete solutions such as MIT ENIGMA.

- *Universal access.* The advantages of secure digital infrastructure are diminished without universal access. The U.S. Government can promote universal access by policies that provide for secure, citizen-controlled personal data stores (PDSs or digital mailboxes) for all citizens in a manner analogous to current physical post office boxes, and promote their use by making government benefits and interactions such as tax transfers and information inquiries conveniently available by mobile devices and web interfaces secured by each citizen's digital identity. Planning by the US Post Office for such universal personal data stores (digital mailboxes) has long been in place, and the secure digital identity infrastructure is already offered by mobile operators and other regulated services.

- *Investment required.* We recommend that the US Government establish a "living lab" to not just test, but actually create, a small-scale deployment of this new ecosystem under real-world conditions with all available and necessary technology in order to obtain citizen and stakeholder feedback. A living lab would prove concept and build citizen confidence towards large-scale deployment and prove viability of technical solutions. We also recommend that the US Government support "microdegrees" leveraging distance education methods (e.g., MOOC, etc.) in order to upgrade the cybersecurity training of the existing workforce. Such continuing education methods have proven quite cost-effective in changing the technology culture within US companies.

The living lab provides a venue where researchers and developers can begin to address challenges around the Internet of Trusted Data, providing them with real-world conditions under which a robust identity system must be deployable with distributed trust authorities, as exemplified by proposals to use blockchain technology. It also permits data sharing to be explored at scale while preserving privacy, where algorithms are sent to existing data repositories based on distributed safe computation. Key to the living lab is universal access to the benefits of the convergence of these new solutions.

INTRODUCTION

Our economies and societies are going through a historical transition from the industrial age of the past two centuries—whose models have been mostly based on physical interactions—to an increasingly digital age based on global, digital interactions. Previous methods for managing identity and data security have proved inadequate in our emerging digital world, and have led to serious cybersecurity breaches.

A number of failure modes emerge at the current transition point:

- While economy and society are becoming digital, identity remains rooted in analog concepts. The consequences of issues such as identity theft include massive fraud, ranging from bank and insurance to tax, and even Uber and AirBnb. A parallel issue emerges of equity and fairness: robust digital identities must be available to all individuals.

- Commercial and government organizations have traditionally built silos of IT systems and datastores that are largely incompatible with each other. In order to move to the next level of a digital economy and to attain the speed and efficiency of business moving at the speed of the network, there must be interoperability and sharing to foster public, private, and individual collaboration on trusted data. It must be efficient and based on universally agreed upon protocols while maintaining security and auditability.

At the same time, our increasingly digital world is opening up opportunities for economic inclusion, improved health care, better financial support, and populations that are more engaged with and supported by their government.

To help address these threats and opportunities, in February 2016 President Barack Obama issued an Executive Order establishing the Commission on Enhancing National Cybersecurity within the Department of Commerce. The Commission was charged with "recommending bold, actionable steps that the government, private sector, and the nation as a whole can take to bolster cybersecurity in today's digital world, and reporting back by the beginning of December."

The Commission invited select members of this working group to participate in a panel on research and development opportunities at a public meeting held in New York City on May 16, 2016. In our testimony to the Commission, we highlighted six key areas where government, technology companies, and academia should work together in order to increase the speed and quality of the two-way information flows that are essential for developing a data-rich society with a holistic approach to cyber protection:

- *Proof of identity.* A new identity management system must be created to replace today's ad-hoc systems.

- *Trustworthy, auditable data provenance.* Systems must automatically track every change that is made to data, so it is auditable and completely trustworthy.

- *Secure, privacy-preserving processing.* We have to enable the entities to engage in transactions and to verify that contracts are being fulfilled but without revealing private or confidential information.

- *Universal access.* Everyone must be able to share in the benefits, and have the protections, of this new trusted data infrastructure.

- *Research and development.* We need to dramatically increase the speed and scale of cyber innovation in both the private and public sector by use of "living lab" field trials.

- *Workforce development.* Companies face a serious shortage of cyber-trained personnel and of management expertise in cybersecurity. We need to increase and maintain the available workforce, which may require greater educational capacity and incentives.

We also emphasized the essential importance of focusing on complete systems, rather than individual technologies or technology layers, and that they be developed and proven in living laboratories with a representative population of users in order to provide feedback about the relevance, efficiency, effectiveness, and ethical dimensions of these new systems.

In discussions with the US Secretary of Commerce, the White House panel on cybersecurity, and the EU VP of Single Digital Market, we were encouraged to create a plan for accomplishing these goals that brought together key players from government, industry, and academia.

On July 11, 2016, we convened a workshop at MIT to start framing our statement of the problem as well as our recommendations. The workshop participants all agreed that we were at a unique point to move forward, much as was the case with the Internet and World Wide Web in the early 1990s. As was the case then, there continues to be a growing consensus on:

1. The problems to be solved:

   - The need to bolster cybersecurity in our increasingly digital economy and society.

   - A requirement for universal, highly secure digital identities covering individuals, private and public institutions, and the Internet of Things (IoT).

   - The need to efficiently access, exchange, and share critical data with full security and privacy protection.

   - The overall systems have to be "fault tolerant" in the presence of "non-trusted" actors, whether they are competitors or other governments you only want to share limited data with, or "bad actors" with malicious intent.

2. The fact that there is a promising evolution of a new set of general technologies and potential solutions to help address these problems, including:

   - Identity, whether personal or organizational, and, moreover, the ability to own and assert identity attributes is a lynchpin concern. There needs to be a kind of "internet of identity" to genuinely enable all other sharing functions.

   - Blockchain networks can provide a single source of auditable truth between organizations and some level of appropriate automation of data processing. However, organizations must decide also on distributed sources of trust for the moderation of such networks. Identity plays a crucial role in enabling blockchain technology to be adopted broadly.

- Overlaying inventions such as personal datastores and secure multi-party computation (see for reference implementations MIT OpenPDS and MIT ENIGMA), we can develop a new digital ecosystem that is secure, trusted, and empowering.

3. The need for the private sector, government, and academia to work together to address these critical problems and leverage these promising technologies to enable and incentivize collaboration and innovation.

At the same time, the population needs to be educated in a coherent fashion about the benefits and role that each individual can play in forming this new system.

Under these circumstances, the question arises: "Are we simply replacing known risks with unknown risks?" Clearly, the shortcomings of existing systems are proving so great that a new approach is needed.

In light of these concerns, we have articulated potential solutions around robust identity and trusted data, which enable the auditability and credibility of both while supporting fair information practice principles.

THE PROMISE OF ROBUST IDENTITY

Our mission in suggesting a robust identity framework focuses on connecting the individual with the digital identity, while protecting privacy. When we say "robust," we mean both reliable and unforgeable.

Benefits include better access to:

- the financial system for the underbanked and unbanked;
- the health care system, in a fashion that reduces medical error and improves care;
- government services;
- other basic services (e.g., making it easier to obtain an apartment or home).

Drivers of Need

A number of problems are driving the need for a robust identity:

- It is fundamental to cybersecurity. Current cybersecurity systems are insufficient to the task, as evidenced by the numerous large-scale data breaches recently experienced by both the private and public sectors globally.

- We all need identity to access services.

- The flaws in translating from a physical proof of identity ("I see you in front of me, I know you are you"), to a digital format ("On the Internet, no one knows you are a dog"), in a robust and portable fashion.

- The question of authority: Who provides the identity?

- The need for identity to be unique, strong, verifiable, and unforgeable.

A Potential Solution

A new paradigm asserts that you are your digital footprint, and you have ownership rights in your data. Just as the Magna Carta established a framework for individual property rights in 1215 CE, so too a new digital social contract needs to provide for digital ownership rights.

The concept of behavioral biometrics is gaining ground in areas such as financial services and digital authentication. Research conducted at MIT and elsewhere has demonstrated that behavior biometrics are much more difficult to fabricate and deliver more than ten times better security than password-based models.[2] With respect to ownership rights, this "New Deal on Data" was first posed by us in collaboration with the World Economic Forum in 2009 and has been expanded since.[3]

Several challenges need to be addressed, including, but not limited to:

- *Big Brother.* The fear of a government using panoptic access for dictatorship.

- *Bad actors*. Whether inside an organization or external, accumulating such data creates risk of misuse by bad actors.

- *Scale and implementation cost*. Implementing such a solution globally will have nontrivial scaling and cost functions (and relatedly, who will pay for it and how?).

- *Undocumented residents*. Deploying such a system creates potential for institutionalizing a digital divide between rich and poor, and introduces new questions around circumstances such as cases where municipalities offer undocumented residents a means of identification even if the Federal government hasn't.

- *Equal protection under the law*. How can we protect someone that the system doesn't acknowledge has an existence?

- *Universal versus siloed data*. Universal data has greater utility, but is generally less secure—siloing can provide a measure of security, but raises issues of interoperability.

- *Regulatory lag*. There is always a gap between a technology innovation and the ability of policymakers and regulators to implement an appropriate framework around it.

Questions also remain as to how this would be developed. Should it be government led, like the EID or India or Estonia? Should it be furnished by industry, similar to how Internet domain name registries are handled? Should it be housed within a nonprofit or academic environment, like the Kerberos Consortium or the World Wide Web Consortium (W3C)? Active dialog with key stakeholders is required to establish the optimal path.

POTENTIAL SOLUTION: CORE IDENTITIES AND PERSONA IDENTITIES

At the heart of digital identities is the concept of the *core identity* of an individual, which inalienably belongs to that individual. The core identity serves as the quantum from which emerges other forms of digitally derived identities (called *personas*), which are practically useful and are legally enforced in digital transactions. An individual must have the freedom to choose to deploy one or more digital personas on the Internet, each used with specific sharing and access permission and tailored to the specific aspect of that individual's life. Each digital personal would carry varying degrees of legal enforceability as relevant to the auditable usage context of that persona.

The individual must be able to use transaction identities derived from his or her relevant persona, without affecting the privacy of their core identity. This derivation process must also allow the relying party (counterparty) in a transaction to validate the source authenticity and strength of provenance of the transaction identity, without affecting the privacy of the core identity of the user. New cryptographic techniques—such as zero knowledge proofs—offer a promising direction in providing solutions for privacy-preserving core identities.

As currently configured, existing business models, legal instruments, and technical implementations are insufficient to support this type of identity ecosystem. This is because something is missing: an architecture for individual ownership of and primacy over one's own core identity that also regulates which entities or relationships have access to attributes of that identity. With such a core identity, it is possible for multiple aliases, accounts, and attributes to be authenticated and authorized in a reliable, privacy-enhancing, and scalable manner. To this end, a viable identity infrastructure provides a way for each person to own their single underlying core identity and to bind several "personas" to that core identity without the need for other parties to access the core identity or be aware of any other personas. With this approach, government issued identity credentials such as driver licenses, passports, professional licenses, birth certificates, etc.) as well as strongly provenanced sources of attributes about a person (e.g., banks for credit scores, etc.) can be leveraged to create a core identity that remains private to the end-user.

A key feature of the new model is that it must allow entities in the ecosystem to: verify the "quality" or security of an identity; assess the relative "freedom" or independence of an identity from any given authority (e.g., government, businesses, etc.); and assess the source of trust for a digital identity.

We believe a new model for digital identities for future blockchain systems is required, which is summarized in the following progressive steps:

1. *Strongly provenanced attributes.* It must be founded on an existing real-world identity that has a high degree of source of trust, where its attributes have a high degree of provenance. This identity maybe issued by an existing identity provider or other trusted third party operating within a legal jurisdiction (e.g., bank, government, service provider, etc.).

2. *Transitive source of trust.* Create a "core identity" based on the existing high-quality identity—that is, use a privacy-preserving algorithm that translates the existing real-world identity with strong provenance into a digital core identity that carries over the source of trust.

3. *Self-issued derived identities as personas.* Provide users with the freedom (and algorithms/tools) to establish personas and to self-issue anonymous but verifiable transaction identities, each of which is cryptographically derived from the user's core identity and each of which carries specific permissioned attributes suitable for the purpose of the transaction identities. The source of trust from the core identity must also be carried over into the derived transaction identity.

4. *Privacy-preserving verification.* Provide the relying parties (counterparties) with a privacy-preserving verification algorithms to validate the source of trust for any given (anonymous) transaction identity. These verification algorithms must allow a relying party to establish a chain of provenance (from the transaction identity all the way back to the origin

attributes and core identity), while preserving the privacy of the owner of the identity.

5. *Legal trust framework (LTF)*. Establish an identity ecosystem for blockchain based on a LTF for core identities, personas, and anonymous transaction identities. Such a legal framework is already in use for identity federation schemes in the industry today, and may be used as the legal basis for this new model.

A legal trust framework is a certification program that enables a party who accepts a digital identity credential (called the relying party or RP) to trust the identity, security, and privacy policies of the party who issues the credential (called the identity service provider), and vice versa. An LTF applies within a given deployment ecosystem, such as an identity federation, or across two partner organizations.

We believe the current LTFs as practiced in the industry can be extended for usage in blockchain systems. New types of entities will be needed specifically for blockchain ecosystems. We denote these as the *Core Identity Provider* and *Transaction Identity Provider*, which extend the current role of the Identity Provider (IdP).

The Core Identity Provider takes a user's existing identity, which has a high degree of source of trust, and converts it using a privacy-preserving function into a private or secret core identity that is maintained as private or secret, and is only supplied to the Transaction Identity Provider. The latter then provides a transaction identity issuance service to the user, as well as a validation service to the relying parties. The user is free to obtain one or more anonymous transaction identities from the Transaction Identity Provider or self-issue a derived transaction identity, all the while maintaining their privacy. The transaction identities can be used on the blockchain system with other users (relying parties) or on the Internet. The validation service offered by the Transaction Identity Provider allows a relying party to inquire about the status and source-grade of a given anonymous transaction identity prior to transacting.

In the context of blockchains, the LTF provides the following:

- *Network scalability.* It allows any two parties to transact on a blockchain without prior engagement, thus achieving network scalability.

- *Provenance assessment.* It allows a relying party (counterparty) to assess the "trustworthiness" (provenance and quality) of an (anonymous) transaction identity prior to commencing the transaction.

- *Cross-jurisdiction interoperability.* It provides a legal foundation for core identities and (anonymous) transaction identities to be recognized in differing legal jurisdictions;

- *New business models.* It incentivizes service providers (including the Core Identity Providers and Transaction Identity Providers) to develop new business models around new scalable services and permissible use of attribute data associated with identities.

- *Risk assessment and risk management.* It provides entities in the ecosystem with a means of assessing risk and of legal recourse in unforeseen circumstances (e.g., attacks to the service, identity leaks, identity data theft, provider negligence, etc.), as specified.

Data is rapidly proliferating from an end-user perspective, without a good solution for managing user data, as well as identities, efficiently. We need a new paradigm for data sharing that preserves user privacy, while allowing data to be shared more globally for the benefit of society.

DATA SHARING

The constituents served by this new system include both enterprises and average consumers. By bringing control of both data and identify back to the consumer, we can drive better outcomes. We can create technology that would enable the simplification and securing of the digital identities through simpler "form factors."

However, questions remain: What exactly does this solution look like? Could it be like Global Entry? Who would manage such a system? In Global Entry's case, it's the TSA.

With respect to R&D, there's a great diversity of work required, and we need to use an approach such as that discussed in the following section. Opportunities created from this solution include the creation of a digital marketplace for personal data that would simultaneously provide assurance of your data.

Key Concepts in a Potential Solution

Data sharing in a privacy-preserving manner requires a new view on data. There are a number of key concepts and design principles that need to be addressed through an evolutionary proof-of-concept (PoC) implementation. Some of these key concepts are as follows:

1. *Moving the algorithm to the data*. The concept here is to perform the algorithm (i.e., query) execution at the location of data (referred to as the data repository). This implies that raw data should never leave its repository, and access to it is controlled by the repository/data owner.

2. *Open algorithms*. Algorithms (i.e., queries or scripts) must be openly published, studied, and vetted by experts to be "safe" from violating the privacy requirements and other requirements stemming from the context of their use.

3. *Permissible use*. When performing computation on attributes or data associated with identities, respect the explicit and implicit permission, or consent, given for use of the data or identity attributes as part of the transaction.

4. *Always return "safe answers" (never raw data)*. When performing computation (e.g., in answering a query), the data repository

must always return "safe answers" and never raw data. This concept seeks to address the issue of data privacy and the potential danger of de-identification (of Personally Identifying Information, or PII) through the correlation of multiple responses.

5. *Data is always in an encrypted state.* Data should be encrypted at all times—namely, at rest, in transit, and during computation. Data should not need to be decrypted prior to computation and then reencrypted afterwards. Advanced cryptographic techniques are now emerging that allow limited forms of computations to be performed on the encrypted data. There two broad scenarios we seek to address:

   • *Computation by individual repository.* Here, computation over encrypted data is performed by a single repository, which may employ a physically distributed set of nodes (e.g., P2P collaboration network) to collaboratively store parts of the data for increased resiliency against attacks. Cryptographic techniques such as secret sharing provide for interesting possibilities in addressing these requirements.

   • *Collaborative computation by multiple parties (multi-party computation).* Some form of queries may require answers to be computed by multiple participants (e.g., repositories) in a collaborative/quorum method while maintain the privacy of data stored at each repository. Each participant may see the final group-computed value, but they must not see each other's raw data. Cryptographic techniques such as multi-party computation (MPC) offer a path forward in solving these scenarios.

6. *Networked collaboration environments and blockchains for audit and accountability.* Peer-to-peer (P2P) networks—such as those underlying the Hyperledger system—offer an attractive solution for data resiliency and scalability, especially when combined with cryptographic techniques such as secret sharing and MPC. The consensus-based ledger mechanism underlying

these blockchain systems offers a way to perform logging, auditing, and accounting of queries executed against data in distributed repositories.

7. *Social and economic incentives.* For privacy-preserving data sharing to scale and be adopted by a wide range of stakeholders, social and economic incentives must be provided, not only for persons or organizations holding "edge data" but also for infrastructure providers. These infrastructure providers are entities who deliver P2P network scalability, as well as efficient edge computing services that yield real-time edge analytics and visibility into the state of data sharing.

The overall goal of any proposed solution should be increased data protection and privacy, together with scalability, performance, and interoperability. In the following sections, we describe different evolutionary phases of a solution, where each phase focuses on one or more of the above key concepts.

Solution, Phase I: Deployed Blockchain

The goal here is to explore the use of a small number of independent data repositories together with P2P nodes and blockchain technology such as Hyperledger:

- *API-driven query/response controls.* The API defined at the data repository provides a "hardwired" query capability. The "querier" performs the query by sending a message to the API at the repository, which in turn sends results to the querier. The API itself defines the type of query accepted and the granularity of answers being returned.

- *Aggregate answers only.* The API will return "safe answers" in the form of aggregate/statistical answers only. This approach conforms to the key principle of never allowing raw data to leave the repository.

- *Multiple repositories.* Multiple data repositories are envisioned, where each repository may store only one kind of data (e.g.,

GPS location) that is constrained through its APIs. To the querier, the nodes on the networked collaboration environment allow the querier to get access to large number data repositories—represented as nodes of the P2P network (i.e., nodes on the blockchain).

- *Metadata for discovery.* Sharing of data presumes that the existence of data is known. A number of nodes on the networked collaboration environment may take the role of "metadata directories," where they can return information regarding the location of nodes with desired data.

- *All access requests/responses logged.* Direct capture of logs into a blockchain is inefficient and does not scale well. Instead, approaches such as those in the Blue Horizon database represent more promising solutions. Each party (the querier and data repository) tracks the API calls, and then hashes the logs. Each party must generate the same hash for the calls, as well as the same hash for data sent/received. These hashes can be written to the blockchain and can be audited by each party only (for privacy preservation).

- *Authorization and identity.* Authorization tokens will be used in conjunction with a basic blockchain identity, with the focus primarily on authorizations to access a data repository through the published APIs. The member services capability of systems such as Hyperledger can begin to be explored in this phase.

Solution, Phase II: Bring Algorithms to the Data

Building on the previous phase, the goal in this phase is to introduce the use of algorithms or scripts that are vetted to be safe for a given classification of data. These vetted algorithms can be signed and published (e.g., at nodes of the networked collaboration environment). Invocation of one of these published algorithms by a querier will require that all the conditions stated be fulfilled (e.g., verified identity of the querier, target data repositories, authorization tokens, etc.). The approach builds on access to APIs from the previous phase, with tighter restrictions expressed through vetting of algorithms. The querier's choice of algorithm can be recorded on the blockchain, with the returned results also being logged and recorded on the blockchain. Furthermore, a published algorithm can be expressed as a smart contract residing in one or more of nodes on the networked collaboration environment.

- *Query control using vetted algorithms/scripts.* Queries are expressed as executable "algorithms" or scripts. The querier sends the algorithm to the relevant endpoints located at the data repositories.

- *Flexible queries.* In this phase the queries have greater flexibility than the API-driven approach in Phase I. Subset SQL or Python may be considered as the query/scripts language.

- *Vetting of safe algorithms.* Algorithms are first vetted by experts for their safety and impact to privacy and to the correctness of returned results. Only aggregate/statistical queries are permitted. Copies of all approved/vetted queries are signed and then stored at a number of nodes on the networked collaboration environment (participating in blockchain) for public verification.

- *Repositories evaluate and execute algorithms.* Each repository must dedicate computational power ("compute engine") to execute/evaluate a received query (in the form of an algorithm) against the available local data. Raw data itself is never returned.

- *Richer data repositories.* Each repository is assumed to store richer sets of data of varying types.

- *Authorization and privacy-preserving identities.* The identity of the querier and the repositories need to be preserved from "leakages" of information through methods such as correlations and others that disclose private information. Basic transaction identities can be deployed, as part of managing identity, privacy, and confidentiality on the network. Some blockchain systems (e.g., Hyperledger) provide a suitable framework for "member services" (i.e., user's core identity and transaction identities).

- *Blockchain used for logs and monitoring.* A blockchain is used to log all access request/responses for audit and postevent traffic analysis.

Solution, Phase III: Basic MPC

This phase introduces more sophisticated cryptographic techniques that support privacy-preserving distributed computations over data. Once such technique is *secure multi-party computation* (SMPC). Here an SMPC cryptographic algorithm is used for computation over data that is stored in plaintext at the repository. A select number of nodes on the blockchain have SMPC capability, and can participate in secure MPC computation instances. Focus is on the performance aspects of a small number of MPC-nodes, including computational performance and network bandwidth measurements. An MPC-node may be implemented as an "overlay" over nodes in a blockchain system. A rudimentary proof-of-MPC-completion maybe recorded on the underlying blockchain.

- *Raw data remains locally at the repositories.* The data remains private, and none of the nodes see each other's raw data. Furthermore, each data item is located at its "home" data repository (i.e., not at a P2P set of nodes).

- *Data at rest in plaintext (not encrypted).* Data at rest in a given repository is in plaintext, and not hidden using secret sharing encryption. This allows focus to be directed to MPC algorithms and their performance.

- *Simple MPC configuration of known nodes.* A small number of repositories (e.g., three nodes) will be used to create a group of parties involved in the MPC computation. Each node in an MPC instance will employ a secure channel (e.g., TLS1.2) to ensure integrity protection from attacks, and each knows the others identity (e.g., via X509 certificate).

- *Predefined simple queries.* Only simple queries will be addressed, possibly as predefined (template) queries. Complex queries (e.g., inner/outer joins of tables) will be left for future work.

- *Metadata service.* Types of data and available simple operations are "advertised" at a special server, to which queries can locate relevant repositories.

- *Rudimentary proof-of-MPC-completion.* MPC-nodes need to record the completion of their MPC computation on the underlying blockchain, with a matching verification/validation mechanism. The proof is to be determined, but may consist of each MPC-node listing its steps and message flows (with other MPC-nodes), and recording these on the blockchain for later replay/verification. This aspect is relevant for providing economic incentives for nodes to participate within a given MPC computation.

Solution, Phase IV: Full MPC with Secret Sharing

This phase employs a combination of two sophisticated cryptographic techniques—namely, the secure MPC technique (from the previous phase) together with data encrypted into pieces (or "shares"). A minimal "threshold" number of shares are required to reconstruct the original data item. A select number of nodes on the blockchain store "shares" of a data item, but never the complete set of shares, providing resiliency against attacks seeking to recover the data item. These are called "shares-nodes." The MPC-nodes are now also responsible for collecting the relevant shares of each data item from the underlying shares-nodes in the blockchain. Each shares-node may hold shares corresponding to different data items, which in turn belong to different owners. The querier sends the algorithm/query to a coordinating node that represents the querier to the MPC-nodes.

- *No centralized data repository.* Data repositories no longer hold any complete data, but only the location of other nodes (shares-nodes) in the decentralized networked collaboration environment that hold data (in the form of encrypted data shares). As the "owner" of a data item, the data repository must perform shares management (i.e., shares creation, distribution, and relocations).

- *Shares distribution, re-collection and management.* Each data repository implements a "standardized" shares location management function that support the creation of shares-coordinates (of all the relevant shares for each data item). The shares-coordinates are then given to the designated MPC-node involved in a given query instance.

- *MPC only nodes.* A new category of nodes will be introduced whose purpose is to participate in and complete an MPC computation instance. This distinction allows for support of an "outsourcing" model whereby the data repository (which now holds no actual data) delegates the MPC computation instance to a given MPC-node.

- *Shares-based primitive operations.* Simple operations (additions and multiplications) over the encrypted data shares.

- *Query-to-primitive translation.* Simple translator from subset SQL into the relevant MPC primitives (e.g., addition and multiplication operations).

- *Authorization for invoking MPC-nodes.* The querier must provide authorization evidence that it is authorized to request the set of MPC-nodes to collect corresponding shares and to perform MPC computation on these shares.

INVESTMENT REQUIRED

R&D investment is needed to implement the solutions suggested herein. In evaluating an R&D plan, what can we leverage what already exists out there, and what would we need to build.

We recommend that the US Government establish a living lab to not just test, but actually deploy, this new paradigm. A living lab would prove concept and build confidence towards a national and international rollout. MIT has employed the living lab model in communities as diverse as Hamburg, Germany, the country of Senegal, and Cambridge, Massachusetts.

We would envision a test starting with 10,000 people, then 100,000+, then 1+ million (roughly logarithmic proof of concept scaling). It could begin with a neighborhood or small community, then a town or larger neighborhood, then a midsize city. It could be deployed to a specific department within the Federal Government. Or, it could be structured on an interest group or common problem area ("affinity-driven"), such as veterans or federal workers.

A competition such as the Department of Transportation Smart City Challenge, with a $50 million prize for the winning proposal, illustrates a viable model for generating a diverse set of perspectives on the problem and potential solutions.

Criteria for Site Selection

1. Town-scale.

2. Proximity to a substantial federal facility.

3. Endpoints: consumers, health system, financial system.

4. Make interoperable with things that are not new?

5. Advisable: strong local university partner.

6. Coordinating "owner" locally.

Geographies that meet these characteristics include Boulder, CO, Austin, TX, Rochester, NY, Hartford, CT, and Boston, MA. Affinity-driven examples include the Veterans Administration or the USPS.

A federally administered competition could stimulate innovation much in the same way that the ARPANET and NSFNET led to the development of the commercial Internet.

Background

The Massachusetts Institute of Technology Connection Science initiative (MIT Connection Science) hosted a working group session on July 11, 2016 in Cambridge, MA to answer the call posed by President Barack Obama's Commission on Enhancing National Cybersecurity, and separately held discussions with then US Secretary of Commerce Penny Pritzker and the European Union's Vice President Andrus Ansip (in charge of the Single Digital Market). This document reflects a distillation of the discussion from the July 11 working group.

Participating were:

- Alex Pentland (Professor, MIT)
- Irving Wladawsky-Berger (MIT Connection Science Fellow)
- David L. Shrier (Managing Director, MIT Connection Science)
- Jerry Cuomo (IBM Fellow and Vice President Blockchain Technologies)
- Steve Davis (Senior Consultant, Payments Innovation, MasterCard)
- Michael Frank (Program Director, Blockchain Technologies, IBM)
- Thomas Hardjono (Chief Technology Officer, MIT Connection Science)
- Guerney Hunt (Research Staff Member, IBM)
- Cameron Kerry (Visiting Scholar, MIT; Distinguished Visiting Fellow, Brookings Institute; formerly General Counsel and Acting Secretary, US Department of Commerce)
- Mark O'Riley (Office of the General Counsel, Government and Regulatory Affair-Technology Policy, IBM)
- Chris Parsons (Vice President Big Data Strategy and Business Development, AT&T)
- Gari Singh (Distinguished Engineer & Blockchain CTO, IBM)

- Anne Shere Wallwork (Senior Counselor for Strategic Policy, Office of Terrorist Financing and Financial Crimes, US Department of the Treasury)
- Rod Walton (Vice President, Qualcomm)
- Irida Xheneti (Entrepreneur in Residence, MIT Connection Science)

REFERENCES

1. Yampolskiy, R., and V. Govindaraju. 2008. "Behavioral Biometrics: A Survey and Classification." *International Journal of Biometrics* 1 (1): 81–113.

2. World Economic Forum. 2009. "The New Deal on Data." http://hd .media.mit.edu/wef_globalit.pdf.

3 CORE IDENTITIES FOR FUTURE TRANSACTION SYSTEMS

Thomas Hardjono, David L. Shrier, and Alex Pentland

INTRODUCTION: THE NEED FOR SCALABLE AND PRIVACY-PRESERVING IDENTITIES

The rise into prominence of blockchain technology[1,2] has rekindled interest in the notion of an identity ecosystem that is not only scalable but also preserves the privacy of individuals and organizations that transact on shared decentralized ledgers and blockchain systems. The call for an identity ecosystem that is privacy-preserving is not new, and was more recently echoed in the NSTIC whitepaper[3] on the *National Strategy for Trusted Identities in Cyberspace*. Specifically, the NSTIC strategy document calls for an identity ecosystem that will minimize the ability to link credential use among multiple service providers, thereby preventing them from developing a complete picture of an individual's activities online. This sentiment is also echoed elsewhere.

Today there are a number of unsolved challenges with regards to digital identities for the Internet and for blockchain systems:

- *Identity tied to specific services.* Most digital "identities" (namely, identifier strings such as email addresses) are created as an adjunct construction to support access to specific services on the Internet. This tight coupling between digital identifiers and services has given rise to the unmanageable proliferation of user accounts on the Internet.

- *Massive duplication of data.* Together with the proliferation of user accounts comes the massive duplication of personal attributes across numerous service providers on the Internet. These service providers are needlessly holding the same set of person-attributes (e.g., name, address, phone, etc.) associated with a user.

- *Lack or absence of user control.* In many cases users have little knowledge about what data is collected by a service provider, how the data was collected, and the actions taken on the data. As such, end users have no control over the other usages of their data beyond what was initially consented to.

- *Diminishing trust in data holders or custodians.* The laxity in safeguarding user data has diminished social trust on the part of users in entities that hold their data. Recent attacks on data repositories and theft of massive amounts of data (e.g., Anthem hack,[4] Equifax attack,[5] etc.) illustrate this ongoing problem.

- *Misalignment of incentives.* Today customer-facing service providers (e.g., online retail) have access only to poor quality user data. Typically, such data is obtained from data aggregators (third parties), many of which collate an incomplete picture of the user through various back-channel means (e.g., "scraping" various Internet sites). The result is a high cost to service providers for new customer on-boarding, coupled with low predictive qualities of the data. Thus, there is a misalignment of incentives among the service providers who want to reach consumers, the third party entities that supply data, and the consumers themselves—who are today bombarded by many misdirected advertising (e.g., spam mail).

- *Increased risk of attacks and increased liability.* Service providers and organizations that hold personal data are increasingly subject to attacks (external as well as internal) that are costly to business. New regulations, such as the General Data Protection Regulation (GDPR) in Europe,[6] increase the legal liability of these service providers in the face of data breaches and identity theft.

- *Inefficient business model.* The current forms of identities (e.g., simple email addresses and cookies) are designed for and operate based on a business model that seeks to understand and harness consumer social behavior, but that relies on inaccurate data. Rather that creating siloes of personal data, businesses and identity providers need to share insights in a privacy-preserving manner. Sharing of data increases its value, especially when data is shared across domains or verticals.

We argue that a scalable identity ecosystem must be developed on a coherent paradigm for privacy-preserving data sharing. The issue of "identity" is about the correct combination of: (1) the digital identifiers representing the individual or organization; (2) the assertions and attributes computed based on relevant strongly provenanced data; and (3) algorithms that are fair and yield accurate results for an intended purpose. In order to get useful insights about an individual or organization, relevant data from various domains may need to contribute into the algorithmic computations. However, having access to various datasets raises the question of privacy. As such, the problem of "identity" expands into the broader question of privacy-preserving sharing of data across different sources.

We believe that an approach such as MIT OPAL[7] for privacy-preserving sharing of insights offers a better foundation for future Internet identities and assertions based on information about a user that has stronger provenance, compared to current approaches.

Furthermore, certain types of data and insights—referred to as core identities—are inherently private or secret to the individual or organization.[8,9] As such, there is a clear need to separate the notion of identifiers (e.g., email address, credit card numbers, etc.) that are short-term and may be replaced, from the notion of core identities, which consist of the set of data and assertions that reveal deep and private insights. These sets of insights may be compartmentalized into personas by the individual or organization to make them accessible to relevant parties only.

CORE IDENTITIES: FUNDAMENTAL CONCEPTS

There are a number of key concepts and principles underlying the notion of core identities, personas, and transaction identifiers. In the following sections, we discuss these in the context of personal data and digital identities on the Internet. The understanding is that these principles may apply to certain kinds of organizations and their data also.

Core Identities, Personas, and Transaction Identifiers

We define identity* as the collective aspect of the set of characteristics or features by which a thing (e.g., human, device, organization) is recognizable and distinguishable from another. In the context of a human person, the individuality of a person plays an important role in that it allows a community of people to recognize the distinct characteristics of an individual person and consider the person as a persisting entity.

- *Core identity.* The collective aspect of the set of characteristics (as represented by personal data) by which a person is uniquely recognizable, and from which a unique core identifier may be generated based on the set of relevant personal data.[8,9]

   Thus, for example, the set of transaction data associated with a person can be collated and used to create a core identity that distinguishes that person from others. Out of this set

---

* Etymology: Middle French *identit*, from Late Latin *identitat-*, *identitas*, probably from Latin *identidem* repeatedly, contraction of *idem et idem*, literally, same and same (Merriam-Webster Dictionary).

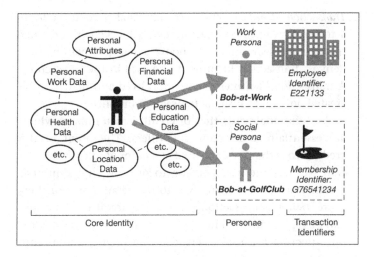

FIGURE 3.1

Core identity as a collective aspect of the set of a person's characteristics.

of transaction data, a transaction identifier may be generated. The core identity pertaining to a person must be kept secret and never be used in any transactions. Figure 3.1 illustrates this concept.

- *Core identifier.* A core identifier is a short practical representation of a core identity derived within the context of a specific collection of data. Like the core identity, a core identifier must be kept secret and never be used in any transactions.

- *Persona.* A persona is defined by and created based on a collection of attributes and assertions relevant in a given context or a given relationship. Thus, a person may have a work-persona, home-persona, social-persona, and others. Each of these personas is context-dependent and involves only the relevant subset of the core identity characteristics of that person. A person may have one or more personas.

- *Transaction identifier.* When an individual seeks to perform a transaction (e.g., on the Internet, a blockchain, or other transacting medium), they choose a relevant persona and derive a transaction identifier to be used in the transaction. A transaction identifier maybe short-lived and may even be created only for that single transaction instance.

  A useful analogy is that of credit card numbers, which are essentially transaction identifiers. The point of the credit card is that it can be used at a point of sale (POS) location without the user needing to provide any additional information about themselves to the retail store. Furthermore, being a transaction identifier, a credit card number can be replaced with a new one (e.g., in case of theft) without affecting the user's personal data (namely, their core identity).

An example is shown in figure 3.1, where a user ("Bob") has two personas (one for work and one for a social golf club), each employing different transaction identifiers. Different data representing different characteristics of the user are employed to create distinct personas. Thus, for example, application for membership in a golf club may not be preconditioned on personal work history data. As such, that aspect of Bob's life does not feature in determining Bob's golf social persona.

Algorithms and Assertions

Following from the previous section on the concepts underlying core identities, data pertaining to individuals or organizations are typically processed before they are made consumable to parties seeking information and insights. During this processing, one or more relevant algorithms may be applied to the suitable data, yielding insights. One way to convey insights is through a construct called assertions.[10]

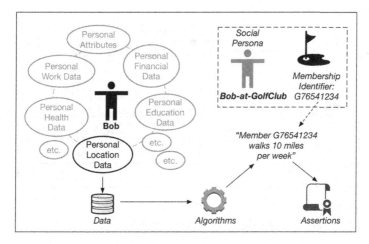

FIGURE 3.2
Example of using data and algorithms to compute assertions.

An example is shown in Figure 3.2. In this example, a set of location data about a user (Bob) is used within an algorithm that computes the average distanced walked by the user within a given time period. The resulting value ("10 miles per week on the golf range") is computed and then linked to a transaction identifier ("G76541234"), and together presented in a digitally signed assertion.

OPAL Principles for Data Privacy

As mentioned previously, in order to get useful insights, relevant data from various domains may need to be included into an algorithmic computation—but having access to these data raises privacy issues.

In this section we briefly review the OPAL principles for privacy-preserving sharing of insights. We believe the OPAL paradigm offers a promising foundation for future Internet identities and assertions. The various aspects of the OPAL principles

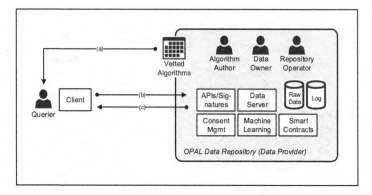

FIGURE 3.3
Overview of Open Algorithms (OPAL) architecture.

have been discussed in-depth in another chapter in this book
and elsewhere.[7,11] They are briefly described in the following:

- *Move the algorithm to the data.* Instead of pulling data from
  various repositories into a centralized location for processing,
  it is the algorithm that should be sent to the data repositories
  for processing there. The goal here is to share insights instead
  of sharing raw data.

- *Data must never leave its repository.* Data must never be exported
  from (or copied from) its repository. This is consistent with
  the previous principle and enforces that principle.

- *Vetted algorithms.* Algorithms should be studied, reviewed,
  and vetted by experts.

  The goal here is to provide all entities in the ecosystem
  with a better understanding and assessment of the quality of
  algorithms from the perspective of bias, unfairness, and other
  possible unintended/unforeseen side effects.

- *Default to safe answers.* The default behavior of data repositories when returning responses should be that of protecting

privacy as the primary goal. This applies to individual, as well as organizational, data privacy.

Additionally, in the context of the data that are used to compute algorithms specifically for identity-related assertions, the following should also be adopted:

- *Trust networks or data federations.* In a group-based information sharing configuration (referred to as a trust network or data-sharing federation), algorithms must be vetted collectively by the trust network members. Individually, each member must observe the OPAL principles and operate on this basis. The operational aspects of the federation should be governed by a legal trust framework (see further discussions below).

- *Consent for algorithm execution.* Data repositories that hold subject data must obtain explicit consent from the subject when this data is to be included in a given algorithm execution. This implies that as part of obtaining a subject's consent, the vetted algorithms should be made available and understandable to subjects. Consent should be unambiguous and retractable (see Article 7 of GDPR[6]). Standards for user-centric authorization and consent management[12,13] exist today in the identity industry, and can be the basis for managing subject consent in data repositories.

- *Decentralized data architectures.* By leaving raw data in its repository, the OPAL paradigm points towards a decentralized architecture for datastores.[14] Decentralized data architectures based on standardized interfaces/APIs should be applicable to personal datastores as legitimate endpoints—that is, the OPAL paradigm should be applicable regardless of the size of the dataset.

User-Centric Consent and Decentralized Control

As mentioned previously, one of the key principles of OPAL is to leave data in its repository, thereby pointing to the need for a decentralized architecture for datastores. Related to this decentralized architecture is the need to empower *data subjects*[6] to consent to their data being included in the execution of an algorithm. Aside from proper informed consent to the subject and remuneration for use of their data, there is the important question of the standard mechanisms used to implement consent management.

The *User-Managed Access* (UMA) standard[12,15] is a set of standard specifications designed to give an individual or organization a *unified control point* for authorizing access to their resources (including data) regardless of their physical location. The UMA standard, based on the OAuth 2.0 framework for authorization,[16] was created to address the common problem today of the user having many of their resources (e.g., files, photos, calendars, etc.) spread at different locations on the Internet and controlled by different service providers.

The UMA architecture provides suitable points in the protocol message flows in which to embed consent-request actions, consent-receipt issuance, and the *terms of use* (terms of service) of the resources being made accessible to the requester. The terms of use can be a legally binding contract issued by the subject whose personal data is being used. The terms can include the limited purpose of use of the data or insights derived, the duration of use, and other aspects such as copyright, licensing, and remuneration to the subject.

A typical example of UMA is the user (Alice) who wishes to share her files as a *protected resource* with another user (Bob). Alice also wishes to share her calendar (another of her protected resource) with her friend Carol. Alice manages these files and calendars on a web application called a *resource server*. The other entities that wish to access Alice's protected resources are called the *requesting parties*. These employ client applications to attempt access. With UMA, Alice can manage all these types of sharing in a unified way, from a single web application point of control called an *authorization server*. She can set policies that guide the authorization server in allowing or disallowing access by clients to protected resources at resource servers.

In the context of OPAL, the consent requested from a subject is a consent for execution of an algorithm, not the general "consent to access" that today typically means permission to copy data to another location or to another entity. We believe the UMA model provides a promising avenue for managing consent for execution. The OPAL paradigm differentiates between two categories of algorithms:

- *Aggregate algorithms*. This refers to an algorithm that by specification returns aggregate answers only. Responses to aggregate queries must never allow identification or re-identification of individuals from the data.

- *Subject-specific algorithms*. This refers to an algorithm that by specification returns identifying information or other insights about a specific individual.

In both types of queries, different degrees of consent will be needed. For aggregate algorithms, the data subject must be properly be informed that a collection of vetted algorithms may be run on a set of data, which includes the subject's personal data. For subject-specific algorithms, an informed consent will be required from the subject (i.e., individual or organization), and a *consent-receipt*[13] must be returned by the subject. Note that in many cases it may be the subjects themselves that initiated a request that necessitated the execution of subject-specific algorithms.

For example, when Alice seeks to obtain a loan (e.g., a home mortgage), it is common for the loan originator (e.g., mortgage company or bank) to perform risk assessment for Alice. This allows the loan originator to make a risk-based decision regarding the loan requested by Alice. As such, Alice may be requested by the loan originator to preauthorize the execution of subject-specific algorithms at multiple data providers (e.g., credit card issuer, bank, telecommunications company, etc.). The point here is to correctly inform Alice of: (1) what the vetted algorithm computes (e.g., average monthly credit card expenditures); (2) the purpose of the execution (e.g., to complete the loan application); (3) the intended recipient of the result (e.g., the mortgage company, Alice's bank, etc.); and (4) the duration of time of keeping the results (e.g., mortgage company needs to keep results for seven years for taxation purposes).

By employing the OPAL paradigm for personal data, coupled with an unambiguous user-centric (rather than access-based) control model, the UMA architecture provides a way to satisfy many regulatory requirements (e.g., GDPR) and answers many of the challenges posed in the 2011 WEF Report[17] regarding personal data as the new asset class.

Chain of Verifiability
An important aspect of using data and algorithms to compute insights is the notion of the provenance and quality of the data (and algorithm) used to derive the insights.[18] There is also the legal aspect of signing an assertion containing an insight. The question pertains as to whether by digitally signing an assertion (e.g., in JSON format) the signer is making a truthful claim about the information in the assertion and whether therefore the signer takes on legal liabilities for issuing the signed assertion. This is particularly relevant as individuals are affected by the assertion.

Therefore, being able to trace back the origins or provenance of all data and all algorithms in the signer's infrastructure or system represents a valuable tool for all entities in the identity ecosystem. Ideally, there need to be mechanisms and protocols that allow the *chain of verifiability* (chain of provenance) to be established for every assertion issued and signed. This chain of verifiability must support tracing back to the various data, algorithms, and processes used to derive the insight that went into the assertion.

A strong chain of verifiability can be achieved using the appropriate combination of: (1) highly private and accurate personal data as held by one of more data providers (e.g., in a data federation or trust network); (2) resilient log and audit mechanisms (e.g., based on blockchains) that keep a truthful history of the use of data, algorithms, processes, and subject consent; (3) the creation of assertions using the OPAL method of safe-answers based on data of known origin in the trust network; and (4) the use of transaction identifiers that have privacy-preserving properties. These components collectively support the establishment of a chain of verifiability that allows not only the relying party to validate the provenance of transaction identifiers and assertions, but also provides entities in the ecosystem a means to satisfy regulatory requirements.

The chain of verifiability or "chain of provenance" is a notion borrowed from both the field of historical analysis and the field of art. In computer technology, the term began to be commonly used in trusted computing[19] in the late 1990s to denote methods or mechanisms to prove the manufacturing origin of hardware and software components, especially components that perform crucial tasks in security-related computations (e.g., digital signatures, encryption). The notion of signed "manifests"[20,21] was used in this context as a means to capture the components that make up a trusted platform.

Privacy-Preserving Identifiers
One open problem with the use of plain transaction identifiers (e.g., within assertions) is the possibility for different transaction identifiers from different personas of a single user to be used to re-identify the user, thereby possibly affecting the personal privacy of the user. A more promising type of digital identifier is one that is cryptographically anonymous but has verifiable properties.[22,23,24,25] A transaction identifier can be said to have strong privacy-preserving properties if it is *unlinkable* across transactions and anonymous but verifiable to be source-authentic.

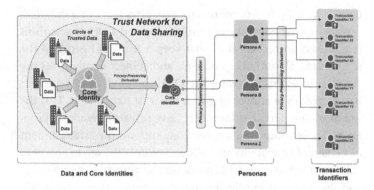

FIGURE 3.4
CoreID and privacy-preserving identifiers.

Over the past two decades there have been several proposed schemes for anonymous identity systems and protocols. One scheme that has been developed into product is the *Enhanced Privacy ID* (EPID) system from Intel corporation.[26] The EPID scheme was intended to provide a certain degree of anonymity for hardware identifiers inside the TPM (v1.2) chip (Trusted Platform Module).[27] The goal was to prevent the tracking of TPM hardware when they are deployed in the field within personal computers and mobile devices.

The basic idea is that N transaction identifiers are generated using a cryptographic protocol that allows the holder (user) to maintain and manage only one set of private keying parameters. Each of these transaction identifiers can then be used publicly by the user, for example, under different personas or for different circumstances. A recipient (counterparty) in a transaction who receives one or more distinct identifiers from this group of N identifiers will not be able to deduce (i.e., link) that these originated from the same group of N identifiers belonging to the same sender (user). Thus, the approach provides anonymity of the user and unlinkability of these identifiers.

The EPID scheme itself is an extension of the *Direct Anonymous Attestation* (DAA)[28] protocol, which is a protocol specifically designed to provide anonymity to the holders of keying material. The EPID protocol can be deployed without TPM hardware, with the option to add and enable a tamper-resistant TPM at a later stage. The intent was to provide service providers with the option to deploy it initially without TPM hardware, and then later add the hardware in a phased approach.[20,29]

EPID is not the only anonymous identity protocol available today. The work of Brickell et al.[28] introduced the first RSA-based DAA protocol in 2004. A related anonymity protocol called *Idemix*[23] employs the same RSA-based anonymous credential scheme as the DAA protocol. Another related protocol called U-Prove[30] can be integrated into the TPMv2.0 hardware.[31] However, the U-Prove protocol has the drawback that it is not multi-show unlinkable,[32] which means that a U-Prove token may only be used once in order to remain unlinkable.

Related to anonymous-verifiable transaction identifiers are anonymous-verifiable attributes.[23,33] This capability allows a user (persona) to present to a counterparty an anonymous transaction identifier coupled with one or more anonymous attribute assertions, and for the counterparty to have reasonable assurance as to the truthfulness of the attribute information stated in the enveloping assertion.

These approaches may be useful for the emerging blockchain technologies that require privacy of parties who are performing a transaction on a shared or public blockchain system.[34] Since the distributed ledger maintained by every node in the blockchain system holds transaction data that are essentially publicly readable (or at best group-readable in a private blockchain), anonymous-verifiable identifiers can at least hide the true identity of the parties involved in the transaction. More sophisticated solutions will be needed to keep the contents of the smart contract agreement just as private.

IDENTITY FEDERATION: A BRIEF HISTORY

Today *Identity and Access Management* (IAM) represents a core component of the Internet. IAM infrastructures allow organizations to maintain entity identifiers (e.g., humans, devices, networks) in order to enable the pursuit of their goals. The IAM industry typically distinguishes between enterprise systems and consumer-facing systems.

Enterprise-IAM (E-IAM) is already a mature product category[35] and E-IAM systems are already well integrated into other enterprise infrastructures, such as directory services for managing employees and corporate assets. The primary goal of E-IAM systems is to authenticate and identify persons (e.g., employees) and devices as they enter the enterprise boundary, and to enforce authorizations (entitlements) and access control driven by corporate policies.

In the case of Consumer-IAM (C-IAM) systems, the primary goal is to reduce friction between the consumer and the online service provider (e.g., merchant) through a mediated-authentication process. The label for this consumer-facing entity that performs mediated-authentication is the "identity provider," which we believe is a misleading label. However, this label has been used widely as accepted terminology by the industry for over two decades now. In reality, an "identity provider" does not create or bequeath an identity to the user. Instead, they issue (transaction) *identifiers* only to the consumers.

Identifiers, Namespaces, and Resolvers

There is a long history of the use of digital identifiers that corresponds to the history of the Internet, and most notably to the history of domain names.[36] Within the area of networking, the use of IEEE802 MAC addresses (a 48-bit *media access control* address) at the physical layer became a necessity when the network interface controller (NIC) for communications became popular with the expansion of IP networking. The 48-bit addressing scheme used for MAC addresses represents an early model of namespaces or scopes.

A *namespace* is way of *logically grouping unique identifiers* or symbols that have meaning only within the context of that namespace. Thus, an identifier defined in a namespace is associated with and meaningful within that namespace only. In other words, it is a technical way to limit the scope of the meaning of an identifier. For example, a 16-digit credit card number has meaning or scope of usage within the card payments industry. The same identifier on its own could be used elsewhere on the Internet (or in computer systems attached to the Internet), but that identifier will only be meaningful in that context or in that namespace. As such, we say that an identifier defined in one namespace has a different meaning as the same identifier defined in another namespace.

As an example, an email address structure consists of the recipient's (person's) identifier followed by the absolute domain name where that email identifier is meaningful. Thus, the email address joe@domain1.com is different from joe@domain2.com because the domains (i.e., the namespaces) of the identifier joe are different. In the design of the Internet, the term *fully qualified domain name* (FQDN)[37] is used to denote a domain name that specifies its exact location in the tree hierarchy of the global Domain Name System (DNS). Similarly, the Universal Resource Identifiers (URIs)[38] and Uniform Resource Locators (URLs)[39] represent a way to uniquely identify resources within namespaces. Other examples include the Digital Object Identifier (DOI),[40] which is a persistent identifier used to uniquely identify objects, and the XML namespace, which is used for providing uniquely named elements and attributes within an XML document.

Some systems employ *resolver* services to map from one name (namespace) to another. For example, the Domain Name Service (DNS) includes a resolver that translates a domain name into an

IP address. Similarly, the *handle* system[41] is a resolver that translates DOIs into other information needed to locate the target object identified by the DOI. More recently, the same notion of unique identifiers and namespaces has been proposed in the Decentralized Identifiers (DID) concept.[42] Similar to X.509 Certificates[43] and X.509 Attribute Certificates,[44] a DID document contains an identifier (in the DID namespace), a public key, an owner-identifier, and pointers to services that can process the DID.

There are several lessons learned from the history of identifiers and namespaces in the Internet. First, identifiers and namespaces are necessary to uniquely distinguish objects, to reach them, and to provide services. There are different forms of identifiers employed in the IP stack (e.g., MAC addresses, IP addresses, user email addresses), each with its own scope of usage or namespace. Second, these identifiers are really transaction identifiers because they do not imply any additional data regarding its owner or assignee (e.g., human person). Third, the history of the Internet has shown that it is good architectural design to separate (1) the scheme to allocate identifiers from (2) the mechanisms used to map an identifier to other contextual data (e.g., attributes of a person, authorization information). Finally, it is also good architectural practice to separate mechanisms for managing identifiers and contextual data from the mechanisms to manage *control* over those constructs and their usage.

Web Single Sign-On and Identity Providers

Historically, the notion of the *Identity Provider* entity (IdP) emerged starting in the late 1990s in response to the growing need to aid users in accessing services online. During this early period, a user would typically create an account and credentials at every new service provider (e.g., online merchant). This cumbersome approach, which is still in practice today, has led to a proliferation of accounts and duplication of the same user attributes across many service providers.

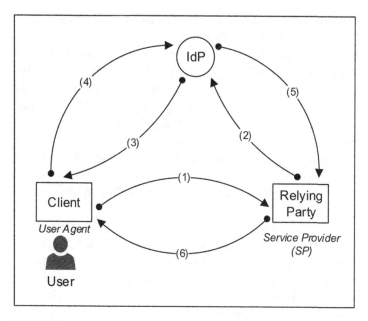

FIGURE 3.5
Overview of Web Single Sign On (Web-SSO).

The solution that emerged became what is known today as *Web Single Sign-On* (Web- SSO).[45] The idea is that a trusted third party referred to as the identity provider would mediate the authentication of the user on behalf of the service provider. This is summarized in Figure 3.5. When a user visits a merchant website (step 1), the user would be redirected to the IdP to perform authentication (steps 2–4). After the completion of a successful authentication event, the IdP would redirect the user's browser back to the calling merchant (step 5), accompanied by an IdP-signed assertion stating that the IdP has successfully authenticated the user. The merchant would then proceed in transacting with the user (step 6).

In order to standardize this protocol behavior, in 2001 an alliance of over 150 companies and organizations formed an industry consortium called the Liberty Alliance Project. The main goal of this consortium was to "establish standards, guidelines and best practices for identity management."[46] Several significant outcomes for the IAM industry resulted from the Liberty Alliance, two among which were: (1) the standardization of the *Security Assertions Markup Language* (SAML 2.0),[47] and (2) the creation of a widely used open source SAML 2.0 server implementation called Shibboleth.[48]

Today SAML 2.0 remains the predominant Web-SSO technology used within Enterprise IAM, which is directly related to the type of authentication protocol dominant in enterprise directory services.[49,50,51]

In the Consumer IAM space, the growth of the web applications industry has spurred the creation of the OAuth 2.0 framework[16] based on JSON web tokens. Similar to the SSO pattern, the purpose of this framework is to authenticate and authorize an "application" to access a user's "resources." The OAuth 2.0 model follows the traditional notion of *delegation* where the user as the resource-owner authorizes an application, such as a web application or mobile application, to access the user's resources (e.g., files, calendar, other accounts, etc.). In contrast to SAML 2.0, which requires the user to be present at the browser to interact with the service provider, in OAuth 2.0 the user can disconnect after he or she authorizes the application to access his or her resources. In effect the user is delegating control to the application (to perform some defined task) in the absence of the user.

Although the OAuth 2.0 design as defined in the RFC lacks details for practical implementation and deployment, a full-fledged system is defined in the OpenID-Connect 1.0 protocol[52] specification based on the OAuth 2.0 model. It is this OpenID-Connect 1.0 protocol (or variations of it) that is today deployed by the major social media platforms in the Consumer-IAM space.

Identity and Authentication Federation

The notion of federation among identity providers arose from a number of practical needs, one being that of the scaling of services. The idea is straightforward and extends from the previous scenario of a user seeking access to a service provider or relying party (e.g., online merchant). This is shown in Figure 3.6. The problem was simply the following: when the relying party

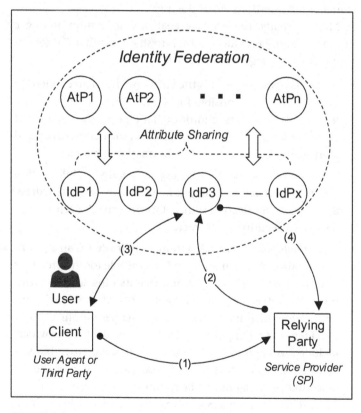

FIGURE 3.6
Classic identity federation and attribute sharing.

directed the user to an IdP with whom the relying party has a business relationship, there was a chance that the user will be unknown to that IdP. As such, the solution is for a group of IdPs to "network together" in such a way that when one IdP is faced with an unknown user, the IdP can inquire with other IdPs in the federation. The federation model opens up other interesting possibilities, including the possible introduction of the so-called *Attribute Provider* (AtP) entity whose primary task is to issue additional useful assertions about the user.

More formally, the primary goal of a federation among a group of identity providers (IdPs) is to share "attribute" information (assertions) regarding a user:[10,53]

- An *identity provider* (IdP) is the entity (within a given identity system) that is responsible for the identification of persons, legal entities, devices, and/or digital objects, the issuance of corresponding identity credentials, and the maintenance and management of such identity information for subjects.

- An *attribute* is a specific category of identifying information about a subject or user. Examples for users include name, address, age, gender, title, salary, health, net worth, driver's license number, Social Security number, etc.

- An *attribute provider* (AtP) is a third party trusted as an authoritative source of information and responsible for the processes associated with establishing and maintaining identity attributes. An attribute provider asserts trusted, validated attribute claims in response to attribute requests from identity providers and relying parties. Examples of attribute providers include a government title registry, a national credit bureau, or a commercial marketing database. An example of the list of attributes or claims can be found in the OpenID-Connect 1.0 core specifications (Section 5.1 on Standard Claims[52]) for federations deploying the OpenID-Connect architecture.

- An *identity federation* is the set of technology, standards, policies, and processes that allow an organization to trust digital identities, identity attributes, and credentials created and issued by another organization. A federated identity system allows the sharing of identity credentials issued, and identity information asserted, by one or more identity providers with multiple relying parties.

• A *relying party or service provider* is system entity that decides to take an action based on information from another system entity. For example, a *Security Assertion Markup Language* (or SAML) relying party depends on receiving assertions from an authoritative asserting party (an identity provider) about a subject.[10]

Although the federated identity model using the SSO flow pattern remains the predominant model today for the browser in the consumer space, there remain several issues with regards to data regarding individuals. One key issue pertains to consent and consent management,[6] and the limited visibility and control users have regarding the flow of their data. Today the user is typically "out of the loop" in terms of consent regarding the information being asserted to by an identity provider or attribute provider. Over the past few years several efforts have sought to address the issue of user control and consent.[12,13,15] The idea here is that not only should the user explicitly consent to his or her attributes being shared, the underlying identity system should also ensure that only minimal disclosure is performed for a constrained use among justifiable parties.[54,55] However, the problem of consent is not only a technical issue, but also a legal and regulatory matter.[56]

OPAL FOR IDENTITY FEDERATION

We believe the OPAL paradigm can provide a foundation for entities in the data ecosystem to share insights associated with an identifier (namely, individuals or organizations) in a privacy-preserving manner, based on both the correct alignment of incentives and strong consent principles.

Data provider organizations should establish OPAL trust networks (circles of trust) for the sharing of insights, as part of the identity-verification workflow. Figure 3.7 provides a high-level illustration, where a querier (e.g., mortgage service) is seeking insights regarding an individual. The querier engages the OPAL trust network (e.g., specializing in financial information) to obtain information about the individual (e.g., credit score). The querier selects the appropriate algorithm(s) from the vetted algorithms collection published by that trust network (figure 3.7, step (a)), and requests the execution of those selected algorithms, possibly accompanied by payments in step (b). After the algorithms have been executed by the relevant data providers in the trust network, a response is provided to the querier in step (c). The response may also include various metadata embellishments, such as the duration of the validity of the response (e.g., for dynamically changing datasets), identification of the datasets used, consent-receipts, timestamps, and so on.

There are a number of interesting aspects to the OPAL trust network as shown in figure 3.7:

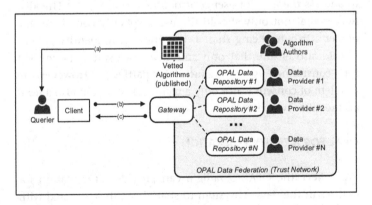

FIGURE 3.7
Trust network based on OPAL.

- *Algorithms instead of attributes.* Rather than delivering static attributes (e.g. "Joe is a resident of NY City") to the relying party, allow instead the relying party (querier) to choose one or more vetted algorithms for a given data domain.

- *Convergence of federations.* Identity federation networks should engage OPAL trust networks in a collaborative manner, with the goal of obtaining higher value for their customers and better services for users (e.g., through more accurate assertions).

    The goal should be to bring together data providers from different domains or verticals (e.g., telecommunications data, health data, finance data, etc.) in such a manner that new insights can be derived about a subject with their consent based on the OPAL paradigm. Research has shown, for example, that combining location data with credit card data offers new insights into the financial wellbeing of a user[57]—with better accuracy than with credit card data alone.

- *Apply correct pricing models for algorithms and data.* For each algorithm and the data to which the algorithm applies, a correct pricing structure needs to be developed by the members of the trust network. This is not only to remunerate the data repositories for managing the datasets and for executing the algorithm (i.e., CPU usage), but also to encourage data owners to develop new business models based on the OPAL paradigm.

    Pricing information could be published as part of the vetted algorithms declaration (e.g., as metadata), offering different tiers of pricing for different sizes of datasets. For example, the price for obtaining insights into the creditworthiness of a subject based solely on their credit card data should be different from the price for obtaining insights based on combined datasets across domains (e.g., appropriate combination of GPS dataset and credit card dataset).[58]

- *Remunerate data subjects.* A correct alignment of incentives must be found for all stakeholders in the ecosystem. Subjects (users) should see some meaningful and measurable return on the use of their data, even if it is in tiny amounts (e.g., pennies or sub-pennies per algorithm execution). The point here is that people will contribute more access to personal data in the OPAL paradigm if they are active participants in the ecosystem and understand the legal protections offered by the legal frameworks that govern the trust network and govern the treatment of their personal data by member data providers.

• *Logs for audit, transparency, and regulatory compliance.* All requests and responses must be logged, together with strong audit capabilities. Emerging technologies such as blockchains and distributed ledgers could be expanded to effect an efficient but immutable log of events. Such a log will be relevant for postevent auditing and for proving regulatory compliance. Logging and audit are also crucial in order to obtain social acceptance and consent from individuals whose data is present within a data repository. Users as stakeholders in the ecosystem must be able to see what data is present within these repositories and to see who is accessing their data through the execution of vetted algorithms.

Currently the OPAL model continues to be deployed in research projects related to MIT Connection Science in the countries of Colombia and Senegal. The first commercial deployment of the OPAL model in the finance industry was launched in 2017 by FortifID.com in Silicon Valley, California.

TRUST FRAMEWORK FOR OPAL FEDERATION

Today legal frameworks for identity management and federation in the United States are based on three types or "layers" of law.[59] The foundational layer is the general commercial law that consists of legal rules that are applicable to identity management systems and transactions. This general commercial law was not created specifically for identity management, but instead is public law written and enacted by governments that applies to all identity systems and their participants—and is thus enforceable in courts.

The second "layer" consists of general identity system law. Such law is written to govern all identity systems within its scope. The intent is to address the various issues related to the operations of the identity systems. The recognition of the need for law at this layer is new, perhaps reflecting the slow pace of development in the legal arena as compared to the technology space. An example of this is the Virginia Electronic Identity Management Act,[60] which was enacted in 2016.

The third "layer" is the set of applicable legal rules and system-specific rules (i.e., specific to the identity system in question). The term "trust framework" is often used to refer to these system rules that have been adopted by the community. A trust framework is needed for a group of entities to govern their collective behavior, regardless whether the identity system is operated by the government or the private sector. In the case of a private sector identity system, the governing body (consisting of the participants in the system) typically drafts rules that take the form of *contracts-based rules*, based on private law.

Examples of trust frameworks for identity federation today are FICAM for federal employees,[61] SAFE-BioPharma Association[62] for the biopharmaceutical industry, and the OpenID-Exchange (OIX)[59] for federation based on the OpenID-Connect 1.0 model.

In order for an OPAL-based information sharing federation to be developed, it should use and expand the current existing legal trust frameworks for identity systems. This is because the overall goal is for entities to obtain richer information regarding a user (subject), and as such it must be bound to the specific identity system rules. In other words, a new set of third layer legal rules and system-specific rules must be devised that must clearly articulate the required combination of technical standards and systems, business processes and procedures, and legal rules that, taken together, establish a trustworthy system[53] for information sharing based on the OPAL model. It is here that system-specific rules regarding the "amount of private information released" must be created by the federation community, involving all stakeholders including the users (subjects).

Taking the parallel of an identity system, an OPAL-based information sharing system must address the following:

- Verifying the correct matching between an identity (connected to a human, legal entity, device, or digital object) and the set of data in a repository pertaining to that identity.

- Providing the correct result from an OPAL-based computation to the party that requires it to complete a transaction.

- Maintaining and protecting the private data within repositories over its lifecycle.

- Defining the legal framework that specifies the rights and responsibilities of the parties, allocates risk, and provides a basis for enforcement.

Similar to—and building upon—an identity system's operating rules, new additional operating rules need to be created for an OPAL-based information sharing system. There are two components to this. The first is the business and technical operational rules and specifications necessary to make the OPAL-based system functional and trustworthy. The second is the contract-based legal rules that (in addition to applicable laws and regulations) define the rights and legal obligations of the parties specific to the OPAL-based system and facilitate enforcement where necessary.

A recent development relevant to the area of personal data and fiduciary relationships is the Vermont Act Related to Blockchain Business Development (S.269, May 2018). The law introduces two completely new types of business entities. The first is a *blockchain-based limited liability company* (BBLLC), and the second a *personal information protection company* (PIPC). The Vermont Act allows blockchain companies to protect owners, managers, and blockchain participants from unwarranted liability by forming BBLLCs. It also gives blockchain companies an enforceable legal framework to create custom blockchain governance structures that perfectly fit their unique technology and circumstances.

The law also creates a legal structure that appeals to companies handling personal information by offering assurances to both consumers and third parties engaged with a PIPC. PIPCs are now required to elevate the interests of consumers providing public information above their own interests. Vermont's law creates a new framework where individuals providing information to PIPCs have assurances through statute and regulation as to the proper use of their personal information.

SELF-ISSUED IDENTIFIERS, PUBLIC KEYS, AND RISK MANAGEMENT

The recent rise of Bitcoin[63] and its use of self-issued and self-asserted public key pairs created an interesting side-effect in the form of public excitement about self-issued identifiers and public keys. This confusion regarding the difference between an identity (in the true sense) versus digital identifiers is reminiscent of a similar confusion in the late 1990s where X.509 certificates were marketed as identities. In reality, public keys (with or without X.509 certificates) used on a blockchain system are simply identifiers that have the extra benefit that the possession of the matching private key can be proven through an authentication protocol (e.g., SSL/TLS) or a common-key establishment protocol (e.g., IKE). The public key itself says nothing about the true identity of its wielder, nor insights about its human owner.[64]

The use of self-issued public keys is not a new concept. It was first proposed and deployed in the mid-1990s in the *Pretty Good*

Privacy (PGP) system,[65] combined with the notion of the *web of trust*. The idea is that instead of relying on a single trusted third party such as a Certificate Authority (CA) to issue X.509 digital certificates[43] a user would simply self-generate the public key pair using the appropriate software tools and then declare the public key (claim ownership) to the user's friends and colleagues.

Some standards organizations, notably the Internet Engineering Task Force (IETF) held (and continue to hold) events called PGP "key signing parties" at every meeting (typically three times per year). In these events, the person issuing the (PGP) public key would go on stage publicly to verbally claim ownership of a public key. In turn, his or her friends and colleagues would vouch in front of the community about person's real-world identity. They would then add the person's public key to their PGP "key ring" (i.e., collection of known and vouched public keys). Today, the PGP system remains in use in some technical communities, notably for email signing (S/MIME) and for software/ firmware authenticity verification (i.e., digital signature).

Although the notion of the web of trust maybe attractive from a technical perspective, what is absent is the crucial notion of *risk assessment* from the perspective of the counterparty who receives objects (e.g., files, transactions, data) signed using a self-issued PGP key. It is the counterparty that has to decide the degree of trustworthiness to be accorded to a received self-issued public key. It is the counterparty that has to decide whether to proceed with the transaction or to decline continuing the engagement flow. Here, the minimal definition of "trustworthiness" means the correct correspondence (mapping) between the public key and its owner (person or organization) in the real world. Most business transactions with high monetary value require a way for both parties to quantify risks associated with this mapping function, as failure in this mapping can mean real monetary loss (e.g., a bogus mapping of a public key to a counterparty leads to theft and monetary loss). It is for this reason the concept of the web of trust failed to gained traction in industry because the vouching of a public key by friends and colleagues was deemed to possess insufficient weight for a business transaction.

In contrast, the model adopted by industry—most notably the financial industry—is that of a *Hierarchical Certificate Authority* model.[66] In the hierarchical CA model, an enterprise or corporation would arrange all its public keys in a hierarchy that often mirrors the organizational divisions, functions, and groups within the organization. At the root of the (inverted) hierarchy tree there would be a *root certificate* (usually in the X.509 standard format), whose private key would be used to sign the other X.509 certificates underneath it in the hierarchy. As such, one could say that all certificates in a hierarchical CA arrangement "chain up" to the root certificate. In the early days of X.509 certificates, many organizations would self-issue and self-sign their root keys and root CA certificate.

Although this model of self-signed root certificates works for intra-enterprise needs, problems arose in cross-enterprise engagements and transactions. For example, when an employee digitally signs a document or email using their employee certificate (i.e., the private key) and sends it outside the organization, the recipient would face difficulty in assessing the trustworthiness of the root certificate that was self-signed by the employee's organization.

In order to solve this acute dilemma, a new breed of services emerged in the early 2000s the goal of which was to bridge this cross-enterprise certificates problem. These services became known as public *Certificate Authorities* (CA) service providers. In this approach, an enterprise would purchase a corporate-level root X.509 certificate that was issued (signed) by the CA service provider. The rest of the intra-enterprise employee certificate issuance followed the same arrangement as before. In its turn, the CA service provider would make its own (self-signed) root CA certificate to be ubiquitously present in as many mediums as possible. This includes the publication of the CA's root certificate in newspapers, website, and software distributions, and its inclusion in browser configurations.

Aside for the service of issuing root certificates for organizations, the CA service provider would also provide a "blacklisting" service for compromised certificates (i.e., any lost or stolen private key of the certificate). For example, when an employee loses the private key of his or her certificate, the employee must immediately notify the CA service provider (who issued the root certificate of the employee's company). This blacklisting service is also known as the *Certificate Revocation List* (CRL).[43] The CRL mechanism provides a way for a recipient of a signed document, email or transaction to first validate the status of the signer's certificate to the CRL service.

A crucial component of the CA service providers model is their role in helping their customers to quantify risks in using the CA-issued public keys and certificates. A mature CA service provider business typically publishes a document referred to as the *Certificate Practices Statement* (CPS).[67] The CPS would specify, among other things: (1) the process and mechanisms used by the CA to issue root certificates; (2) the mechanisms used to protect stored copies (if any) of customer's private keys (e.g., using hardware security modules); (3) other protection mechanism to guard relevant keying material; (4) the performance level of their CRL service; (5) third-party audit process for the CA infrastructure; and (6) the warranties and liabilities (in dollar value) of the CA service should any private key in the possession of the CA is compromised (e.g., "maximum liability of USD $10 million for loss of private key of enterprise root certificate for companies with 50,000 employees or less"). It is this last aspect of placing dollar value liabilities on the CA that allows a CA's customers to perform risk management and even obtain insurance against the loss of private keys.

It is precisely this CPS aspect that was missing from the original web of trust model in the mid-1990s that prevented the model from being adopted in industry. Similarly, any effort today of rebooting the web of trust model, either using blockchain technology or otherwise, must address this risk and liabilities question before it will be adopted by industry and businesses.

SUMMARY: CALL TO ACTION

There are number of steps that can be initiated today towards engineering the building blocks of digital identity technologies for the future:

- *Personal data, core identity, personas, and identifiers.* There needs to be a conscious effort on the part of technical communities, technologists, standards organizations, "identerati," and industry in general to use appropriate concepts and correct terminology in the context of digital identity and personal data.

- *Open Algorithms for preserving privacy.* Refine and deploy the OPAL principles in various industry verticals for data relevant in that domain. Data providers need to see that their data increases in value when combined with relevant data from different but compatible domains. The OPAL paradigm provides a way forward to combine data from different domains while preserving privacy and complying with regulatory requirements.

- *Trust networks for data federation for identity.* Data providers can establish new sources of revenue by establishing industry trust networks based on the OPAL principles, creating assertions about individuals and organizations in a transparent manner with the consent of subjects.

- *User-centric control.* An important aspect in the success of trust networks is the proper inclusion of individuals as equal stakeholders in the ecosystem. Empowering individuals to control usage of their personal data while providing shared revenue for the use of their data provides a good basis for the development of new incentive models for the trust network ecosystem.

- *New legal trust frameworks for personal data.* New legal frameworks for sharing insights based on the OPAL paradigm need to be developed and refined. Such legal frameworks could be based on and extend existing trust frameworks that are already in use in industry. Such frameworks must address not only personal data rich in Personal Identifying Information (PII), but also corporate data that may need to be shared within a trust network in a privacy-preserving manner.

  Here, we believe that a number of industry verticals (e.g., finance and banking, health, etc.) are suitably positioned to establish these new legal frameworks, which will in turn benefit the trust network members by introducing new kinds of insights previously unattainable.

- *New incentive models for ecosystem participants.* New models of incentives need to be developed that embrace the user/consumer as a stakeholder in the ecosystem and that incentivize them to share higher quality data in a privacy-preserving manner.

  With the emergence of IoT devices and the growth in data generated from consumer IoT devices (e.g., home appliances, medical devices, etc.), the need for consumer privacy and therefore consent and buy-in from consumers will become pressing matters.

REFERENCES

1. Haber, S., and W. S. Stornetta. 1991. "How to Time-Stamp a Digital Document." In *Advances in Cryptology—Proceedings of CRYPTO'90* (LNCS 537), edited by A. J. Menezes and S. A. Vanstone, 437–455. Berlin, Heidelberg: Springer.

2. Bayer, D., S. Haber, and W. Stornetta. 1993. "Improving the Efficiency and Reliability of Digital Time-Stamping." In *Sequences II: Methods in Communication, Security and Computer Science*, edited by R. Capocelli, A. DeSantis, and U. Vaccaro, 329–334. New York: Springer-Verlag.

3. The White House. 2011. "National Strategy for Trusted Identities in Cyberspace: Enhancing Online Choice, Efficiency, Security, and Privacy." http://www.whitehouse.gov/sites/default/files/rssviewer/NSTIC-strategy 041511.pdf.

4. Abelson, R., and M. Goldstein. 2015. "Millions of Anthem Customers Targeted in Cyberattack." *New York Times*, February 5. https://www .nytimes.com/2015/02/05/business/hackers-breached-data-of-millions -insurer-says.html.

5. Bernard, T. S., T. Hsu, N. Perlroth, and R. Lieber. 2017. "Equifax Says Cyberattack May Have Affected 143 Million in the U.S," *New York Times*, September 7. https://www.nytimes.com/2017/09/07/business/equifax -cyberattack.html.

6. European Commission. 2016. "Regulation (EU) 2016/679 of the European Parliament and of the Council of 27 April 2016 on the Protection of Natural Persons with Regard to the Processing of Personal Data and on the Free Movement of Such Data (General Data Protection Regulation)." *Official Journal of the European Union* L119: 1–88.

7. Hardjono, T., and A. Pentland. 2018. "Open Algorithms for Identity Federation." In *Proceedings of the IEEE Future of Information and Communication Conference*, Singapore, April. https://arxiv.org/pdf/1705.10880.pdf.

8. Hardjono, T., D. Greenwood, and A. Pentland. 2013. "Towards a Trustworthy Digital Infrastructure for Core Identities and Personal Data Stores." Presented at ID360 Conference on Identity, University of Texas, April.

9. The Jericho Forum. "Identity Commandments." 2011. The Open Group. Available on www.opengroup.org.

10. OASIS. March 2005. "Glossary for the OASIS Security Assertion Markup Language (SAML) V2.0." http://docs.oasis-open.org/security/saml /v2.0/samlglossary-2.0-os.pdf.

11. Pentland, A., D. Shrier, T. Hardjono, and I. Wladawsky-Berger. 2016. "Towards an Internet of Trusted Data: Input to the Whitehouse Commission on Enhancing National Cybersecurity." In *Trust::Data—A New Framework for Identity and Data Sharing*, edited by T. Hardjono, A. Pentland, and D. Shrier, 21–49. Boston: Visionary Future.

12. Hardjono, T., E. Maler, M. Machulak, and D. Catalano. April 2015. "User-Managed Access (UMA) Profile of OAuth 2.0—Specification Version 1.0." Kantara Initiative, Kantara Published Specification. https://docs.kantarainitiative.org/uma/rec-uma-core.html.

13. Lizar, M., and D. Turner, 2017. "Consent Receipt Specification Version 1.0," March. https://kantarainitiative.org/confluence/display/infosharing/Home.

14. Pentland, A. 2014. "Saving Big Data from Itself." *Scientific American*, August, 65–68.

15. Maler, E., M. Machulak, and J. Richer. 2017. "User-Managed Access (UMA) 2.0." Kantara Initiative, Kantara Published Specification, January. https://docs.kantarainitiative.org/uma/ed/uma-core-2.0-10.html.

16. Hardt, D. 2012. "The OAuth 2.0 Authorization Framework." RFC6749, October. http://tools.ietf.org/rfc/rfc6749.txt

17. World Economic Forum. 2011. "Personal Data: The Emergence of a New Asset Class." http://www.weforum.org/reports/personal-data-emergence-new-asset-class.

18. Hardjono, T., and A. Pentland. 2016. "On Privacy-Preserving Identity within Future Blockchain Systems." W3C Workshop on Distributed Ledgers on the Web. Cambridge, MA: W3C, June. https://www.w3.org/2016/04/blockchain-workshop.

19. Trusted Computing Group. 2003. "TPM Main—Part 1 Design Principles—Specification Version 1.2." TCG Published Specification, October. http://www.trustedcomputinggroup.org/resources/tpm_main_specification.

20. Hardjono, T., and N. Smith, eds. 2005. "TCG Infrastructure Reference Architecture for Interoperability (Part 1)—Specification Version 1.0 Rev 1.0," June. http://www.trustedcomputinggroup.org/resources.

21. Hardjono, T., and N. Smith, eds. 2006. "TCG Infrastructure Working Group Architecture (Part 2)—Integrity Management—Specification Version 1.0 Rev 1.0," November. http://www.trustedcomputinggroup.org /resources.

22. Brands, S. 1993. "Untraceable Off-Line Cash in Wallets with Observers." In *CRYPTO'93 Proceedings of the 13th Annual International Cryptology*, 302–318. Berlin: Springer-Verlag.

23. Camenisch, J., and E. Van Herreweghen. 2002. "Design and Implementation of the Idemix Anonymous Credential System." In *Proceedings of the 9th ACM conference on Computer and Communications Security*, 21–30. Washington, DC: ACM.

24. Hardjono, T., and A. Pentland. 2016. "Verifiable Anonymous Identities and Access Control in Permissioned Blockchains." Unpublished manuscript. arXiv:1903.04584. http://arxiv.org/abs/1903.04584

25. Hardjono, T., and N. Smith. 2016. "Cloud-Based Commissioning of Constrained Devices Using Permissioned Blockchains." In *Proceedings of the 2nd ACM International Workshop on IoT Privacy, Trust, and Security* (IoTPTS 2016), 29–36. Xi'an, China: ACM.

26. Brickell, E., and J. Li. 2012. "Enhanced Privacy ID: A Direct Anonymous Attestation Scheme with Enhanced Revocation Capabilities." *IEEE Transactions on Dependable and Secure Computing* 9 (3) 345–360.

27. Trusted Computing Group. 2003. "TPM Main—Specification Version 1.2." TCG Published Specification, October. http://www.trusted computinggroup.org/resources/tpmmainspecification.

28. Brickell, E., J. Camenisch, and L. Chen. 2004. "Direct Anonymous Attestation." In *Proceedings of the 11th ACM Conference on Computer and Communications Security CCS2004*, 132–145. Washington, DC: ACM.

29. Hardjono, T. 2004. "Infrastructure for Trusted Computing." In *Proceedings of ACSAC Workshop on Trusted Computing*, December. https:// www.acsac.org/2004/workshop/Thomas-Hardjono.pdf.

30. Microsoft Corporation. 2014. "U-Prove Cryptographic Specification v1.1 (Rev 3)." http://research.microsoft.com/en-us/projects/u-prove.

31. Chen, L., and J. Li. 2013. "Flexible and Scalable Digital Signatures in TPM 2.0." In *Proceedings of the 2013 ACM SIGSAC Conference on Computer and Communications Security* CCS2013, 37–48. Berlin: ACM.

32. Chen, L., and R. Urian. 2015. "DAA-A: Direct Anonymous Attestation with Attributes." In *Trust and Trustworthy Computing, Proceedings of 8th International Conference, TRUST 2015* (LNCS 9229), 228–245. Berlin: Springer-Verlag.

33. ABC4Trust. 2015. "ABC4Trust: Attribute-Based Credentials for Trust." https://abc4trust.eu.

34. Hardjono, T., and E. Maler. 2017. "Blockchain and Smart Contracts Report." Kantara Initiative, Report, June. https://kantarainitiative.org /confluence/display/BSC/Home.

35. Gartner, Inc. 2016. "2017 Planning Guide for Identity and Access Management." Report, October.

36. Mockapetris, P. 1983. "Domain Names: Concepts and Facilities." RFC0882, November. http://tools.ietf.org/rfc/rfc0882.txt.

37. Mockapetris, P. 1987. "Domain Names—Implementation and Specification." RFC1035, November. http://tools.ietf.org/rfc/rfc1035 .txt.

38. Berners-Lee, T. 1994. "Universal Resource Identifiers in WWW: A Unifying Syntax for the Expression of Names and Addresses of Objects on the Network as Used in the World-Wide Web." RFC1630, June. http:// tools.ietf.org/rfc/rfc1630.txt.

39. Berners-Lee, T., L. Masinter, and M. McCahill. 1994. "Uniform Resource Locators (URL)." RFC1738, December. http://tools.ietf.org/rfc /rfc1738.txt

40. Kahn, R., and R. Wilensky. 1995. "A Framework for Distributed Digital Object Services." *D-Lib Magazine*, May. http://www.cnri.reston.va.us /home/cstr/arch/k-w.html.

41. Sun, S., L. Lannom, and B. Boesch. 2003. "Handle System Overview." RFC3650, November. http://tools.ietf.org/rfc/rfc3650.txt.

42. Reed, D., and M. Sporny. 2018. "Decentralized Identifiers (DIDs) v0.11." W3C, Draft Community Group Report 09 July 2018. https://w3c -ccg.github.io/did-spec/.

43. Housley, R., W. Polk, W. Ford, and D. Solo. 2002. "Internet X.509 Public Key Infrastructure Certificate and Certificate Revocation List (CRL) Profile."RFC3280, April. http://tools.ietf.org/rfc/rfc3280.txt.

44. Farrell, S., and R. Housley. 2002. "An Internet Attribute Certificate Profile for Authorization." RFC3281, April. http://tools.ietf.org/rfc /rfc3281.txt.

45. OASIS. 2005. "Profiles for the OASIS Security Assertion Markup Language (SAML) V2.0," March. https://docs.oasis-open.org/security/saml /v2.0/saml-profiles-2.0-os.pdf.

46. "Liberty Alliance" (2001–2009). Accessed May 29, 2017. https://en .wikipedia.org/wiki/LibertyAlliance.

47. OASIS. 2005. "Assertions and Protocols for the OASIS Security Assertion Markup Language (SAML) V2.0," March. http://docs.oasisopen.org /security/saml/v2.0/saml-core-2.0-os.pdf.

48. Morgan, R. L., S. Cantor, S. Carmody, W. Hoehn, and K. Klingenstein. 2004. "Federated Security: The Shibboleth Approach." *EDUCAUSE Quarterly* 27 (4): 1217.

49. Neuman, C., T. Yu, S. Hartman, and K. Raeburn. 2005. "The Kerberos Network Authentication Service (V5)." RFC4120, July. http://tools .ietf.org/rfc/rfc4120.txt.

50. Zhu, L., P. Leach, K. Jaganathan, and W. Ingersoll. 2005. "The Simple and Protected Generic Security Service Application Program Interface (GSS-API) Negotiation Mechanism." RFC4178, October. http://tools.ietf .org/rfc/rfc4178.txt.

51. Jaganathan, K., L. Zhu, and J. Brezak. 2006. "SPNEGO-Based Kerberos and NTLM HTTP Authentication in Microsoft Windows." RFC4559, June. http://tools.ietf.org/rfc/rfc4559.txt.

52. Sakimura, N., J. Bradley, M. Jones, B. de Medeiros, and C. Mortimore. 2014. "OpenID Connect Core 1.0." OpenID Foundation, Technical

Specification v1.0—Errata Set 1, November. http://openid.net/specs/openid-connect-core-10.html.

53. American Bar Association. 2012. "An Overview of Identity Management: Submission for UNCITRAL Commission 45th Session." ABA Identity Management Legal Task Force, May. http://meetings.abanet.org/webupload/commupload/CL320041/relatedresources/ABA-Submission-to-UNCITRAL.pdf.

54. Cameron, K. 2004. "The Laws of Identity." http://www.identityblog.com/stories/2004/12/09/thelaws.html.

55. Cavoukian, A. 2006. "7 Laws of Identity—the Case for Privacy-Embedded Laws of Identity in the Digital Age." Office of the Information and Privacy Commissioner of Ontario, Canada, Tech. Rep., October. http://www.ipc.on.ca/index.asp?navid=46&fid1=470.

56. Kerry, C. F. 2018. "Why Protecting Privacy Is a Losing Game Today—and How to Change the Game." Brookings Institution, Report—Center for Technology Innovation, July. https://www.brookings.edu/research/why-protecting-privacy-is-a-losing-game-today-and-how-to-change-the-game.

57. Singh, V. K., B. Bozkaya, and A. Pentland. 2015. "Money Walks: Implicit Mobility Behavior and Financial Well-Being." *PLOS ONE* 10 (8): 1–17, https://doi.org/10.1371/journal.pone.0136628.

58. Pentland, A. 2015. *Social Physics: How Social Networks Can Make Us Smarter*. New York: Penguin Books.

59. Makaay, E., T. Smedinghoff, and D. Thibeau. 2017. "OpenID Exchange: Trust Frameworks for Identity Systems." http://www.openidentityexchange.org/wp-content/uploads/2017/06/OIX-White-PaperTrust-Frameworks-for-Identity-SystemsFinal.pdf.

60. State of Virginia. 2015. "Virginia Electronic Identity Management Act," March. VA Code 2.2–436 2.2–437; VA Code 59.1–550 59.1–555. https://lis.virginia.gov/cgi-bin/legp604.exe?151+ful+CHAP0483.

61. US General Services Administration. 2013. "U.S. Federal Identity, Credential and Access Management (FICAM) Program." http://info.idmanagement.gov.

62. SAFE-BioPharma Association. 2016. "SAFE-BioPharma FICAM Trust Framework Provider Approval Process (FICAM-TFPAP)." https://www .safe-biopharma.org/SAFETrustFramework.html.

63. Nakamoto, S. 2008. "Bitcoin: A Peer-to-Peer Electronic Cash System." https://bitcoin.org/bitcoin.pdf.

64. Pentland, A., and T. Hardjono. 2018. "Digital Identity Is Broken. Here's a Way to Fix It." *Wall Street Journal*, April 3. https://blogs.wsj.com /cio/2018/04/03/digitalidentityisbro-kenheresawaytofixit/.

65. Atkins, D., W. Stallings, and P. Zimmermann. 1996. "PGP Message Exchange Formats," August, RFC1991. http://tools.ietf.org/rfc/rfc1991.txt.

66. Ford, W., and M. S. Baum. 2000. *Secure Electronic Commerce: Building the Infrastructure for Digital Signatures and Encryption*. Upper Saddle River, NJ: Prentice-Hall.

67. Chokhani, S., and W. Ford. 1999. "Internet X.509 Public Key Infrastructure Certificate Policy and Certification Practices Framework," March, RFC2527. http://tools.ietf.org/rfc/rfc2527.txt.

4 MIT OPEN ALGORITHMS

Thomas Hardjono and Alex Pentland

OPEN ALGORITHMS: A NEW PARADIGM FOR SHARING INSIGHTS

The *Open Algorithms* (OPAL) paradigm seeks to address the increasing need for individuals and organizations to share data in a privacy-preserving manner.[1] Data is crucial to the proper functioning of communities, businesses, and governments. Previous research has indicated that data increases in value when it is combined. Better insight is obtained when different types of data from different areas or domains are combined.[2] These insights allows communities to begin addressing the difficult social challenges of today, including better urban design, containing the spread of diseases, detecting factors that impact the economy, and other challenges of our data-driven society.[3,4]

Today there are a number of open challenges with regards to the information sharing ecosystem:

- *Data is siloed.* Today data is siloed within organizational boundaries, and the sharing of raw data with parties outside the organization remains unattainable, either due to regulatory constraints or due to business risk exposures.

- *Privacy is inadequately addressed.* The 2011 World Economic Forum (WEF) report[5] on personal data as a new asset class finds that the current ecosystems that access and use personal data are fragmented and inefficient.

For many participants, the risks and liabilities exceed the economic returns, and personal privacy concerns are inadequately addressed. Current technologies and laws fall short of providing the legal and technical infrastructure needed to support a well-functioning digital economy. The rapid rate of technological change and commercialization in using personal data is undermining end-user confidence and trust.

- *Regulatory and compliance requirements.* The introduction of the EU General Data Protection Regulations (GDPR)[6] will impact global organizations that rely on the Internet for trans-border flow of raw data. This includes cloud-based processing sites that are spread across the globe.

Thus, we are facing an interesting dilemma with regards to data-driven decision-making for individuals, organizations, and communities. On one hand, individuals, organizations, and communities need "access to data" in order to perform computations as part of decision-making. The promise is that better insights can be obtained by combining data from different domains in interesting and innovative ways. On the other hand, however, there is considerable risk to privacy when "data is shared" across entities. The WEF report[5] clearly points to inadequate care given today to personal data; and evidence abounds with regard to theft or misuse of personal data reported in the media.[7,8,9] It is with this backdrop that an open algorithms model is put forward as an alternative paradigm in which to view and treat data.

In this chapter we discuss the OPAL principles and put forward the architecture developed at MIT to implement these principles. We discuss the issue of authorization and consent in the context of "consent to execute a vetted algorithm" and contrast this with the prevailing interpretation of consent as being "consent to copy and move data." We also briefly put forward a basic model for multiple data providers to collaborate in a trust network founded on the principles of open algorithms.

OPEN ALGORITHMS PRINCIPLES

The concept of Open Algorithms (OPAL) evolved from several research projects over the past decade within the Human Dynamics Group at the MIT Media Lab, particularly the thesis work of Yves-Alexandre de Montjoye (now at Imperial College) and Guy Zyskind (now CEO and founder of Enigma.co). From various research results it was increasingly becoming apparent that an individual's privacy could be affected through the correlation of just small amounts of data.[10,11]

One noteworthy seed project was *OpenPDS*, which sought to develop further the concept of personal datastores (PDS),[12,13,14] by incorporating the idea of analytics on personal data and the notion of "safe answers" as being the norm for responses generated by a personal datastore.

However, beyond the world of personal datastores there remains the pressing challenges around how large datastores can be enabled to secure their data, safeguard privacy, and comply with regulations (e.g., GDPR[6])—while at the same time enabling productive collaborative data sharing. The larger the data repository, the more attractive it would become to hackers and attackers. As such, it became evident that the current mindset of performing data analytics at a centralized location needed to be replaced with a new paradigm for thinking about data sharing in a distributed manner.

The following are the fundamental principles of open algorithms and the treatment of data:

- *Move the algorithm to the data.* Instead of pulling data from various repositories into a centralized location for processing, it is the algorithm that should be sent to the data repositories for processing there. The goal here is to share insights instead of sharing raw data.

- *Data must never leave its repository.* Data must never be exported from (or copied from) its repository. This is consistent with the previous principle and enforces that principle.

  Exceptions to this rule are when the user requests a download of their data, or when there is a legally valid court order to obtain a copy of the data.

- *Vetted algorithms.* Algorithms should be studied, reviewed, and vetted by experts.

  The goal here is to provide all entities in the ecosystem with a better understanding and assessment of the quality of algorithms from the perspective of bias, unfairness, and other possible unintended/unforeseen side effects.

- *Default to safe answers.* The default behavior of data repositories when returning responses should be that of protecting privacy as the primary goal. This applies to individual as well as organizational data privacy.

  For aggregate computations, data repositories should place additional filters on responses to detect and resolve potential privacy leakages. For subject-specific computations (i.e., about a specific individual or organization), data repositories should obtain explicit and informed consent from the subject. We believe this principle is consistent with Article 7 of the GDPR.[6]

There are a number of corollary principles to the above principles that enhance the protection of data and therefore enhance privacy:

- *Data is always in an encrypted state.* Data must remain encrypted during computation and in storage.

  The notion here is that in order to protect data repositories from attacks and theft (e.g., theft by an insider), data should never be decrypted. This implies that algorithms sent to a data repository must be executed by the repository on its encrypted data without first decrypting it into plaintext. We believe that in the future this principle will be crucial and unavoidable from the perspective of infrastructure cybersecurity.

There are a number of emerging technologies—such as homomorphic encryption[15] and secure multi-party computation[16,17,18]—that may provide the future foundations to address this principle.

- *Decentralized data architectures.* Data repositories should adopt decentralized and distributed data architectures for infrastructure security and resiliency.

  Cryptographic techniques such as secret sharing[19] can be applied to data, to yield multiple encrypted "shards" of the data. These shards can in turn be distributed physically across a network of repositories belonging to the same data provider.[11] This approach increases the resiliency of the data provider infrastructure because an attacker would need to compromise a minimal number of repositories (N out of M nodes) in the data provider's network before the attacker can obtain access to the data item. This approach increases the attack surface, and makes the task of attacking considerably harder. Combining this approach with secure multi-party computation (e.g., MIT Enigma[20]) provides a possible future direction for the infrastructure resiliency of data providers.

The open algorithm principles also apply to individual personal datastores (PDS)[12,13,14,21] independent of whether the PDS is operated by the individual or by a third-party service provider (e.g., hosted model). The basic idea is that in order to include the individual citizen in the open algorithms ecosystem, they must have sufficient interest, empowerment, and incentive to be a participant.[22] The ecosystem must therefore respect personal datastores as legitimate OPAL data repository endpoints. New models for computations across highly distributed personal data repositories need to be developed following the open algorithms principles.

Furthermore, new service provisioning architecture must be envisaged that allows individuals to automatically relocate their OPAL personal datastores from one operator to another. One such proposal[23] uses smart-contract technologies together with legally binding terms to ensure that the service provider does not retain copies of the data embedded within the portable PDS. For communities of individuals and for organizations, the notion of *decentralized autonomous organizations*[24] can be further developed to become the basis for *community datastores* (CDS). A community datastore combines individual data belonging to multiple community members, and operates under a well-defined governance model and legal trust framework.[25,26,27] The financial credit union model in the United States may provide a suitable legal model for community datastores,[28] one in which the community as a legal entity has *information fiduciary obligations* to its individual members.[29,30]

THE MIT OPAL DESIGN

In the following sections we describe the OPAL development project at MIT that implements the open algorithms paradigm. The high-level design of MIT OPAL is summarized in figure 4.1, and consists of the following entities, services, and functions:

- *OPAL data service*. The OPAL data service is the service that allows a caller (querier) to request algorithm(s) to be executed on data located at the data provider.

  The data service makes available a description of the algorithms and the schema of the datasets available at the backend data providers. Additionally, in some deployment situations the data service may perform the task of collating and merging responses from various data providers.

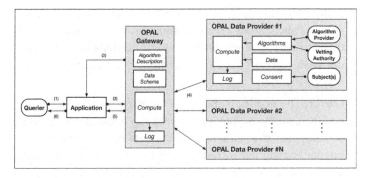

FIGURE 4.1
Overview of the Open Algorithms (OPAL) ecosystem.

Note that in the single data provider scenario, the data service may be owned and operated by the data provider, and may even be collapsed into the data provider's infrastructure. In the case of a consortium of data providers, they may collectively own and operate the data service.

- *Data provider*: The data provider represents the data repository that holds the relevant data and algorithms.

  The source of the data and algorithms can be the data provider itself, or the data provider may have obtained the data and algorithms from external sources. The data provider may publish (directly or through the data service) the data schemas of its available data and algorithm descriptions of its algorithms.

- *Algorithm provider*. The algorithm provider is the entity that supplies algorithms specifically for data held at the data provider.

  In some cases, the algorithm provider may not a separate entity from the data provider (i.e., the data provider authors its own algorithms). In other situations, the algorithm provider could be an outsourced entity whose task is to create custom algorithms for the data provider. The algorithm provider is called out as a separate function in figure 4.1 because there are some circumstances in which the data provider may not wish to create or own algorithms due to liabilities that may be incurred.

- *Querier.* The querier is the entity wishing to obtain information or insights by having (requesting) a specific algorithm be computed over data held by the data provider entity. The querier is assumed to remunerate the data service operator and the data provider in some manner (i.e., fees).

- *Application.* The application is the tool or system used by the querier to interact with the OPAL data service.

    The application may be owned and operated by a single data provider, by a consortium of data providers, or by an independent third-party service provider. This last case of a third-party operated application is the basis for many current web applications,[31] where the web application is often referred to as the "client."

- *Data subject.* The data subject is the legal individual or organization whose data is present within the larger data collection held by the data provider. The data subject is the entity providing consent for the algorithm execution over the dataset that may contain their data.

- *Vetting authority.* The vetting authority is the entity that provides assurance regarding the quality of a given algorithm intended for a specific data. The vetting authority provides expert review based on a well-defined fairness criterion that is relevant to the data provider, data subject(s), and the querier.

The general interaction flow among the entities is shown in figure 4.1. The querier (individual or organization) seeking information employs the application in step 1 to select one or more algorithms and their intended data (step 2). The querier uses the application to convey these selections to the data service in step 3. Payment may accompany this request from the querier. The data service interacts with the relevant data providers in step 4 in order to complete the request. The data service returns the response to the application and querier in step 5.

As mentioned previously, an algorithm intended for a given data must be vetted by experts in order to obtain some measure of fairness of the algorithm as used for that data. Although the topic of fairness is outside the scope of the current work, it is worthwhile to mention specific challenges that are relevant. The term "fair" is used loosely to denote a set of broad categories of issues, and not any specific technical approaches. As AI and machine learning approaches become more widely adopted in the real world, their impact will affect different parts of society in different ways.

Also outside the scope of this work, but associated with algorithmic fairness, are the issues of *transparency* and *accountability*. In OPAL, transparency refers to the history of transactions— namely, the precise tracking of *which algorithm* was executed on *which data*, by *which entity* at *which moment* in time for *what purposes*. This tracking information should be visible to data subjects (individuals and organizations) whose data is involved. Authentic information regarding tracking should be the basis for accountability.

Today the OPAL architecture is being deployed at national scale in Senegal and Colombia, by the DataPop Alliance, Imperial College, the authors here at MIT, and the French telecom company Orange. These deployments are supported by the French Development Agency (AFD), Orange, the governments of Colombia and Senegal, and the telecommunications providers Sonatel and Telefonica.

AUTHORIZATION AND CONSENT MANAGEMENT

Within the MIT OPAL design, we used the notion of consent for execution in contrast to the usual ambiguous concept of "consent to access." Consent for execution means permission to execute a given vetted algorithm over data for a duration of time for a stated purpose, without moving the data from its repository. We believe this approach is substantially different from the usual "consent for access," which is most commonly interpreted as permission to read (copy) data—something that violates the open algorithms principles. In order for a subject (individual or organization) to have a meaningful understanding of the implications of "consent," sufficient, clear, and unambiguous notice must be provided to the subject. This notice must never be modified postevent without the subject's re-consent.

In addressing the issue of consent, the MIT OPAL design considers the following three models for consent:

- *Subject's consent for data participation.* Here the subject is giving permission to the data provider to include the subject's data within the broader dataset for algorithm execution. This question of inclusion is separate from (but may be dependent on the questions of: (1) whether the algorithm computes aggregates only and (2) whether the subject is allowing themselves to be re-identified as a result.

- *Subject's consent for execution.* Here the subject is giving permission to the data provider to run a specific algorithm on a dataset, within which the subject's data resides. A key aspect is the subject's own understanding of what the algorithm computes, and whether the algorithm has been vetted by entities accepted (trusted) by the subject.

- *Subject's consent for delegation.* Here the subject is giving permission to another entity to make decisions regarding consent for data participation and consent for execution. This aspect is relevant in cases when the subject does not have the capacity to decide on a per-execution basis (e.g., medical situation) or in the case when the subject is deceased (e.g., personal data bequeathed to a trust).

The technical construct used in the MIT OPAL design is the classic access ticket (access token) that was first popularized in the 1980s by the MIT Kerberos authentication system,[32,33,34] and which is now the basis for the majority of token-based access control systems in industry. In the context of web applications, the same notion of tickets or tokens is used in the XACML standard,[35] as well as in the OAuth 2.0 authorization framework.[31] For consent management, the MIT OPAL design follows closely the authorization model of the User-Managed Access (UMA) standard.[36,37] UMA extends the OAuth 2.0 framework by introducing new functions and services, which contribute in the following ways:

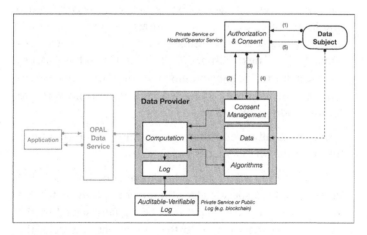

FIGURE 4.2
Authorization and consent in MIT OPAL.

- *Recognition of service operators as third-party legal entities.* An important contribution of UMA is the recognition that in the real-world deployments of services there are entities that provide services to the user and the data/resource owner but that may be "opaque" to them in that they have not provided consent for these service operators to gain access to data and information handled by or routed through the operator. This problem becomes acute when the data or resource is of high value. For example, UMA recognizes that the OAuth 2.0 client entity is typically a third-party service that is owned and operated by a legal entity with which the resource owner (subject or data owner) does not have any relationship.

- *Service endpoints as legally binding points of access.* Another important contribution of UMA is the recognition that a given service endpoint (e.g., REST API) and the transaction flow provide a natural point to bind transacting entities (and their service operators) into a legal agreement. More specifically, in a given transaction handshake (e.g., between Alice and Bob), consisting of several transaction flows (i.e., atomically inseparable set of messages), there is a point where continuing to the next transaction flow implies to both parties the acceptance of legally binding outcomes. Thus, the technical implementation of access service endpoints gives rise to legally binding obligations.

More specifically, we further distinguish the following types of tokens in the MIT OPAL design:

- *Execution consent token.* This token represents the permission granted to run a specific algorithm over a specific data for a specific purpose. This token must be digitally signed by the grantor of the permission. In the case of personal data, the grantor is the individual data subject and the grantee is the data provider. In the case of organizational data owned by a legal organization, the grantor and grantee may be persons (e.g., employees, principals) inside the organization. In such cases, the token may be part of an internal broader privileges management system (e.g., Microsoft PAC structure[38]).

- *Delegation token.* This token represents permission by a data subject to another party to perform decision-making (on behalf of the subject) with regard to the execution of a specific algorithm on a specific data. The delegation token must be digitally signed by the subject and ideally should indicate a time duration of validity.

The notion of delegation tokens or tickets has been explored extensively in different systems (e.g., *proxiable* and *forwardable tickets* in Kerberos[33,38,39] and more recently in the eXtensible Access Control Markup Language or XACML standard[35]).

The authorization and consent flows are summarized in figure 4.2. In step 1, the subject registers the existence, availability, and location of data. This registration is performed at an Authorization and Consent Service, which may be a service or system operated by the subject, operated by the data provider, or a hosted service operated by a third party. Here it is important to note that no data is exported to Authorization and Consent Service. A data provider must obtain an execution consent token from the subject to include the subject's data within a given algorithm execution. This request is shown as step 2 in figure 4.2, with the issuance of the execution consent token in step 3. In turn the data provider must issue an execution consent receipt in step 4 and step 5.

With regards to receipts, one promising construct that has been standardized is the *Consent Receipt*[40] structure. This receipt is signed by the data provider, and in effect it gives the subject a record of what the subject has consented to. Related to consent, figure 4.2 also shows an audit log that is external to the data provider entity. The purpose of this log is to allow the subject and other relevant entities to obtain insight as to which algorithms were executed on which data at which point in time (i.e., transparency and accountability).

ENABLING DATA PROVIDER COMMUNITIES IN INDUSTRY

Data increases in value when it is combined across different domains or verticals, yielding insights that were previously unattainable.[2,3] Data is crucial for the running of communities, businesses, societies, and governments. The key challenge is how different entities in a community can share insights meaningfully, without compromising the privacy of individuals and organizations.

We believe that the open algorithms paradigm points to a new direction in which the sharing of insights among organizations and institutions can be achieved at scale. We refer to groups of entities sharing insights as data provider communities or data communities (or "circle of trust"). The idea is that a group of data providers across relevant data domains agree to create a "consortium" that operates following clear rules, with privacy as a major requirement (see figure 4.3). The idea is not new, and has been used in smaller scale in fixed-attribute sharing among a federated group of identity providers.[41,42]

In the context of open algorithms, there are a number of important aspects to the notion of data communities:

- *Adherence to open algorithms principles.* Members of a data community must agree to adhere to the principles of open algorithms, emphasizing the need for preserving the privacy of individuals and organizations whose data are held by the members.

- *Collaborative creation of new algorithms.* New insights can only be obtained by creating new algorithms that analyze data from different domains. Members of a data community should invest resources towards this end in order for them to realize the benefits of collaboration.

- *Mutual agreement to execute algorithms.* Depending on the composition of membership, the members of a data community

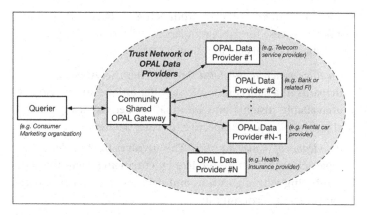

FIGURE 4.3
Data provider communities based on Open Algorithms.

should agree to honor the request from other members to execute group-shared algorithms against data in their respective repositories.

- *Governance by systems rules.* Members of a data community must operate by adhering to system rules that define the various dimensions of operations based on the open algorithms principles.

- *Common auditability.* Part of the system rules of the data community must address the function and implementation of common audit of actions and transactions occurring among the members. Such auditability will be needed to avoid potential conflicts from occurring when the membership consists of competing entities (e.g., competing businesses).

- *Enforceable legal obligations and liabilities.* The governance of the data community must be based on legal contracts that clearly define the obligations of each member, as well as liabilities in cases of non-adherence to the systems rules.

In order for a group of data providers to collaborate as an OPAL-based data community, there must be sufficient and clear business advantages and gains from doing so. That is, there must be a business case for data providers to collaborate. Some examples of these benefits are as follows:

- *Creation of new data-related services.* These services allow participants in a data community to offer unique and previously unavailable insights and information derived using shared algorithms on their respective (private) datasets.

- *Broadening of market adoption.* This involves the broadening of a participant's existing services by enhancing them through combining with algorithms and datasets from other participants in a data community.

- *Standardization of technical or functional operations.* Standardization allows for improved reusability and more efficient certification, thus lowering cost burdens (for participants and their customers).

More formally, we define system rules for OPAL-based data communities as follows:

> The set of rules, methods, procedures and routines, technology, standards, policies, and processes, applicable to a group of participating entities, governing the collection, verification, storage, exchange of algorithms (for specific datasets) that provide information and insights about an individual, a community, or organization under their consent for the purpose of facilitating risk-based decisions.

There are two broad purposes of system rules in the context of OPAL. The first is *achieving functionality* that allows the shared system to operate, while the second is *establishing trustworthiness of the system* as a whole among the members of the community of data providers. The first purpose of systems rules—namely, to achieve functionality—refers to the technical aspects of the operations of a data community:

- *Proper operations.* The system rules provide some form of governance to ensure the system functions properly for its intended purpose (i.e., it works).

- *Compliance.* In this context, compliance means to ensure that the system and its participants operate in accordance with the requirements of any applicable law. In the OPAL case, this includes the various privacy regulations in the jurisdiction within which the community of data providers operate.

The second purpose of systems rules—namely, to establish trustworthiness—refers to the ability of parties participating in a data community to obtain a measurable degree of certainty as a function of risk management:

- *Risk management.* The system rules allow entities to address and manage risks inherent in participating in the OPAL-based data community system.

- *Legal certainty and predictability.* The system rules address the legal rights, responsibilities, and liabilities of the participants, and thus eliminate the uncertainty of the application of existing law not written for OPAL-based data community systems.

- *Transparency.* The availability of system rules makes the terms of the specifications, rules, and agreements comprising the system rules to be accessible to all participants.

THE PERSONAL INFOMEDIARY

As mentioned previously, the MIT OPAL Project grew out of several projects that sought to address the question of privacy in this big data world. One such project was *OpenPDS*,[14] which sought to develop further the concept of personal datastores (PDS).[12,13] In OpenPDS, the idea was for individuals to install an agent software on mobile devices that would retain copies of all data sent and received by the user on that device. Seeing that mobile devices typically have limited memory/storage, the data would be periodically downloaded to some personal datastore (e.g., home storage server, storage in the cloud, etc.). The data in the personal datastore could then be made accessible

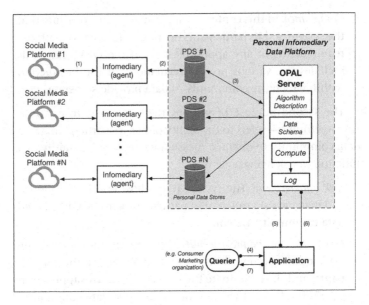

FIGURE 4.4
The Personal Infomediary based on OPAL.

to external queriers, where local analytics would always return "safe answers." This configuration is illustrated in figure 4.4.

Currently, an extension to the basic OpenPDS concept is being developed based on the OPAL concept, and which is referred to as the OPAL Personal Infomediary (or simply "infomediary"). We define the personal infomediary as an active software agent that acts as a two-way proxy between the user (owner of the infomediary) and a given social media platform with which the user interacts on a daily basis. For simplicity, we assume there will be a unique infomediary for each social media platform or other interactive data sources.

In being an active proxy to the social media platform (or other interactive data sources), the goal of the MIT personal infomediary is as follows:

- *Intelligent personal mediation.* Provide an intelligent agent that mediates interaction between the user and the social media platform. The agent can be enhanced to incorporate various advanced AI and machine learning techniques to enhance the user experience.

- *Personal data collection.* Collect copies of all traffic between the user and the social media platforms. The user is free to deploy one infomediary for multiple social media platforms (One-to-Many), or one infomediary for each social media platform. Data from the infomediaries are connected into the user's personal data store.

- *Personal analytics.* Provide a source of user-owned data such that the user can perform analytics (e.g., using software tools) in order to: (a) gain insight about the user's behavior for a given social media platform; (b) gain insight about the user's behavior across multiple social media platforms; and (c) gain insight about the behavior of the social media platform and detect possible unfair targeting feeds from the social media platform.

- *Personal revenue.* Provide a source of revenue for the individual user by providing OPAL-based access to the user's data collected in the various personal datastores.

Cooperatives such as credit unions or other trusted third parties may act as information fiduciaries,[29] offering to host infomediary services for their community. By aggregating user data for the benefit of the users, such a fiduciary service can act as a "data union," analogous to a labor union, balancing the power of large corporations.

CONCLUSIONS

The goal of this chapter has been to present and discuss the open algorithms (OPAL) paradigm, discuss its key principles, and provide an example of an implementation in the form of the MIT OPAL Project.

Society is currently facing an interesting dilemma with regards to data-driven decision-making. On one hand, individuals, organizations, and communities need access to data in order to perform computations as part of decision-making. On the other hand, however, there is considerable risk to privacy when data is shared (copied) across entities. The open algorithm paradigm seeks to address this by changing the way we view data processing and privacy-preserving computations.

The key principles—move the algorithm to the data, data must never leave its repository, and the use of vetted algorithms—are very much in line with the goals of the GDPR regulations, notably in placing emphasis on individual data privacy. We have discussed the MIT OPAL design as an example of an implementation of the open algorithms principles. The design recognizes a number of entities in the OPAL ecosystem, with specific roles that together must meet the goals of the OPAL principles. From the user consent perspective, the OPAL paradigm simplifies consent by requesting consent for algorithm execution over the user's data. This is considerably better than the current norm in industry where "consent to access" is interpreted as permission to copy/move raw data.

Data increases in value when it is combined across different domains or verticals, yielding insights that were previously unattainable. To this end we believe that a trust network of data providers—operating based on a common legal framework—provides a promising avenue for data providers in industry to collaborate while maintaining data privacy. Integral to this legal framework are the system rules that define the legal obligations and liabilities of each entity in the trust network.

Finally, we venture into the future by presenting the MIT personal infomediary project that builds on OPAL. The personal infomediary is an active software agent that acts as a two-way proxy between the user (owner of the infomediary) and a given social media platform with which the user interacts on a daily basis. The infomediary collects copies of all traffic between the user and the social media platforms, and provides a source of user-owned data such that the user can perform analytics in order to gain insight about the interactions of the user with the various social media platforms. When a trusted third party offers to host user infomediaries as a fiduciary service, the result can be a "data union" or "data cooperative" that can balance the power of large corporations.

REFERENCES

1. Pentland, A., D. Shrier, T. Hardjono, and I. Wladawsky-Berger. 2016. "Towards an Internet of Trusted Data: Input to the Whitehouse Commission on Enhancing National Cybersecurity." In *Trust::Data—a New Framework for Identity and Data Sharing*, edited by T. Hardjono, A. Pentland, and D. Shrier, 21–49. Boston: Visionary Future.

2. Singh, V. K., B. Bozkaya, and A. Pentland. 2015. "Money Walks: Implicit Mobility Behavior and Financial Well-Being." *PLOS ONE* 10 (8): 1–17. https://doi.org/10.1371/journal.pone.0136628.

3. Pentland, A. 2015. *Social Physics: How Social Networks Can Make Us Smarter*. New York: Penguin Books.

4. Pentland, A., T. Reid, and T. Heibeck. 2013. "Big Data and Health—Revolutionizing Medicine and Public Health: Report of the Big Data and Health Working Group 2013." World Innovation Summit for Health, Qatar Foundation, Tech. Rep., December. http://www.wish-qatar.org/app/media/382.

5. World Economic Forum. 2011. "Personal Data: The Emergence of a New Asset Class." http://www.weforum.org/reports/personal-data-emergence-new-asset-class.

6. European Commission. 2016. "Regulation (EU) 2016/679 of the European Parliament and of the Council of 27 April 2016 on the Protection

of Natural Persons with Regard to the Processing of Personal Data and on the Free Movement of Such Data (General Data Protection Regulation)." *Official Journal of the European Union* L119: 1–88.

7. Abelson, R., and M. Goldstein. 2015. "Millions of Anthem Customers Targeted in Cyberattack." *New York Times*, February 5. https://www.nytimes.com/2015/02/05/business/hackers-breached-data-of-millions-insurer-says.html.

8. Bernard, T. S., T. Hsu, N. Perlroth, and R. Lieber. 2017. "Equifax Says Cyberattack May Have Affected 143 Million in the U.S." *New York Times*, September 7. https://www.nytimes.com/2017/09/07/business/equifax-cyberattack.html.

9. Gramville, K. 2018. "Facebook and Cambridge Analytica: What You Need to Know as Fallout Widens." *New York Times*, March 19. https://www.nytimes.com/2018/03/19/technology/facebook-cambridge-analytica-explained.html.

10. de Montjoye, Y. A., J. Quoidbach, F. Robic, and A. Pentland. 2013. "Predicting Personality Using Novel Mobile Phone-Based Metrics." In *Social Computing, Behavioral-Cultural Modeling and Prediction* (LNCS Vol. 7812), 48–55. New York: Springer.

11. Pentland, A. 2014. "Saving Big Data from Itself." *Scientific American*, August, 65–68.

12. Hardjono, T., and J. Seberry. 1996. "Strongboxes for Electronic Commerce." In *Proceedings of the Second USENIX Workshop on Electronic Commerce*. Berkeley, CA: USENIX Association.

13. Hardjono, T., and J. Seberry. 1997. "Secure Access to Electronic Strongboxes in Electronic Commerce." In *Proceedings of 2nd International Small Systems Security Conference* (IFIP WG 11.2), edited by J. Eloff and R. von Solms, 1–13. Copenhagen: IFIP.

14. de Montjoye, Y.A., E. Shmueli, S. Wang, and A. Pentland. 2014. "openPDS: Protecting the Privacy of Metadata through SafeAnswers." *PLOS ONE* 9 (7): 13–18. https://doi.org/10.1371/journal.pone.0098790.

15. Gentry, C. 2009. "Fully Homomorphic Encryption using Ideal Lattices." In *Proceedings of the 41st Annual ACM Symposium on Theory of Computing* (STOC'09), 169–178. New York: ACM.

16. Yao, A. C. 1982. "Protocols for Secure Computations." In *Proceedings of the 23rd Annual Symposium on Foundations of Computer Science*, ser. SFCS '82, 160–164. Washington, DC: IEEE Computer Society.

17. Yao, A. C.-C. 1986. "How to Generate and Exchange Secrets." In *Proceedings of the 27th Annual Symposium on Foundations of Computer Science*, ser. SFCS '86, 162–167. Washington, DC: IEEE Computer Society.

18. Goldreich, O., S. Micali, and A. Wigderson. 1987. "How to Play Any Mental Game." In *Proceedings of the Nineteenth Annual ACM Symposium on Theory of Computing*, ser. STOC '87, 218–229. New York: ACM.

19. Shamir, A. 1979. "How to Share a Secret." *Communications of the ACM* 22 (11): 612–613.

20. Zyskind, G., O. Nathan, and A. Pentland. 2015. "Decentralizing Privacy: Using Blockchain to Protect Personal Data." In *Proceedings of the 2015 IEEE Security and Privacy Workshops*. San Jose, CA: IEEE Computer Society.

21. Mitchell, A., I. Henderson, and D. Searls. 2008. "Reinventing Direct Marketing with VRM Inside." *Journal of Direct, Data and Digital Marketing Practice* 10 (1): 3–15.

22. Searls, D. 2012. *The Intention Economy*. Boston: Harvard Business Review Press.

23. Hardjono, T. 2017. "Decentralized Service Architecture for OAuth 2.0." Internet Engineering Task Force, February. https://tools.ietf.org/html/draft-hardjono-oauth-decentralized-00.

24. Bollier, D., and J. H. Clippinger. 2013. "The Next Great Internet Disruption: Authority and Governance." In *From Bitcoin to Burning Man and Beyond*, edited by D. Bollier and J. Clippinger, 21–28. Amherst, MA: ID3 & Off the Commons Books.

25. Hardjono, T., P. Deegan, and J. Clippinger. 2013. "The ID3 Open Mustard Seed Platform." In *From Bitcoin to Burning Man and Beyond*, edited by D. Bollier and J. Clippinger, 143–159. Amherst, MA: ID3 & Off the Commons Books.

26. Hardjono, T., P. Deegan, and J. Clippinger. 2014. "On the Design of Trustworthy Compute Frameworks for Self-Organizing Digital

Institutions." In *Proceedings of the 6th International Conference on Social Computing and Social Media and 6th International Conference on Human-Computer Interaction* (LNCS 8531), edited by G. Meiselwitz, 342–353. Berlin: Springer-Verlag.

27. Hardjono, T., P. Deegan, and J. Clippinger. 2014. "Social Use Cases for the ID3 Open Mustard Seed Platform." *IEEE Technology and Society Magazine* 33 (3): 48–54.

28. Greenwood, D., A. Stopczynski, B. Sweatt, T. Hardjono, and A. Pentland. 2014. "The New Deal on Data: A Framework for Institutional Controls." In *Privacy, Big Data and the Public Good: Frameworks for Engagement*, edited by J. Lane, V. Stodden, S. Bender, and H. Nissenbaum, 192–210. New York: Cambridge University Press.

29. Balkin, J. M. 2016. "Information Fiduciaries and the First Amendment." *UC Davis Law Review* 49 (4): 1183–1234.

30. Kerry, C. F. 2018. "Why Protecting Privacy Is a Losing Game Today—and How to Change the Game." Brookings Institution, Report—Center for Technology Innovation, July. https://www.brookings.edu/research/why-protecting-privacy-is-a-losing-game-today-and-how-to-change-the-game.

31. Hardt, D. 2012. "The OAuth 2.0 Authorization Framework." RFC 6749 (Proposed Standard), Internet Engineering Task Force, October. http://www.ietf.org/rfc/rfc6749.txt.

32. Steiner, J. G., C. Neuman, and J. I. Schiller. 1988. "Kerberos: An Authentication Service for Open Network Systems." In *Proceedings of USENIX*, 191–202. Dallas, TX: USENIX Association.

33. Kohl, J., and C. Neuman. 1993. "The Kerberos Network Authentication Service (V5)." RFC 1510 (Historic), Internet Engineering Task Force, September, obsoleted by RFCs 4120, 6649. http://www.ietf.org/rfc/rfc1510.txt.

34. Hardjono, T. 2010. "OAuth 2.0 Support for the Kerberos v5 Authentication Protocol." Internet Engineering Task Force, draft-hardjono-oauth-kerberos-01, December. https://tools.ietf.org/html/draft-hardjono-oauth-kerberos-01.

35. OASIS. 2013. "eXtensible Access Control Markup Language (XACML) Version 3.0." http://docs.oasis-open.org/xacml/3.0/xacml-3.0-core-spec -os-en.html.

36. Hardjono, T., E. Maler, M. Machulak, and D. Catalano. 2015. "User-Managed Access (UMA) Profile of OAuth 2.0—Specification Version 1.0." Kantara Initiative, Published Specification, April. https://docs .kantarainitiative.org/uma/rec-uma-core.html.

37. Maler, E., M. Machulak, and J. Richer. 2017. "User-Managed Access (UMA) 2.0." Kantara Initiative, Published Specification, January. https:// docs.kantarainitiative.org/uma/ed/uma-core-2.0–10.html.

38. Microsoft Corporation. 2014. "Microsoft Privilege Attribute Certificate Data Structure." MS-PAC Specification v20140502, May.

39. Microsoft Corporation. 2014. "Microsoft Kerberos Protocol Extensions." MS-KILE Specification v20140502, May.

40. Lizar, M., and D. Turner. 2017. "Consent Receipt Specification Version 1.0." https://kantarainitiative.org/confluence/display/infosharing /Home.

41. Hardjono, T., and A. Pentland. 2016. "On Privacy-Preserving Identity within Future Blockchain Systems." W3C Workshop on Distributed Ledgers on the Web (Cambridge, MA, June). https://www.w3.org/2016 /04/blockchain-workshop.

42. Hardjono, T., and A. Pentland. 2018. "Open Algorithms for Identity Federation." In *Proceedings of IEEE Future of Information and Communication Conference* (Singapore, April). https://arxiv.org/pdf/1705.10880.pdf.

5 BUILDING A DATA-RICH SOCIETY

Alex Pentland

The wide adoption of Internet access, earth-imaging satellites, mobile phones with cameras, social media and similar technologies has dramatically changed our ability to understand our neighborhoods, cities, and countries: now there are data about the world and about each of us everywhere. Recent research studies have shown that this exponential increase in the volume and types of available data is opening unprecedented possibilities for understanding global patterns of human behavior and for helping decision-makers to tackle problems of societal importance, such as: monitoring socioeconomic deprivation[2,6,10,11, 12] and crime levels,[3,13,14] mapping the propagation of diseases,[1,9,14, 15,16] and understanding the impact of natural disasters, environmental risks, and other emergencies,[4,5,7,8,17,18] etc. These successes have encouraged the UN to identify these new data methods as the "data revolution" that will allow countries to measure progress toward the seventeen Sustainable Development Goals (SDGs), including the goals of zero poverty, zero hunger, good health, clean water and energy, gender equality, sustainable cities, quality education, etc., by 2030[6] (see also Appendix B).

With data at this scale and granularity, you can get a picture of society that was unimaginable only a few years ago. This ability to see human behavior continuously and quantitatively has kicked off a new science (according to articles in *Nature*,

Science, and other leading journals) called computational social science, and it is beginning to transform traditional social sciences. This is akin to when Dutch lensmakers created the first practical lenses: microscopes and telescopes created broad new scientific vistas. Today, the new technology of living labs—observing human behavior by collecting a community's digital breadcrumbs—is beginning to give researchers a more complete view of life in all its complexity. This, I believe, is not only the future of social science, but also the future of policymaking and practical governance.

What does this new, data-rich view of society look like? How will it change the way we think about government, and about ourselves? My lab at MIT has deployed "Open Algorithms" (OPAL) data experiments in several countries and with a wide variety of collaborators. In this chapter, I will try to give you a sample of what sort of insights we can obtain by using these new data resources, using data from a wide variety of cities in the United States, the European Union, and Asia, and also consider how we can use new data resources to build better civic systems, using the city of Beijing as a specific example.

A NEW UNDERSTANDING OF HUMAN NATURE

The foundations of modern Western society, and of rich societies everywhere, were laid in the 1700s in Scotland by Adam Smith, John Locke, and others. The understanding of ourselves that this early social science created is that humans are rational individuals and independent thinkers who are driven by self-interest. This viewpoint is built into every part of our society now—we use markets, we take direct democracy as our ideal of government, and our schools focus on training students to have better analytical skills.

But this rational individual model is much too simple—and it is not just the rational "self-interested" part that is questionable, but more importantly the part about humans acting as individuals who are independent of everyone else. Our behavior is strongly influenced by those around us and, as we will see, is the source of most of our wisdom. Our ability to thrive is due to learning from other people's experiences. We are not individuals but rather members of a social species.

The idea of "rational individuals" reached its current form when mathematicians in the 1800s tried to make sense of Adam Smith's observation that people "...are led by an invisible hand to...advance the interest of the society, and afford means to the multiplication of the species." These mathematicians found that they could make the invisible hand work if they used a very simplified model of human nature: people act only to benefit themselves (they are "rational"), and they act alone, independent of others (they are "individuals").

Today, the mathematics of most economies and of most governing systems assume that people make up their minds independently and they don't influence each other. While this may not be a bad first approximation, it fails in the end because it is people influencing each other, peer-to-peer, that causes financial bubbles, cultural change, and (as we will see) it is this peer-to-peer influence that is the source of innovation and growth.

Furthermore, the idea of "rational individuals" is not what Adam Smith said created the invisible hand. Instead, Adam Smith thought: "It is human nature to exchange not only goods but also ideas, assistance, and favors...it is these exchanges that guide men to create solutions for the good of the community." Interestingly, Karl Marx said something similar—namely, that society is the sum of all our social relationships.

The norms of society, the solutions for society, come from peer-to-peer communication—not from markets, not from individuals. We should focus on interaction between individuals, not individual genius. Until recently, though, we didn't have data to prove how our society really works, nor did we have the right sort of mathematics model networks of peer-to-peer interaction. Now we have both the math and the data to better understand and govern ourselves, and we can begin to understand ourselves much more clearly.

WEALTH COMES FROM FINDING NEW OPPORTUNITIES

What do these new data and math tools show? Are we really creatures of our social networks? To answer the question of who we really are, we now have data available from huge numbers of people in most every society on earth and can approach the question using very powerful statistical techniques. For instance, figure 5.1 shows data from a sample of 100,000 randomly selected people in a mid-income country and compares their ability to hear about new opportunities (measured by how closed or open their social networks are) to their income.

The answer is that people who have more open networks make more money. Moreover, this is not just an artifact of the way we measured their access to opportunities, because you can get the same result looking at the diversity of jobs of the people they interact with, or the diversity of locations of the people they interact with. Shockingly, if you compare people who have a sixth grade education to illiterate people, this curve moves only a little to the left. If you look at people with college educations, the curve moves only a little bit to the right. The variation that has to do with education is trivial when compared with the variation that has to do with diversity of interaction.

You may wonder if greater network diversity causes greater income or whether it is the other way around. The answer is that greater network diversity indeed causes greater income on average (this is the idea of weak ties bringing new opportunities), but it is also true that greater income causes social networks to be more diverse. This is not the standard picture that we have in our heads when we design society and policy.

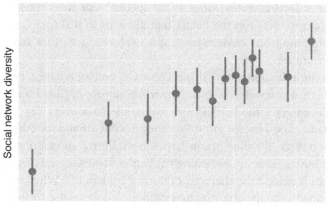

FIGURE 5.1
As people interact with more diverse communities, their income
increases (100,000 randomly chosen people in mid-income
country).[19]

In Western society, we generally assume that individual features far outweigh social network factors. While this assumption
is incorrect, nevertheless it influences our approach to many
things. Consider how we design our schools and universities. My
research group has worked with universities in several different
countries and measured their patterns of social interactions. We
find that social connections are dramatically better predictors of
student outcome than personality, study patterns, previous training, grades, or other individual traits. Performance in school, in
school tests, has more to do with the community of interactions
that you have than with the things that the "rational individual"
model leads us to assume are important. It's shocking.

It is better to conceive of humans as a species who are on
a continual search for new opportunities, for new ideas, and
their social networks serve as a major, and perhaps the greatest, resource for finding opportunities. The bottom line is that

humans are like every other social species. Our lives consist of a balance between the habits that allow us to make a living by exploiting our environment and exploration to find new opportunities.

In the animal literature this is known as *foraging behavior*. For instance, if you watch rabbits, they will come out of their holes, they'll go get some berries, they will come back every day at the same time—except some days they'll scout around for other berry bushes. It's the tension between exploring, in case your berry bush goes away, and eating the berries while they are there.

This is exactly the character of normal human life. When we examined data for one hundred million people in the United States, we can see that people are immensely predictable. If I know what you do in the morning, I can know, with a 90% plus odds of being right, what you will be doing in the evening and with whom. But every once in a while, people break loose and they explore people and places that they visit only very occasionally and this behavior is extremely unpredictable.

Moreover, when you find individuals who do not show this pattern, they are almost always sick or stressed in some way. You can tell whether a person's life is healthy in a general sense—both mentally and physically—by whether they show this most basic biological rhythm or not. In fact, this tendency is regular enough that one of the largest health services in the U.S. is using this to keep track of at-risk patients.

If you combine this idea of foraging for novelty with the idea that diverse networks bring greater opportunities and greater income, you would expect that cities that facilitate connecting with a wide range of people would be wealthier. So, we gathered data from 150 cities in the United States and 150 cities in the European Union, and examined the patterns of physical interactions between people.

If your city facilitates more diverse interactions, then you likely have more diverse opportunities and over the long term you will

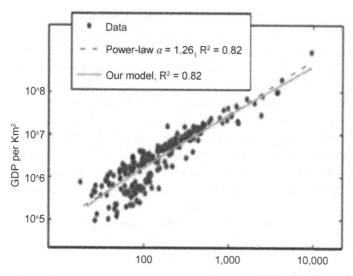

FIGURE 5.2

As face-to-face communication within a city allows interaction between more diverse communities, the city wealth increases. Data from 150 cities in the United States and 150 in the European Union.[20]

make more money. From the figure above, you can see this model predicts GDP per square kilometer extremely accurately, in both the United States and the European Union. What that says is that the factors that we usually think about—investment, education, infrastructure, institutions—may be epiphenomenal. Instead of being the core of growth and innovation, they may make a difference primarily because they help or hinder the search for new opportunities. The main driver of progress in society may be the search for new opportunities and the search for new ideas—as opposed to skills in people's heads or capital investment.

Summary: OPAL-style data systems (as described in previous chapters) that produce census-like descriptions of society by combining data from mobile phone operators, banks, and governments provide a safe, powerful method of developing quantitative models of cities and their civic systems. This new computational social science understanding of human behavior and society in terms of networks, the search for new opportunities, and the exchange of ideas might best be called Social Physics, a name coined two centuries ago by Auguste Comte, the founder of sociology. His concept was that certain ideas shaped the development of society in a regular manner. While his theories were in many ways too simplistic, the recent successes of computational social science show that he was going in the right direction. It is the flow of ideas and opportunities between people that drives society, providing quantitative results at scales ranging from small groups, to companies, cities, and even entire countries.

OPTIMIZING OPPORTUNITY

Once we understand ourselves better, we can build better societies. If the search for new opportunities and ideas is the core of human progress, then we should ask how best to accomplish this search. To optimize opportunity, I will turn to the science of financial investment, which provides clear, simple, and well-developed examples of the tradeoff between exploiting known opportunities and exploring for new ones.

In particular, I will look at Bayesian portfolio analysis. These methods are used to choose among alternative actions when the potential for profit is unknown or uncertain. Many of the best hedge funds and the best consumer retail organizations use this type of method for their overall management structure.

The core idea associated with these analysis methods is that when decision-makers are faced with a wide range of alternative actions, each with unknown payoff, they must select actions to discover those that lead to the best payoffs and at the same time exploit the actions that are currently believed to be the best in order to remain competitive against opponents. This is the same idea as animals foraging for food, or people searching for new opportunities while still making a living.

In a social setting the payoff for each potential action can be easily and cheaply determined by observing the payoffs of other members of a decision-maker's social network. This use of social learning dramatically improves both overall performance and reduces the cognitive load placed on the human participants. The ability to rapidly communicate and observe other decisions across the social network is one of the key aspects of optimal social learning and exploration for opportunity.

As an example, my research group recently examined how top performers maximize the sharing of strategic information within a social-network stock-trading site where people can see the strategies that other people choose, discuss them, and copy them. The team analyzed some 5.8 million transactions and found that the groups of traders who fared the best all followed a version of this social learning strategy called distributed Thompson sampling. It was calculated that the forecasts from groups that followed the distributed Thompson sampling formula reliably beat the best individual forecasts by a margin of almost 30%. Furthermore, when the results of these groups were compared to results obtained using standard AI techniques, the humans that followed the distributed Thompson sampling methodology reliably beat the standard AI techniques!

It is important to emphasize that this approach is qualitatively the same as that used by Amazon to configure its portfolio of products as well as its delivery services. A very similar approach is taken by the best financial hedge funds. Fully dynamic and interleaved planning, intelligence gathering, evaluation, and action selection produce a powerfully optimized organization.

This social learning approach has one more advantage that is both unique and essential for social species: the actions of the individual human are in their best interest and in the best interest of everyone in the social network. Furthermore, the alignment of individuals' incentives and the organization's incentives are visible and understandable. This means that it is easy, in terms of both incentives and cognitive load, for individuals to act in the best interests of the society: optimal personal and societal pay-offs are the same, and the individual can learn optimal behavior just by observing others.

SOCIAL BRIDGES IN CITIES: PATHS TO OPPORTUNITY

Cities are a great example of how the process of foraging for new opportunities shapes human society. Cities are major production centers of society, and as we have already seen, cities where it is easy to search for new opportunities are wealthier. Long-term economic growth is primarily driven by innovation in the society, and cities facilitate human interaction and idea exchange needed for good ideas and new opportunities.

These new opportunities and new ideas range from changes in means of production or product types to the most up-to-the-minute news. For example, success on Wall Street often involves knowing new events minutes before anyone else. In this environment, the informational advantages of extreme spatial proximity become very high. This may explain why Wall Street remains in a tiny physical area in the tip of Manhattan. The spatial concentration of economic actors increases productivity at the firm level by increasing the flow of new ideas, both within and across firms.

Our evidence suggests that bringing together people from diverse communities will be the best way to construct a vibrant, wealthy city. When we examine flows of people in real cities, however, we find that mixing is much more limited than we normally think. People who live in one neighborhood work mostly with people from only a couple of other neighborhoods and they shop in a similarly limited number of areas.

Physical interaction is mostly limited to a relatively small number of social bridges between neighborhoods. It is perhaps unsurprising that people who spend time together, whether at work or at play, learn from each other and adopt very similar behaviors. When I go to work, or to a store, I may see someone wearing a new style of shoe, and think: "Hey, that looks really cool. Maybe I'll get some shoes like that." Or, perhaps I go to the restaurant that I always like, and somebody nearby orders something different, and I think: "Oh, that looks pretty good. Maybe I'm going to try that next time." When people spend time together they begin to mimic each other, they learn from each other, and they adopt similar behaviors and attitudes.

In fact, what you find is that all sorts of behaviors, such as what sort of clothes they buy, how they deal with credit cards, even diseases of behavior (like drug addiction or alcoholism) flow mostly within groups connected by social bridges. They don't follow demographic boundaries nearly as much. In a recent study of a large European city, for instance, we found that social bridges were 300% better at predicting people's behaviors than demographics including age, gender, income, and education.

Groups of neighborhoods joined by rich social bridges form local cultures. Consequently, by knowing a few places that a person hangs out in, you can tell a huge amount about them. This is very important in both marketing and politics. The process of learning from each other by spending time together means that ideas and behaviors tend to spread mostly within the cluster, but not further. A new type of shoe, a new type of music, a political viewpoint, will spread within a cluster of neighborhoods joined by social bridges, but will tend not to go across cluster boundaries to other places. Advertisers and political hacks talk about influencers changing people's minds. What I believe is that it is more the social bridges, people hanging out, seeing each other, interacting with each other, that determine the way ideas spread.

Privacy is an important question in terms of using social bridges data to engineer civic systems. Data about individuals must be treated specially to preserve privacy, and, of course, any sort of data brings the dangers associated with cyberattacks. To address these issues, we worked in collaboration with civic systems experts from many different fields (health, transportation, power, etc.), to determine the proper tradeoff between usefulness and risk to privacy through re-identification. The results are shown in the figure below; across use domains there was a smooth tradeoff between resolution (e.g., city scale, district scale, or individual scale), time (e.g., year, month, day, or seconds), and utility. The scale typically used by the national census and city planners turns out to be optimal: data that are averaged to the district (neighborhood) level have the best tradeoff between risk and utility. As a consequence, all of our social

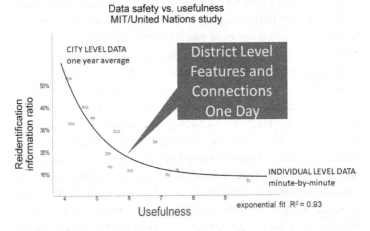

FIGURE 5.3
OPAL-style data systems that aggregate data to the district and daily level provide a safe means for designing civic systems without undue threat to personal privacy.[21]

bridges measurements were averaged down to the district-by-district level and no individual-level data were used.

Summary: What Adam Smith said about people exchanging ideas—that it is the peer-to-peer exchanges that determine norms and behaviors—is exactly true. But what is truly stunning is that because we hold onto the "rational individual" model of human nature, we assume that preferences are best described by individual demographics—age, income, gender, race, education and so forth—and that is wrong. The way to think about society is in terms of these behavior groups. Whom do they associate with? What are those other people doing? The idea of social bridges is a far more powerful concept than demographics, because social bridges are the most powerful way that people influence each other. By understanding these social bridges, we can begin to build a smarter, more harmonious society.

DIVERSITY AND PRODUCTIVITY

As an example, consider the OPAL-style data experiment I created with Professors Guan and Chen of Beijing Normal University. Using mobile phone data to determine the social bridges caused by physical interactions between people provides a way to estimate behavioral effects of social learning through observation (e.g., what clothes to wear or what food to order) and through intermediary interactions (e.g., word of mouth, mutual friends). To infer these social bridge interactions between people, a network of aggregated interactions was first obtained based on proximity. Physical proximity has been shown to increase the likelihood of face-to-face conversations and this increase in interaction strength is widely used to help city planning and placement of city amenities.[23]

The social bridges idea is based on the observation that individuals can commonly be identified as part of a community with relatively homogeneous behavior based on where they live,

work, and shop. Where you invest your most valuable resource—
time—reveals your preferences. Each community typically has
access to different pools of information, opportunities, or offers
different perspectives. Diverse interactions should then increase
a population's access to the opportunities and ideas required for
productive activity and economic growth.

When we apply this logic to the cities in the United States, Asia,
and Europe, we find that the effect of diversity on GDP growth
is comparable to that of changes in population density. In other
words, the effect on GDP of diversity of idea flow via the social
bridges is about the same as the effect on GDP of the number of
individuals in the region. If we compare the explanatory strength
of interaction diversity with other variables, such as average age
or percentage of residents who received a tertiary education, we
find that these traditional measures are much weaker at explain-
ing economic growth than social bridge diversity. This means
that models and civil systems that depend only on population
and education are missing the main effects.

FIGURE 5.4
Interaction diversity (left) and economic growth (right) for the
city of Beijing comparing the effects of interaction diversity
and economic growth. These maps show that they are highly
correlated.[22]

CONCLUSION

MIT's mission is to solve humanity's greatest challenges, particularly via advancing the frontier of human knowledge. The OPAL and ENIGMA style data systems described in this book, which provide unprecedented views of the human condition, can be key to achieving these goals. The example presented in this chapter, from my Beijing City Innovation Lab, shows how the structure of social bridges predicts productivity and GDP growth. This prediction capability shows how such a data system can support both the theory and practice of city planning and enable government to better promote economic growth and innovation.

In creating living labs such as the one in Beijing, we draw on interdisciplinary expertise across several of MIT's schools (Engineering, Management, Science, and Architecture & Planning / MIT Media Lab), as well as our research collaborators from dozens of universities around the world.

While we are by no means the only researchers using the living lab methodology, we are world leaders in both data architecture and analytics infrastructure. As living labs continue to proliferate around the world, I see our role as being the leading global provider of state-of-the-art tools that can be used to improve the human experience.

We continue to seek out new partners who can help us on the journey of exploration of the potential of data-enabled living labs. We hope to transform societies and help companies to better engage their stakeholders. To make this possible, we need to build systems that follow the Trust::Data framework described in this book, and advocates and evangelists who raise awareness of, and enhance the capabilities of, these powerful new tools. Please join us in building this better tomorrow.

REFERENCES

1. Bengtsson, L., J. Gaudart, X. Lu, S. Moore, E. Wetter, K. Sallah, S. Rebaudet, and R. Piarroux. 2015. "Using Mobile Phone Data to Predict the Spatial Spread of Cholera." *Scientific Reports* 5:8923.

2. Blumenstock, J., G. Cadamuro, and R. On. 2016. "Predicting Poverty and Wealth from Mobile Phone Metadata." *Science* 350 (6264): 1073–1076.

3. Bogomolov, A., B. Lepri, J. Staiano, N. Oliver, F. Pianesi, and A. Pentland. 2014. "Once Upon a Crime: Towards Crime Prediction from Demographics and Mobile Phone Data." In *Proceedings of the 16th International Conference on Multimodal Interaction* (ICMI 2014), 427–434. New York: ACM.

4. Gundogdu, D., O. D. Incel, A. A. Salah, and B. Lepri. 2016. "Countrywide Arrhythmia: Emergency Event Detection Using Mobile Phone Data." *EPJ Data Science* 5 (1): 1–19. https://doi.org/10.1140/epjds/s13688 -016-0086-0.

5. Jean, N., M. Burke, M. Xie, W. M. Davis, D. B. Lobell, and S. Ermon. 2016. "Combining Satellite Imagery and Machine Learning to Predict Poverty." *Science* 353 (6301): 790–794.

6. Independent Expert Advisory Group on a Data Revolution for Sustainable Development. 2014. "A World That Counts: Mobilising the Data Revolution for Sustainable Development." UN Data Revolution Group. http://www.undatarevolution.org/wp-content/uploads/2014/11 /A-World-That-Counts.pdf.

7. Lu, X., L. Bengtsson, and P. Holme. 2012. "Predictability of Population Displacement after the 2010 Haiti Earthquake." *PNAS* 109: 11576–11581.

8. Pastor-Escuerdo, D., Y. Torres Fernandez, J. M. Bauer, A. Wadhwa, C. Castro-Correa, L. Romanoff, J. G. Lee, A. Rutherford, V. Frias-Martinez, N. Oliver, E. Frias-Martinez, and M. Luengo-Oroz. 2014. "Flooding through the Lens of Mobile Phone Activity." In *IEEE Global Humanitarian Technology Conference* (GHTC 2014), 279–286. San Jose, CA: IEEE Computer Society. DOI: 10.1109/GHTC.2014.6970293

9. Ruktanonchai, N. W., D. Bhavnani, A. Sorichetta, L. Bengtsoon, K. H. Carter, R. C. Cordoba, A. Le Menach, X. Lu, E. Wetter, E. zu

Erbach-Schoenberg, and A. J. Tatem. 2016. "Census-Derived Migration Data as a Tool for Informing Malaria Elimination Policy." *Malaria Journal* 15: 273.

10. Smith-Clarke, C., A. Mashhadi, and L. Capra. 2014. "Poverty on the Cheap: Estimating Poverty Maps Using Aggregated Mobile Communication." In *Proceedings of the SIGCHI Conference on Human Factors in Computing Systems* (CHI 2014), 511–520. New York: ACM.

11. Soto, V., V. Frias-Martinez, J. Virseda, and E. Frias-Martinez. 2011. "Prediction of Socioeconomic Levels Using Cell Phone Records." In *Proceedings of the International Conference on User Modeling, Adaptation, and Personalization* (UMAP 2011), 377–388. Berlin: Springer-Verlag. DOI: 10.1007/978-3-642-22362-4.

12. Steele, J. E., P. R. Sundsøy, C. Pezzulo, V. A. Alegana, T. J. Bird, J. Blumenstock, J. Bjelland, K. Engø-Monsen, Y.-A. de Montjoye, A. M. Iqbal, K. N. Hadiuzzaman, X. Lu, E. Wetter, A. J. Tatem, and L. Bengtsson. 2017. "Mapping Poverty Using Mobile Phone and Satellite Data." *Journal of the Royal Society Interface* 14 (127): 1–10. https://doi.org/10.1098/rsif.2016.0690.

13. Traunmueller, M., G. Quattrone, and L. Capra. 2014. "Mining Mobile Phone Data to Investigate Urban Crime Theories at Scale." In *Proceedings of the International Conference on Social Informatics* (SocInfo 2014), 396–411. Berlin: Springer-Verlag.

14. Wang, H., D. Kifer, C. Graif, and Z. Li. 2016. "Crime Rate Inference with Big Data." In *Proceedings of the ACM SIGKDD Conference on Knowledge Discovery and Data Mining* (KDD 2016), 635–644. New York: ACM.

15. Wesolowski, A., N. Eagle, A. J. Tatem, D. L. Smith, A. M. Noor, R. W. Snow, C. O. Buckee. 2012. "Quantifying the Impact of Human Mobility on Malaria." *Science* 338 (6104): 267–270.

16. Wesolowski, A., C. J. E. Metcalf, N. Eagle, J. Kombich, B. T. Grenfell, O. N. Bjørnstad, J. Lessler, A. J. Tatem, and C. O. Buckee. 2015. "Quantifying Seasonal Population Fluxes Driving Rubella Transmission Dynamics Using Mobile Phone Data." *PNAS* 112 (35): 11114–11119.

17. Wesolowski, A., T. Qureshi, M. F. Boni, P. R. Sundsøy, M. A. Johansson, S. B. Rasheed, K. Engø-Monsen, and C. O. Buckee. 2015. "Impact of

Human Mobility on the Emergence of Dengue Epidemics in Pakistan."
PNAS 112 (38): 11887–11892.

18. Wilson, R., E. zu Erbach-Schoenberg, M. Albert, D. Power, M. Gonzalez, S. Guthrie, H. Chamberlain, C. Brooks, C. Hughes, L. Pitonakova, C. O. Buckee, X. Lu, E. Wetter, A. J. Tatem, and L. Bengtsson. February 4, 2016. "Rapid and Near Real-Time Assessments of Population Displacement Using Mobile Phone Data Following Disasters: The 2015 Nepal Earthquake." *PLOS Currents* 8. DOI: 10.1371/currents.dis.d073fbece328 e4c39087bc086d694b5c.

19. Jahani, Eaman, Pål Sundsøy, Johannes Bjelland, Linus Bengtsson, Alex 'Sandy' Pentland, and Yves-Alexandre de Montjoye. 2017. "Improving Official Statistics in Emerging Markets Using Machine Learning and Mobile Phone Data." *EPJ Data Science* 6 (3). https://doi.org/10.1140/epjds/s13688-017-0099-3.

20. Pan, Wei, Gourab Ghoshal, Coco Krumme, Manuel Cebrian, and Alex Pentland. 2013. "Urban Characteristics Attributable to Density-Driven Tie Formation." *Nature Communications* 4 (1961). https://doi.org/10.1038/ncomms2961.

21. "Mapping the Risk-Utility Landscape of Mobile Data for Sustainable Development & Humanitarian Action." 2015. http://unglobalpulse.org.

22. Chong, Shi-Kai, M. Baharami, H. Chen, S. Balcisoy, B. Bozkaya, and A. Pentland. Forthcoming. "Economic Outcomes Predicted by Diversity in Cities."

23. Pentland, A. 2015. *Social Physics: How Social Networks Can Make Us Smarter*. New York: Penguin Books.

II POLICY

6 THE NEW DEAL ON DATA

Daniel "Dazza" Greenwood,
Arkadiusz Stopczynski, Brian Sweatt,
Thomas Hardjono, and Alex Pentland

INTRODUCTION

In order to realize the promise of a Data for Good society and to reduce the potential risk to individuals, institutions are updating the operational frameworks that govern the business, legal, and technical dimensions of their internal organizations. In this chapter, we outline ways to support the emergence of such a society within the framework of the New Deal on Data, and describe future directions for research and development. In our view, the traditional control points relied on as part of corporate governance, management oversight, legal compliance, and enterprise architecture must evolve and expand to match operational frameworks for big data. These controls must support and reflect greater user control over personal data, as well as large-scale interoperability for data sharing between and among institutions. The core capabilities of these controls should include responsive rule-based systems governance and fine-grained authorizations for distributed rights management.

THE NEW DEAL ON DATA

The digital breadcrumbs we leave behind are clues to who we are, what we do, and what we want. This makes personal data—data about individuals—immensely valuable, both for public good and for private companies. The ability to see the details of so many interactions is also immensely powerful and can be used for good or for ill. Therefore, protecting personal privacy and freedom is critical to our future success as a society. We need to enable more data sharing for the public good; at the same time, we need to do a much better job of protecting the privacy of individuals.

A successful data-driven society must be able to guarantee that our data will not be abused—perhaps especially that government will not abuse the power conferred by access to such fine-grained data. There are many ways in which abuses might be directly targeted—from imposing higher insurance rates based on individual shopping history,[11] to creating problems for the entire society by limiting user choices and enclosing users in information bubbles.[12] To achieve the potential for a new society, we require the New Deal on Data, which describes workable guarantees that the data needed for public good is readily available while at the same time protecting the citizenry.[13]

The key insight behind the New Deal on Data is that our data is worth more when shared. Aggregate data—averaged, combined across population, and often distilled to high-level features—can be used to inform improvements in systems such as public health, transportation, and government. For instance, we have demonstrated that data about the way we behave and where we go can be used to minimize the spread of infectious disease.[14] Our research has also shown how digital breadcrumbs can be used to track the spread of influenza from person to person on an individual level. And the public good can be served as a result: if we can see it, we can also stop it. Similarly, if we are worried about global warming, shared, aggregated data can reveal how patterns of mobility relate to productivity.[15] This, in turn, equips us to design cities that are more productive and, at the same time, more energy efficient. However, to obtain these results and make a greener world, we must be able to see people moving around; this depends on having many people willing to contribute their data, if only anonymously and in aggregate. In addition, the Big Data transformation can help society find efficient means of governance by providing tools to analyze and understand what needs to be done, and to reach consensus on how to do it. This goes beyond simply creating more communication platforms; the assumption that more interaction between users will produce better decisions may be very misleading— although in recent years, we have seen impressive uses of social networks for better organization in society (e.g., during political protests).[16] We are far from even starting to reach consensus about the big problems: epidemics, climate change, pollution— big data can help us achieve such goals.

However, to enable the sharing of personal data and experiences, we need secure technology and regulation that allow individuals to safely and conveniently share personal information with each other, with corporations, and with government. Consequently, the heart of the New Deal on Data must be to provide both regulatory standards and financial incentives enticing owners to share data, while at the same time serving the interests of individuals and society at large. We must promote greater idea flow among individuals, not just within corporations or government departments.

Unfortunately, today most personal data are siloed in private companies and therefore largely unavailable. Private organizations collect the vast majority of personal data in the form of mobility patterns, financial transactions, and phone and Internet communications. These data must not remain the exclusive domain of private companies, because they are then less likely to contribute to the common good; private organizations must be key players in the New Deal on Data. Likewise, this data should not become the exclusive domain of the government. The entities who should be empowered to share and make decisions about their data are the people themselves: users, participants, citizens.

We cannot only involve experts, but must also use the wisdom of crowds—users themselves interested in improving society.

PERSONAL DATA: EMERGENCE OF A NEW ASSET CLASS

One of the first steps to promoting liquidity in land and commodity markets is to guarantee ownership rights so that people can safely buy and sell. Similarly, a first step toward creating more ideas and greater flow of ideas—idea liquidity—is to define ownership rights. The only politically viable course is to give individual citizens key rights over data that are about them, the type of rights that have undergirded the European Union's Privacy Directive since 1995.[17] We need to recognize personal data as a valuable asset of the individual, which can be given to companies and government in return for services.

We can draw the definition of ownership from English common law on ownership rights of possession, use, and disposal:

- You have the right to possess data about yourself. Regardless of what entity collects the data, the data belong to you, and you can access your data at any time. Data collectors thus play a role akin to a bank, managing data on behalf of their "customers."

- You have the right to full control over the use of your data. The terms of use must be opt in and clearly explained in plain language. If you are not happy with the way a company uses your data, you can remove the data, just as you would close your account with a bank that is not providing satisfactory service.

- You have the right to dispose of or distribute your data. You have the option to have data about you destroyed or redeployed elsewhere.

Individual rights to personal data must be balanced with the need of corporations and governments to use certain data-account activity, billing information, and the like to run their day-to-day operations. The New Deal on Data therefore gives individuals the right to possess, control, and dispose of copies of these required operational data, along with copies of the incidental data collected about the individual, such as location and similar context. These ownership rights are not exactly the same as literal ownership under modern law; the practical effect is that disputes are resolved in a different, simpler manner than would be the case for land ownership disputes, for example.

In 2007, one of the authors of this chapter (Alex Pentland) first proposed the New Deal on Data to the World Economic Forum.[18] Since then, this idea has run through various discussions and eventually helped to shape the 2012 Consumer Data Bill of Rights in the United States, along with a matching declaration on Personal Data Rights in the European Union.

The World Economic Forum (WEF) echoed the European Consumer Commissioner, Meglena Kuneva, in dubbing personal data the "new oil" or new resource of the twenty-first century.[19] The "personal data sector" of the economy today is in its infancy, its state akin to the oil industry during the late 1890s. Productive collaboration between government (building the state-owned freeways), the private sector (mining and refining oil, building automobiles), and the citizens (the user-base of these services) allowed developed nations to expand their economies by creating new markets adjacent to the automobile and oil industries.

If personal data, as the new oil, is to reach its global economic potential, productive collaboration is needed between all stakeholders in the establishment of a personal data ecosystem. A number of fundamental uncertainties exist, however, about privacy, property, global governance, human rights—essentially about who should benefit from the products and services built on personal data.[20] The rapid rate of technological change and commercialization in the use of personal data is undermining end-user confidence and trust.

The current personal data ecosystem is feudal, fragmented, and inefficient. Too much leverage is currently accorded to service providers that enroll and register end-users. Their siloed repositories of personal data exemplify the fragmentation of the ecosystem, containing data of varying qualities; some are attributes of persons that are unverified, while others represent higher quality data that have been cross-correlated with other data points of the end-user. For many individuals, the risks and liabilities of the current ecosystem exceed the economic returns. Besides not having the infrastructure and tools to manage personal data, many end-users simply do not see the benefit of fully participating. Personal privacy concerns are thus addressed inadequately at best, or simply overlooked in the majority of cases. Current technologies and laws fall short of providing the legal and technical infrastructure needed to support a well-functioning digital economy.

Recently, we have seen the challenges, but also the feasibility, of opening private big data. In the Data for Development (D4D) Challenge (http://www.d4d.orange.com), the telecommunication company, Orange, opened access to a large dataset of call detail records from the Ivory Coast. Working with the data as part of a challenge, teams of researchers came up with life-changing insights for the country. For example, one team developed a model for how disease spreads in the country and demonstrated that information campaigns based on one-to-one phone conversations among members of social groups can be an effective countermeasure.[21] Data release must be carefully done, however; as we have seen in several cases, such as the Netflix Prize privacy disaster[22] and other similar privacy breaches,[23] true anonymization is extremely hard—recent research by de Montjoye et al. and others[24,25] has shown that even though human beings are highly predictable, we are also unique. Having access to one dataset may be enough to uniquely fingerprint someone based on just a few data points, and this fingerprint can be used to discover their true identity. In releasing and analyzing the D4D data, the privacy of the people who generated the data was protected not only by technical means, such as removal of personally identifiable information (PII), but also by legal means, with the researchers signing an agreement that they would not use the data for re-identification or other nefarious purposes. Opening data from the silos by publishing static datasets—collected at some point and unchanging—is important, but it is only the first step. We can do even more when data is available in real time and can become part of a society's nervous system. Epidemics can be monitored and prevented in real time,[26] underperforming students can be helped, and people with health risks can be treated before they get sick.[27]

The report of the World Economic Forum[28] suggests a way forward by identifying useful areas on which to focus efforts:

- *Alignment of key stakeholders.* Citizens, the private sector, and the public sector need to work in support of one another. Efforts such as NSTIC[29] in the United States—albeit still in its infancy—represent a promising direction for global collaboration.

- *Viewing data as money.* There needs to be a new mindset, in which an individual's personal data items are viewed and treated in the same way as their money. These personal data items would reside in an "account" (like a bank account) where they would be controlled, managed, exchanged, and accounted for just as personal banking services operate today.

- *End-user centricity.* All entities in the ecosystem need to recognize end-users as vital and independent stakeholders in the co-creation and exchange of services and experiences. Efforts such as the User-Managed Access (UMA) initiative[30] provide examples of system design that are user-centric and managed by the user.

ENFORCING THE NEW DEAL ON DATA

How can we enforce this New Deal? The threat of legal action is important, but not sufficient; if you cannot see abuses, you cannot prosecute them. Enforcement can be addressed significantly without prosecution or public statute or regulation. In many fields, companies and governments rely on rules governing common business, legal, and technical (BLT) practices to create effective self-organization and enforcement. This approach holds promise as a method by which institutional controls can form a reliable operational framework for big data, privacy, and access.

One current best practice is a system of data sharing called a "trust network," a combination of networked computers and legal rules defining and governing expectations regarding data. For personal data, these networks of technical and legal rules keep track of user permissions for each piece of data and act as a legal contract, specifying what happens in case of a violation. For example, in a trust network all personal data can have attached labels specifying where the data come from and what they can and cannot be used for. These labels are exactly matched by the terms in the legal contracts between all of the participants, stating penalties for not obeying them. The rules can—and often do—reference or require audits of relevant systems and data use, demonstrating how traditional internal controls can be leveraged as part of the transition to more novel trust models. A well-designed trust network, comprised of elegantly integrated computer and legal rules, allows automatic auditing of data use and allows individuals to change their permissions and withdraw data.

The mechanism for establishing and operating a trust network is to create system rules for the applications, service providers, data, and the users themselves. System rules are sometimes called "operating regulations" in the credit card context, "trust frameworks" in the identity federation context, or "trading partner agreements" in a supply value chain context. Several multi-party shared architectural and contractual rules create binding obligations and enforceable expectations on all participants in scalable networks. Furthermore, the design of the system rules allows participants to be widely distributed across heterogeneous business ownership boundaries, legal governance structures, and technical security domains. However, the parties need not conform in all or even most aspects of their basic roles, relationships, and activities in order to connect to a trust network. Cross-domain trusted systems must—by their nature—focus enforceable rules narrowly on commonly agreed items in order for that network to achieve its purpose.

For example, institutions participating in credit card and automated clearing house networks are subject to profoundly different sets of regulations, business practices, economic conditions, and social expectations. The network rules focus on the topmost agreed items affecting interoperability, reciprocity, risk, and revenue allocation. The knowledge that fundamental rules are subject to enforcement action is one of the foundations of trust and a motivation to prevent or address violations before they trigger penalties. A clear example of this approach can be found in the Visa Operating Rules, which cover a vast global real-time network of parties agreeing to rules governing their roles in the system as merchants, banks, transaction processors, individual or business card holders, and other key system roles.

Such rules have made the interbank money transfer system among the safest systems in the world and the backbone for daily exchanges of trillions of dollars, but until recently those were only for the "big guys."[31] To give individuals a similarly safe method of managing personal data, the Human Dynamics group at MIT, in partnership with the Institute for Data Driven Design (co-founded by John Clippinger and author Alex Pentland) have helped to build an open Personal Data Store (open-PDS).[32] The openPDS is a consumer version of a personal cloud trust network now being tested with a variety of industry and government partners. The aim is to make sharing personal data as safe and secure as transferring money between banks.

When dealing with data intended to be accessible over networks—whether big, personal, or otherwise—the traditional container of an institution makes less and less sense. Institutional controls apply, by definition, to some type of institutional entity such as a business, governmental, or religious organization. A synopsis of all the business, legal, and technical (BLT) facts and circumstances surrounding big data is necessary in order to know what access, confidentiality, and other expectations exist; the relevant contextual aspects of big data at one institution are often profoundly different from those at another. As more and more organizations use and rely on big data, a single formula for institutional controls will not work for increasingly heterogeneous BLT environments.

The capacity to apply appropriate methods of enforcement for a trust network depends on clear understanding and agreement among the parties about the purpose of the system and the respective roles or expectations of those connecting as participants. Therefore, some contextual anchor is needed to have a clear basis for establishing an operational framework and institutional controls appropriate for big data.

TRANSITIONING END-USER ASSENT PRACTICES

The way users grant authorization to share their data is not a trivial matter. The flow of personal information such as location data, purchases, and health records can be very complex. Every tweet, geotagged picture, phone call, or purchase with credit card provides the user's location not only to the primary service, but also to all the applications and services that have been authorized to access and reuse these data. The authorization may come from the end-user or be granted by the collecting service, based on umbrella terms of service that cover reuse of the data. Implementation of such flows was a crucial part of the Web 2.0 revolution, realized with RESTful APIs, mashups, and authorization-based access. The way personal data travels between services has arguably become too complex for a user to handle and manage.

Increasing the range of data controlled by the user and the granularity of this control is meaningless if it cannot be exercised in an informed way. For many years, a poor model has been provided by End-User License Agreements (EULAs), long incomprehensible texts that are accepted blindly by users trusting they have not agreed to anything that could harm them. The process of granting meaningful authorization cannot be too complex, as it would prevent a user from understanding her decisions. At the same time, it cannot be too simplistic, as it may not sufficiently convey the weight of the privacy-related decisions it captures. It is a challenge in itself to build end-user assent systems that allow users to understand and adjust their privacy settings.

This gap between the interface—single click—and the effect can render data ownership meaningless; one click may wrench people and their data into systems and rules that are antithetical to fair information practices, as is prevalent with today's end-user licenses in cloud services or applications. Managing the long-term tensions fueled by "old deal" systems operating simultaneously with the New Deal is an important design and migration challenge during the transition to a big data economy. During this transition, and after the New Deal on Data is no longer new, personal data must continue to flow in order to be useful. Protecting the data of people outside of directly user-controlled domains is very hard without a combination of cost-effective and useful business practices, legal rules, and technical solutions.

We envision "living informed consent," where the user is entitled to know what data is being collected about her by which entities, empowered to understand the implications of data sharing, and finally put in charge of the sharing authorizations. We suggest that readers ask themselves a question: Which services know which city I am in today? Google? Apple? Twitter? Amazon? Facebook? Flickr? Some app I authorized a few years ago to access my Facebook check-ins and have since forgotten about? This is an example of a fundamental question related to user privacy and assent, and yet finding an accurate answer can be surprisingly difficult in today's ecosystem. We can hope that most services treat data responsibly and according to user authorizations. In the complex network of data flows, however, it is relatively easy for data to leak to careless or malicious services.[33] We need to build solutions that help users to make well-informed decisions about data sharing in this environment.

BIG DATA AND PERSONAL DATA INSTITUTIONAL CONTROLS

The concept of "institutional controls" refers to safeguards and protections implemented through legal, policy, governance, and other measures that are not solely technical, engineering, or mechanical. Institutional controls in the context of big data can perhaps best be understood by examining how such controls have been applied to other domains, most prevalently in the field of environmental regulation. A good example of how this concept supports and reflects the goals and objectives of environmental regulation can be found in the policy documents of the Environmental Protection Agency (EPA), which gives the following definition in its Institutional Controls Glossary:

> *Institutional controls.* Non-engineering measures intended to affect human activities in such a way as to prevent or reduce exposure to hazardous substances. They are almost always used in conjunction with, or as a supplement to, other measures such as waste treatment or containment. There are four categories of institutional controls: governmental controls; proprietary controls; enforcement tools; and informational devices.[34]

The concept of an "institutional control boundary" is especially clarifying and powerful when applied to the networked and digital boundaries of an institution. In the context of Florida's environmental regulation, the phrase is applied when a property owner's risk management and cleanup responsibilities extend beyond the area defined by the physical property boundary. For example, a recent University of Florida report on cleanup target levels (CTLs) states, "in some rare situations, the institutional control boundary at which default CTLs must be met can extend beyond the site property boundary."[35]

When institutional controls apply to "separately owned neighboring properties" a number of possibilities arise that are very relevant to management of personal data across legal, business, and other systemic boundaries. Requiring the party responsible for site cleanup to use "best efforts" to attain agreement from the neighboring owners to institute the relevant institutional controls is perhaps the most direct and least proscriptive approach. When direct negotiated agreement is unsuccessful, then use of third-party neutrals to resolve disagreements regarding institutional controls can be required. If necessary, environmental regulation can force the acquisition of neighboring land by compelling the party responsible to purchase the other property or by purchase of the property directly by the EPA.[36]

In the context of big data, institutional controls are seldom, if ever, imposed through government regulatory frameworks such as are seen in environmental waste management oversight by the EPA.[37] Rather, institutions applying measures constituting institutional controls in the big data and related information technology and enterprise architecture contexts will typically employ governance safeguards, business practices, legal contracts, technical security, reporting, audit programs, and various risk management measures.

Inevitably, institutional controls for big data will have to operate effectively across institutional boundaries, just as environmental waste management must sometimes be applied across real property boundaries and may subject multiple different owners to enforcement actions corresponding to the applicable controls. Short of government regulation, the use of system rules as a general model is one widely understood, accepted, and efficient method for defining, agreeing, and enforcing institutional and other controls across BLT domains of ownership, governance, and operation.

Following on from the World Economic Forum's recommendation to treat personal data stores in the manner of bank accounts,[38] a number of infrastructure improvements need to be realized if the personal data ecosystem is to flourish and deliver new economic opportunities:

- *New global data provenance network.* In order for personal datastores to be treated like bank accounts, origin information regarding data items coming into the datastore must be maintained.[39] In other words, the provenance of all data items must be accounted for by the IT infrastructure on which the personal datastore operates. The databases must then be interconnected in order to provide a resilient, scalable platform for audit and accounting systems to track and reconcile the movement of personal data from different datastores.

- *Trust network for computational law.* For trust to be established between parties who wish to exchange personal data, some degree of "computational law" technology may have to be integrated into the design of personal data systems. This technology should not only verify terms of contracts (e.g., terms of data use) against user-defined policies but also have mechanisms built in to ensure non-repudiation of entities who have accepted these digital contracts. Efforts such as the UMA initiative are beginning to bring better evidentiary proof and enforceability of contracts into technical protocol flows.[40]

- *Development of institutional controls for digital institutions.* Currently, a number of proposals for the creation of virtual currencies (e.g., Bitcoin,[41] Ven[42]) have underlying systems with the potential to evolve into self-governing "digital institutions."[43] Such systems and the institutions that operate on them will necessitate the development of a new paradigm to understand aspects of institutional control within their context.

SCENARIOS OF USE IN CONTEXT

Developing frameworks for big data that effectively balance economic, legal, security, and other interests requires an understanding of the relevant context and applicable scenarios within which the data exists.

A sound starting point from which to establish the applicable scenarios of use is to enumerate the institutions involved with a given set of big data, and develop a description of how or why they hold, access, or otherwise intermediate the data. Although big data straddles multiple BLT boundaries, one or more institutions are typically able to, or in some situations required to, manage and control the data. The public good referred to in the introduction of this book can be articulated as design requirements or even as certification criteria applicable to those institutions that operate the systems through which the big data is computed or flows.

It may be also be necessary to narrowly define certain aspects of the scenario in which the data exist in order to establish the basic ownership, control, and other expectations of the key parties. For example, describing a transaction as a financial exchange may not provide enough relevant detail to reveal the rights, obligations, or other outcomes reasonably expected by the individuals and organizations involved. The sale of used cars via an app, the conduct of a counseling session via Google Hangout, and the earning of a master's degree via an online university all represent scenarios in which the use case of a financial exchange takes place. However, each of these scenarios occurs in a context that is easily identifiable: the sale of goods and deeper access to financial information if the car is financed; the practice of therapy by a licensed professional accessing and creating confidential mental health data; or e-learning services and protected educational records and possibly deeper financial information if the program is funded by scholarship or loans. The scenarios can also identify the key elements necessary to establish existing consumer rights—the people (a consumer and a used car dealer), the transaction (purchase of a used car), the data (sales and title data, finance information, etc.), and the systems (the third-party app and its relevant services or functions, state DMV services, credit card and bank services, etc.). The rights established by relevant state lemon laws, the Uniform Commercial Code, and other applicable rules will determine when duties arise or are terminated, what must be promised, what can be repudiated, by whom data must be kept secure, and other requirements or constraints on the use of personal data and big data. These and other factors differ when a transaction that seems identical operates within a different scenario, and even scenarios will differ depending on which contexts apply. In order to define high-level goals and objectives, it is critical that we answer the following four basic questions:

1. Who are the people in the scenario? (Who are the parties involved and what are their respective roles and relationships?)

2. What are the relevant interactions? (What transactions or other actions are conducted by or with the people involved?)

3. What are the relevant data and datasets? (What types of data are created, stored, computed, transmitted, modified, or deleted?)

4. What are the relevant systems? (What services or other software are used by the people, for the transactions, or with the data?)

Inspired by common law, the New Deal on Data sets out general principles of ownership that both guide and inform basic relationships and expectations. However, the dynamic bundle of recombinant rights and responsibilities constituting "ownership" interests in personal data and the expectations pertaining to big data vary significantly from context to context, and even from one scenario to another within a given general context. Institutional controls and other system safeguards are important methods to ensure that there are context-appropriate outcomes that are consistent with clearly applicable system scenarios as well as the contours and foundations for a greater public good. The New Deal on Data can be achieved in part by sets of institutional controls involving governance, business, legal, and technical aspects of big data and interoperating systems. Reference scenarios can be used to reveal signature features of the New Deal on Data in various contexts and can serve as anchors in evaluating what institutional controls are well aligned to achieve a balance of economic, privacy, and other interests.

The types of requirements and rules governing participation by individuals and organizations in trust networks vary depending on the facts and circumstances of the transactions, data types, relevant roles of people, and other factors. Antecedent but relevant networks such as credit card systems, trading partner systems, and exchange networks are instructive not only for their many common elements but also as important examples of how vastly different they are from one another in their contexts, scenarios, legal obligations, business models, technical processes, and other signature patterns. Trust networks that are formed to help manage big data in ways that appropriately respect personal data rights and other broader interests will similarly succeed to the extent they can tolerate or promote a wide degree of heterogeneity among participants for BLT matters that need not be uniform or directly harmonized. In some situations, new business models and contexts will emerge that require fresh thinking and novel combinations of roles or types of relationships among transacting parties. In these cases, understanding the actual context and scenarios is critical in customizing acceptable and sustainable BLT rules and systems. Example scenarios can describe deeper fact-based situations and circumstances in the context of social science research involving personal data and big data.[44] The roles of people, their interactions, the use of data, and the design of the corresponding systems reflect and support the New Deal on Data in ways that deliberately provide greater immediate value to stakeholders than is typically expected.

The New Deal on Data is designed to provide good value to anyone creating, using, or benefiting from personal data, but the vision need not be adopted in its entirety before its value becomes apparent. Its principles can be adopted on a large scale in increments—one economic sector, transaction type, or data type at a time. Adopting the New Deal on Data in successive phases helps to address typical objections to change based on cost, disruption, or overregulation. Policy incentives can further address these objections, for example, by allowing safe harbor protections for organizations operating under the rules of a trust network.

Predesigned use cases can provide benchmarks for determining whether given uses of personal data are consistent with measurable criteria. Such criteria can be used to establish compliance with the rules of a trust network and for certification by government for the right to safe harbor or other protections. Because the New Deal on Data is rooted in common law and the social compact, the appropriate set of rights and expectations covering privacy and other personal data interests can be enumerated, debated, and agreed upon in ways that fit the given use cases.

CONCLUSIONS

Society today faces unprecedented challenges and meeting them will require access to personal data, so we can understand how society works, how we move around, what makes us productive, and how everything from ideas to diseases spread. The insights must be actionable and available in real time, thus engaging the population, creating the nervous system of the society. In this chapter we have reviewed how big data collected in institutional contexts can be used for the public good. In many cases, although the data needed to create a better society has already been collected, it sits in the closed silos of companies and governments. We have described how the silos can be opened using well-designed and carefully implemented sets of institutional controls, covering business, legal, and technical dimensions. The framework for doing this—the New Deal on Data—postulates that the primary driver of change must be recognizing that ownership of personal data rests with the people that data is about. This ownership—the right to use, transfer, and remove the data—ensures that the data is available for the public good, while at the same time protecting the privacy of citizens.

The New Deal on Data is still new. We have described here our efforts to understand the technical means of its implementation, the legal framework around it, its business ramifications, and the direct value of the greater access to data that it enables. It is clear that companies must play the major role in implementing the New Deal, incentivized by business opportunities, guided by legislation, and pressured by demands from users. Only with such orchestration will it be possible to modernize the current system of data ownership and put immense quantities and capabilities of collected personal data to good use.

See Appendix A for the WEF whitepaper on "Personal Data: The Emergence of a New Asset Class."

ATTRIBUTION

This material has been published as chapter 9 in the book *Privacy, Big Data, and the Public Good* edited by Julia Lane, Victoria Stodden, Stefan Bender, and Helen Nissenbaum, and is reproduced by permission of Cambridge University Press. For more information on this book, please see Cambridge University Press (http://dx.doi .org/10.1017/CBO9781107590205 and http://www.cambridge.org

/9781107637689) and the amazon.com book page (http://www.amazon.com/Privacy-Big-Data-Public-Good/dp/1107637686).

REFERENCES

1. Woetzel, Jonathan et al. 2009. "Preparing for China's Urban Billion." McKinsey Global Institute, March. http://www.mckinsey.com/insights/urbanization/prepar-ing_for_urban_billion_in_china.

2. Lazer, David, Alex 'Sandy' Pentland, Lada Adamic, Sinan Aral, Albert Laszlo Barabasi, Devon Brewer, Nicholas Christakis, Noshir Contractor, James Fowler, and Myron Gutmann. 2009. "Life in the Network: The Coming Age of Computational Social Science." *Science* 323: 721–723.

3. Aral, Sinan, and Dylan Walker. 2012. "Identifying Influential and Susceptible Members of Social Networks." *Science* 337: 337–341; Mislove, Alan, Sune Lehmann, Yong-Yeol Ahn, Jukka-Pekka Onnela, and J. Niels Rosenquist. Pulse of the Nation: U.S. Mood throughout the Day Inferred from Twitter (website). Accessed November 22, 2013. http://www.ccs.neu.edu/home/amislove/twittermood/; Vitak, Jessica, Paul Zube, Andrew Smock, Caleb T. Carr, Nicole Ellison, and Cliff Lampe. 2011. "It's Complicated: Facebook Users' Political Participation in the 2008 Election." *Cyberpsychology, Behavior, and Social Networking* 14: 107–114.

4. Madrigal, Alexis. 2013. "Dark Social: We Have the Whole History of the Web Wrong." *The Atlantic*, October 12. http://www.theatlantic.com/technology/archive/2012/10/dark-social-we-have-the-whole-history-of-the-web-wrong/263523/.

5. Eagle, Nathan, and Alex Pentland. 2006. "Reality Mining: Sensing Complex Social Systems." *Personal and Ubiquitous Computing* 10: 255–268; Pentland, Alex. 2009. "Reality Mining of Mobile Communications: Toward a New Deal on Data." The Global Information Technology Report 2008–2009, 75–80. Geneva: World Economic Forum.

6. Pentland, Alex, David Lazer, Devon Brewer, and Tracy Heibeck. 2009. "Using Reality Mining to Improve Public Health and Medicine." *Studies in Health Technology and Informatics* 149: 93–102.

7. Singh, Vivek K., Laura Freeman, Bruno Lepri, and Alex 'Sandy' Pentland. 2013. "Classifying Spending Behavior Using Socio-Mobile Data." *HUMAN* 2: 99–111.

8. Pan, Wei, Yaniv Altshuler, and Alex 'Sandy' Pentland. "Decoding Social Influence and the Wisdom of the Crowd in Financial Trading Network." In *2012 International Conference on Social Computing* (Social-Com), 203–209. Washington, DC: IEEE Computer Society. DOI: 10.1109/SocialCom-PASSAT.2012.133.

9. Greene, Kate. 2008. "Reality Mining." *MIT Technology Review*, March/April. http://pubs.media.mit.edu/pubs/papers/tr10pdfdownload.pdf.

10. Kuneva, Meglena. 2009. European Consumer Commissioner, "Keynote Speech," in Roundtable on Online Data Collection, Targeting and Profiling, March 31. http://europa.eu/rapid/press-release_SPEECH-09-156_en.htm.

11. Gittleson, Kim. 2013. "How Big Data Is Changing the Cost of Insurance." BBC News, November 14. http://www.bbc.co.uk/news/business-24941415.

12. Hannak, Aniko, Piotr Sapiezynski, Kakhki Arash Molavi, Balachander Krishnamurthy, David Lazer, Alan Mislove, and Christo Wilson. 2013. "Measuring Personalization of Web Search." In *Proceedings of 22nd International Conference on World Wide Web* (WWW 2013), 527–538. New York: ACM.

13. Pentland, "Reality Mining of Mobile Communications."

14. Madan, Anmol, Manuel Cebrian, David Lazer, and Alex Pentland. 2010. "Social Sensing for Epidemiological Behavior Change." In *Proceedings of the 12th ACM International Conference on Ubiquitous Computing* (Ubicomp), 291–300. New York: ACM.

15. Pan, Wei, Gourab Ghoshal, Coco Krumme, Manuel Cebrian, and Alex Pentland. 2013. "Urban Characteristics Attributable to Density-Driven Tie Formation." *Nature Communications* 4: article 1961.

16. Grossman, Lev. 2009. "Iran Protests: Twitter, the Medium of the Movement." *Time Magazine*, June 17; Barry, Ellen. 2009. "Protests in Moldova Explode, with Help of Twitter." *New York Times*, April 8.

17. "Directive 95/ 46/ EC of the European Parliament and of the Council of 24 October 1995 on the Protection of Individuals with Regard to the Processing of Personal Data and on the Free Movement of Such Data." 1995. *Official Journal L281* (November 23): 31–50.

18. World Economic Forum. 2011. "Personal Data: The Emergence of a New Asset Class," January. http://www.weforum.org/reports/personal -data-emergence-new-asset-class.

19. Ibid.

20. Ibid.

21. Lima, Antonio, Manlio De Domenico, Veljko Pejovic, and Mirco Muso-lesi. 2013. "Exploiting Cellular Data for Disease Containment and Informa-tion Campaign Strategies in Country-Wide Epidemics." School of Computer Science Technical Report CSR-13–01, University of Birmingham (May).

22. Narayanan, Arvind, and Vitaly Shmatikov. 2008. "Robust De-Anonymization of Large Sparse Datasets." In *Proceedings of the 2008 IEEE Symposium on Security and Privacy* (SP), 111–125. Washington, DC: IEEE Computer Society. DOI: 10.1109/SP.2008.33.

23. Sweeney, Latanya. 2000. "Simple Demographics Often Identify Peo-ple Uniquely." Data Privacy Working Paper 3, Carnegie Mellon Univer-sity, Pittsburgh.

24. de Montjoye, Yves-Alexandre, Samuel S. Wang, and Alex Pentland. 2012. "On the Trusted Use of Large-Scale Personal Data." *IEEE Data Engi-neering Bulletin* 35 (4): 5–8.

25. Song, Chaoming, Zehui Qu, Nicholas Blumm, and Albert-Laszlo Barabasi. 2010. "Limits of Predictability in Human Mobility." *Science* 327: 1018–1021.

26. Pentland et al., "Using Reality Mining."

27. Tacconi, David, Oscar Mayora, Paul Lukowicz, Bert Arnrich, Cornelia Setz, Gerhard Troster, and Christian Haring. 2008. "Activity and Emo-tion Recognition to Support Early Diagnosis of Psychiatric Diseases." In *Proceedings of the 2nd International ICST Conference on Pervasive Computing*

Technologies for Healthcare, 100–102. Washington, DC: IEEE Computer Society. https://doi.org/10.1109/PCTHEALTH.2008.4571041.

28. World Economic Forum, "Personal Data."

29. The White House. 2011. "National Strategy for Trusted Identities in Cyberspace: Enhancing Online Choice, Efficiency, Security, and Privacy." Washington, DC, April.

30. Hardjono, Thomas. 2013. "User-Managed Access UMA Profile of OAuth2.0." Internet draft. http://docs.kantarainitiative.org/uma/draft -uma-core.html.

31. A Creative Commons licensed example set of integrated business and technical system rules for the institutional use of personal data stores is available at https://github.com/HumanDynamics/SystemRules.

32. See http://openPDS.media.mit.edu for project information and https://github.com/HumanDynamics/openPDS for the open source code.

33. Bilton, Nick. 2012. "Girls around Me: An App Takes Creepy to a New Level." *New York Times,* Bits (blog), March 30. http://bits.blogs.nytimes .com/2012/03/30/girls-around-me-ios-app-takes-creepy-to-a-new-level.

34. US Environmental Protection Agency, RCRA Corrective Action Program. 2007. "Institutional Controls Glossary," Washington, DC. http:// www.epa.gov/epawaste/hazard/correctiveaction/resources/guidance/ics /glossary1.pdf.

35. University of Florida, Center for Environmental & Human Toxicology. 2005. "Development of Cleanup Target Levels (CTLs) for Chapter 62–777, F.A.C." Technical report, Florida Department of Environmental Protection, Division of Waste Management, February. http://www .dep.state.fl.us/waste/quick_topics/publications/wc/FinalGuidanceDocu -mentsFlowCharts_April2005/TechnicalReport2FinalFeb2005.

36. US Environmental Protection Agency. 2012. "Institutional Controls: A Guide to Planning, Implementing, Maintaining, and Enforcing Institutional Controls at Contaminated Sites," OSWER 9355.0–89, Washington, DC, December. https://www.epa.gov/fedfac/institutional-controls-guide -planning-implementing-maintaining-and-enforcing-institutional.

37. DeMeo, Ralph A., and Sarah Meyer Doar. 2011. "Restrictive Cove-
nants as Institutional Controls for Remediated Sites: Worth the Effort?"
Florida Bar Journal 85 (2). https://www.floridabar.org/the-florida-bar-journal
/restrictive-covenants-as-institutional-controls-for-remediated-sites-worth
-the-effort/; Florida Department of Environmental Protection, Division
of Waste Management. 2012. "Institutional Controls Procedures Guidance." Tallahassee, June. http://www.dep.state.fl.us/waste/quick_topics
/pub-lications/wc/csf/icpg.pdf; University of Florida. "Development of
Cleanup Target Levels."

38. World Economic Forum, "Personal Data."

39. Hardjono, Thomas, Daniel Greenwood, and Alex Pentland. 2013.
"Towards a Trustworthy Digital Infrastructure for Core Identities and
Personal Data Stores." Presented at the ID360 Conference on Identity,
University of Texas.

40. Hardjono, Thomas, and Eve Maler. 2013. "User-Managed Access
UMA Profile of OAuth 2.0, Binding Obligations on User-Managed Access
(UMA) Participants." Internet Draft. http://docs.kantarainitiative.org
/uma/draft-uma-trust.html.

41. Barber, Simon, Xavier Boyen, Elaine Shi, and Ersin Uzun. 2012. "Bitter
to Better—How to Make Bitcoin a Better Currency." In *Proceedings of the
Financial Cryptography and Data Security Conference*, LNCS 7397, 399–414.
Berlin: Springer-Verlag.

42. Stalnaker, Stan. "About [Ven Currency]." Accessed January 16, 2014.
http://www.ven.vc.

43. Hardjono, Thomas, Patrick Deegan, and John Clippinger. 2014. "On
the Design of Trustworthy Compute Frameworks for Self-Organizing
Digital Institutions." In *Proceedings of the 6th International Conference
on Social Computing and Social Media and 6th International Conference on
Human-Computer Interaction* (LNCS 8531), edited by G. Meiselwitz, 342–
353. Berlin: Springer-Verlag.

44. See, e.g., the study SensibleDTU (https://www.sensible.dtu.dk
/?lang=en). This study of one thousand freshman students at the

Technical University of Denmark gives students mobile phones in order to study their networks and social behavior during an important change in their lives. It uses not only data collected from the mobile phones (such as location, Bluetooth-based proximity, and call and SMS logs), but also from social networks and questionnaires filled out by participants.

7 THE RISE OF DECENTRALIZED PERSONAL DATA MARKETS

Jacopo Staiano, Guy Zyskind,
Bruno Lepri, Nuria Oliver,
and Alex Pentland

The almost universal adoption of mobile phones, the exponential increase in the use of Internet services, social media platforms, and credit cards, and the proliferation of wearable devices and connected objects (Internet of Things) have resulted in a massive production of human behavioral data that characterize many aspects of daily life with extremely fine temporal and spatial granularities.[9] Such ubiquitous collection of personal data represents an invaluable resource for designing and building systems that are able to understand the needs and activities of both individuals and communities—so as to, for example, provide personalized, context-aware feedback and services.[8] Consequently, many public services of societal interest (e.g., city planning, public health, emergency response) could be greatly improved by the analysis of this data. Similarly, many commercial services, such as Waze or recommendation engines, require personal data such as location, purchase, or browsing history.

This scenario, however, raises unprecedented privacy challenges and concerns derived from the collection, storage, and usage of vast amounts of personal data.[1,16] At the same time, people are becoming more aware of the value and the risks associated with their personal data, most especially around location data.[22,27] This increased concern is reflected in new privacy regulations for mobile phone data (http://ec.europa.eu/justice/data

-protection/individuals/index_en.htm) and in research studies and debates about the difficulty of anonymization for these sorts of data.[6,11]

The core problem, then, is how can an individual share sensitive data for a public service (e.g., city planning) or a desired commercial service (e.g., traffic and driving advice) and be sure that the data will only be used for the intended purpose? This question implicitly recognizes the risks in terms not only of possible abuses in the usage of the personal data but also of the "missed chance for innovation" that is inherent in the current dominant paradigm of siloed data collection, management, and exploitation—which precludes participation to a wide range of actors, most notably the very producers of personal data (i.e., the users).

Recently, new user-centric models for personal data management have been proposed, in order to empower individuals with more control of their own data's lifecycle.[14] To this end, researchers and companies are developing repositories that implement medium-grained access control to different kinds of personally identifiable information (PII), such as, for example, passwords, social security numbers, health data,[23] location,[10,12] and personal data collected by means of smartphones or connected devices.[12]

Previous work has also introduced the concept of personal data markets in which individuals sell their own personal data to entities interested in buying it.[2] While personal data markets might be the next natural step in designing technology to support a transparent and privacy-preserving use of personal data, they are still at a research stage due to a number of technological and regulatory challenges. In order to implement a market, it is necessary to connect potential buyers (demand) with sellers (offer) and provide a trustworthy mechanism for the exchange of goods or value between buyers and sellers. In a personal data market, the sellers are individuals (who own their personal data), the buyers are corporations, researchers, governments, etc., and the mechanism for the exchange of "goods" is still to be defined.

Moreover, research works have consistently found that technology users are increasingly concerned about their privacy related to personal data sharing.[16,22] In order to realize the vision of personal data markets, we believe that humans should be placed at the center. Therefore, beyond technological implementations of enabling platforms, it is of paramount importance to carry out user-centric studies to shed light on human factors related to personal data markets, such as personal preferences, sensitivities, and valuations of personal data.

In a recent study,[19] we investigated, in a living lab setting,[5] the monetary value that people assign to different kinds of personal data as collected by their mobile phone, including location and communication information. Five major insights related to how our participants valued their mobile personal data emerged:

1. *Bulk mobile personal information is perceived as most valuable, when compared to individual mobile personal data points* (e.g., the total of all locations collected throughout the study was considered to be more valuable than a single location). Interestingly, the values obtained during our study are found to be lower that those reported in a similar study, which focused on the valuation of personal web browsing information.[4]

2. *Location, location, location!* We observed the highest valuation to be consistently associated with location information, which also emerged as the most opted-out category of mobile PII. Several participants also expressed that they did not want to be geolocalized and considered location information to be highly sensitive and personal. Moreover, we found statistically significant correlations between mobility behaviors (e.g., mean daily distance traveled, daily radius of gyration, etc.) and valuations of personal data. Not all users value their personal data equally: the more someone travels on a daily basis, the more s/he values not only her/his location information but also her/his communication and application usage information.

These insights may have an impact on the design of commercial location sharing applications. While users of such applications might consent at install time to share their location with the app, our work suggests that when explicitly asked about either individual or bulk location data, 17% of users decide not to share their location information. In addition, mobility behaviors will influence the valuations of PII. Tsai et al.[21] conducted an online survey with more than five hundred American subjects to evaluate their own perceptions of the likelihood of several location sharing scenarios along with the magnitude of the harm or benefit of each scenario (e.g., being stalked or finding people in an emergency). The majority of the participants found the risks of using location sharing technologies to be higher than the benefits. However, today a significant number of very popular mobile apps, such as Foursquare and Facebook Places, make use of location data. These popular commercial location sharing apps seem to mitigate their users' privacy concerns by allowing them to selectively report their location using check-in functionalities instead of tracking them automatically.

3. *Sociodemographic characteristics do not dictate value—behavior does.* When we correlated bid values against sociodemographic characteristics of the participants in our study, we did not find any significant correlations. On the other hand, we found statistically significant correlations between behavior (particularly mobility and app usage) and valuations of bids. From our findings it seems that personal differences in valuations of mobile PII are associated with behavioral differences rather than demographic differences. Most notably, findings show that the larger the daily distance traveled and radius of gyration, the higher is the valuation of PII. Conversely, the more apps a person uses, the lower the valuation of PII. A potential reason for this correlation is due to the fact that savvy app users have accepted that mobile apps collect their

mobile PII in order to provide their service and therefore consider their mobile PII to be less valuable.

4. *Trust yourself, not the government!* From both our study and Carrascal et al.,[4] it clearly emerges that individuals mainly trust themselves to handle their own personal data. Despite this finding, note that most users today do not have the tools to be able to handle their personal data in a secure, transparent, and user-friendly way. This result supports the adoption of a decentralized and user-centric architecture for personal data management.

5. *Unusual days lead to higher bids.* While analyzing the data collected during our study, we noticed that the bids—in all categories—for two specific days were significantly higher than for the rest of the days. One of these highly valued days was a holiday and the other was characterized by extremely strong winds causing multiple roadblocks and incidents. This suggests that not all personal data, even within the same category and level of complexity, is valued equally by our participants. This finding has a direct implication for personal data markets and for services that monetize mobile personal data.

To sum up, our findings show how: (1) location-related, behavioral, and bulk PII are the most sensitive and valued types of personal data; and (2) users manifest a desire to control both access and usage of their personal data. These results highlight privacy concerns that individuals have shown in real-world experiments.

On this topic, Orange commissioned an independent research agency, Loadhouse, to conduct 2028 online interviews of mobile phone users in the United Kingdom, France, Spain, and Poland to understand consumer attitudes related to personal data usage.[25] The goal was to uncover the extent and nature of trust between consumers and a variety of service providers, what value consumers assign to their personal data, and the factors that influence this value. Interestingly, European consumers seem to struggle for have control over their own personal data while companies are becoming more sophisticated in capturing and using these data. In addition, the results of the study show that customers understand that their own data has value to businesses and this value is variable based on the type of information and the relationship with the organization. More specifically, there are three types of data that customers identify when it comes to their willingness to share their data with an organization: (1) data related to friends and other contacts or data related to private information (such as their income); (2) behavioral data, including information such as location or mobile purchase history; and (3) basic demographic data, such as name, date of birth, mobile number, or marital status.

While these research works support the creation of a personal data market from a user-centric perspective, it also uncover a key technological challenge that still would need to be addressed in order to realize such a personal data market: a method for secure data sharing that would guarantee both data privacy and data integrity. Combined with a lack of existing tools to securely enable personal data markets, such findings led us to develop Enigma, a computational framework that addresses these privacy concerns while enabling applications of both commercial and societal interest to leverage personal information in a trusted manner. In the next section we describe Enigma and illustrate how it could be used to implement a personal data market.

ENIGMA: A DECENTRALIZED PLATFORM FOR SECURE PERSONAL DATA SHARING

As we discussed in chapter 1, ENIGMA is a decentralized platform that uses at its core a blockchain protocol to enable secure data sharing such that it removes the need for a trusted third party and enables the autonomous control of personal data.[26]

Given the properties of blockchain, Enigma users are able for the first time to share and sell their personal data with cryptographic guarantees regarding their privacy.

ENIGMA leverages the recent technological trend of decentralization: advances in the fields of cryptography and decentralized computer networks have resulted in the emergence of a novel technology—known as the blockchain—which has the potential to reduce the role of one of the most important actors in our society—the middle man.[3,7] By allowing people to transfer a unique piece of digital property or data to others, in a safe, secure, and immutable way, this technology can create: digital currencies (e.g., Bitcoin) that are not backed by any governmental body;[13] self-enforcing digital contracts, called smart contracts, whose execution does not require any human intervention (e.g., Ethereum);[20] and decentralized marketplaces that aim to operate free from regulations.[7] Hence, ENIGMA tackles the challenge of providing a secure and trustworthy mechanism for the exchange of goods in a personal data market.

In a personal data market scenario, buyers are likely to be companies, public institutions, and researchers, while sellers are individuals who receive compensation for sharing their own data. The ENIGMA system allows any type of computation to be outsourced to the cloud while guaranteeing the privacy of the underlying data and the correctness of the result. A core feature in the system is that it allows the data owners to define and control who can query it, thus ensuring that only approved parties learn the output. Moreover, no data leaks during the process to any other party.

ENIGMA itself is comprised of a network of computers that store and execute queries. Using secure multi-party computation (sMPC or MPC), each computer only sees random pieces of the data, a fact that prevents information leaks. Furthemore, queries carry a micropayment for the computing resources as well as a micropayment to those users whose data is queried, thus providing the foundation for the rise of a data market.

When owners share data, the data is split into several random pieces called shares. Shares are created in a process of secret-sharing[18] and perfectly hide the underlying data while maintaining some necessary properties allowing them to later be queried in this masked form. Since users in ENIGMA are owners of their data, we need a trusted database to publicly store a proof of who owns which data. ENIGMA makes use of a blockchain as a decentralized secure database that is not owned by any party. Our solution is based on Zyskind et al.,[24,26] which also allows an owner to designate which services can access its data and under what conditions. This way, when a service requests a computation, parties can query the blockchain and ensure that it holds the appropriate permissions. In addition to being a secure and distributed public database, the blockchain is also used to facilitate payments from services to computing parties and owners, while enforcing correct permissions and verifying that queries execute correctly.

In the context of a secure market for personal mobile data, ENIGMA serves as the underlying enabling technology for selling and buying personal data. The owners of the data would have access to an interface where they could select which mobile personal data (automatically collected by their mobile phones) would be uploaded into the system and which services could issue queries against their data. In exchange for enabling their personal data to be used by services, the owners would be digitally reimbursed. Their raw data would never be exposed or seen by any service or user.

The ENIGMA system offers owners not only full control of their personal data, but also transparency on which services are accessing their data and for what purposes. Service providers would be able to monetize the personal data available in the system without ever having access to the raw data. They would have to pay the owners of the data a fair price that would be proportional to the value such data brings to their business. Finally, thanks to ENIGMA's blockchain technology, all transactions would take place while preserving data integrity and privacy.

CONCLUSION

Current transformations of the "data ecology" are substantially due to the exponential growth of mobile and ubiquitous computing, together with big data analysis. These shifts are undeniably having a dramatic impact on people's personal data sharing awareness, sensitivities and desires. The first wave of social media, geosocial, and Web 2.0 applications have exploited personal data as a market opportunity with little participation by the producers of the data: the end-users. However, today we have reached critical mass in privacy concerns and awareness on the use of personal data, partially due to media exposure of breaches and intelligence scandals. This critical mass is increasingly demanding "a new deal on data"[15] where transparency, control, and privacy are at the core of any data-driven service.

The surge of connected sensors in both private and public spaces is expected to further exacerbate this tension, thus potentially limiting both the business and societal impact that the next generation of data-driven applications could have (for instance, in smart city scenarios). A multidisciplinary effort, comprising sociologists, lawyers, technologists, and policymakers, is therefore needed to address the problem of personal data access and control. A user-centric Personal Data Market approach (coupled with cryptographic guarantees on data access and usage, as presented in this article) represents a possible answer to resolving such tension, which we plan to empirically validate in the future.

We envision a world where technology serves as a means both to business innovation and societal progress, rather than an obstacle or a tool for undermining people and ultimately democracies: mindful citizens, supported by technology that respects their rights and fulfills their needs, are in our vision key to build the smart and data-driven societies of tomorrow.

REFERENCES

1. Acquisti, A., L. Brandimarte, and G. Loewenstein. 2015. "Privacy and Human Behavior in the Age of Information." *Science* 347 (6221): 509–514. DOI: 10.1126/science.aaa1465.

2. Adar, E., and B. Huberman. 2001. "A Market for Secrets." *First Monday* 6 (8). http://firstmonday.org/issues/issue6_8/adar/index.html.

3. Benkler, Y. 2006. *The Wealth of Networks*. New Haven, CT: Yale University Press.

4. Carrascal, J. P., C. Riederer, V. Erramilli, M. Cherubini, and R. de Oliveira. 2013. "Your Browsing Behavior for a Big Mac: Economics of Personal Information Online." In *Proceedings of the 22nd International Conference on World Wide Web* (Rio de Janeiro, Brazil, May 13–17), 189–200. New York: ACM Press.

5. Centellegher, S., M. De Nadai, M. Caraviello, C. Leonardi, M. Vescovi, Y. Ramadian, N. Oliver, F. Pianesi, A. Pentland, F. Antonelli, and B. Lepri. 2016. "The Mobile Territorial Lab: A Multilayered and Dynamic View on Parents' Daily Lives." *EPJ Data Science* 5 (3). https://doi.org/10.1140/epjds/s13688-016-0064-6.

6. Cvrcek, D., M. Kumpost, V. Matyas, and G. Danezis. 2006. "A Study on the Value of Location Privacy." In *Proceedings of the 5th ACM workshop on Privacy in Electronic Society* (Alexandria, VA, October 30), 109–118. New York: ACM Press.

7. De Filippi, P. 2015. "The Interplay between Decentralization and Privacy: The Case of Blockchain Technologies." *Journal of Peer Production* 7.

8. Lathia, N., V. Pejovic, K. Rachuri, C. Mascolo, M. Musolesi, and P. J. Rentfrow. 2014. "Smartphones for Large-Scale Behavior Change Interventions." *IEEE Pervasive Computing* 12 (3): 2–9.

9. Lazer, D., A. Pentland, L. Adamic, S. Aral, A.-L. Barabasi, D. Brewer, N. Christakis, N. Contractor, J. Fowler, M. Gutmann, T. Jebara, G. King,

M. Macy, D. Roy, and M. Van Alstyne. 2009. "Computational Social Science." *Science* 323 (5915): 721.

10. Mun, M., S. Hao, N. Mishra, K. Shilton, J. Burke, D. Estrin, M. Hansen, and R. Govindan. 2010. "Personal Data Vaults: A Locus of Control for Personal Data Streams." In *Proceedings of the 6th ACM International COnference*, Co-NEXT'10 (Philadelphia, PA, November 30–December 3), 1–12. New York: ACM Press.

11. de Montjoye, Y.-A., C. Hidalgo, M. Verleysen, and V. Blondel. 2013. "Unique in the Crowd: The Privacy Bounds of Human Mobility." *Scientific Reports* 3 (1376). https://doi.org/10.1038/srep01376.

12. de Montjoye, Y.-A., E. Shmueli, S. Wang, and A. Pentland. 2014. "OpenPDS: Protecting the Privacy of Metadata through SafeAnswers." *PLOS ONE* 9 (7): e98790. https://doi.org/10.1371/journal.pone.0098790.

13. Nakamoto, S. 2008. "Bitcoin: A Peer-to-Peer Electronic Cash System." Accessed March 26, 2019. https://bitcoin.org/bitcoin.pdf.

14. Pentland, A. "Society's Nervous System: Building Effective Government, Energy, and Public Health Systems." *IEEE Computer* 45 (1): 31–38.

15. Pentland, A. 2008. "Reality Mining of Mobile Communications: Toward a New Deal on Data." World Economic Forum Global IT Report, chapter 1.6, 75–80.

16. Rainie, L., and M. Duggan. 2016. "Privacy and Information Sharing." Pew Research Center. http://www.pewinternet.org/2016/01/14/privacy-and-information-sharing/(2016).

17. Schneier, B. 2015. *Data and Goliath: The Hidden Battles to Collect Your Data and to Control Your World*. New York: Norton and Company.

18. Shamir, A. 1979. "How to Share a Secret." *Communications of the ACM* 22 (11): 612–613.

19. Staiano, J., N. Oliver, B. Lepri, R. de Oliveira, M. Caraviello, and N. Sebe. 2014. "Money Walks: A Human-Centric Study on the Economics of Personal Mobile Data." In *Proceedings of the 2014 ACM International Joint Conference on Pervasive and Ubiquitous Computing* (Seattle, WA, September 13–17), 583–594. New York: ACM Press.

20. Szabo, N. 1997. "Formalizing and Securing Relationships on Public Networks." *First Monday* 2 (9). https://ojphi.org/ojs/index.php/fm/article/view/548/469.

21. Tsai, J., P. Kelley, L. Cranor, and N. Sadeh. 2010. "Location Sharing Technologies: Privacy Risks and Controls." *I/S: A Journal of Law and Policy for the Information Society* 6 (2): 119–151.

22. Urban, J. M., C. J. Hoofnagle, and S. Li. 2012. "Mobile Phones and Privacy." BLCTResearch Paper Series, July 11.

23. Want, R., T. Pering, G. Danneels, M. Kumar, M. Sundar, and J. Light. 2002. "The Personal Server: Changing the Way We Think about Ubiquitous Computing." In *Proceedings of 4th International Conference on Ubiquitous Computing* (Goteborg, Sweden, September 29–October 1), 194–209. New York: ACM Press.

24. Zyskind, G., Oz Nathan, and Alex Pentland. 2015. "Decentralizing privacy: Using Blockchain to Protect Personal Data." In *Proceedings of 2015 IEEE Symposium on Security and Privacy Workshops*, 180–184. Washington, DC: IEEE Computer Society.

25. "The Future of Digital Trust: A European Study on the Nature of Consumer Trust and Personal Data." 2014. http://www.orange.com/en/content/download/21358/412063/version/5/file/Orange+Future+of+Digital+Trust+Report.pdf.

26. Zyskind, Guy, Oz Nathan, and Alex Pentland. 2015. "Enigma: Decentralized Computation Platform with Guaranteed Privacy." arXiv:1506.03471.

27. Danezis, G., S. Lewis, and R. J. Anderson. 2005. "How Much Is Location Privacy Worth?" Presented at the 4th Workshop on the Economics of Information Security (Cambridge, MA, June 2–3). https://econinfosec.org/weis-archive/.

8 ENABLING HUMANITARIAN USE OF MOBILE PHONE DATA

Yves-Alexandre de Montjoye,
Jake Kendall, and Cameron F. Kerry

Mobile phones are now ubiquitous in developing countries, with eighty-nine active subscriptions per one hundred inhabitants.[1] Though many types of population data are scarce in developing countries, the metadata generated by millions of mobile phones and recorded by mobile phone operators can enable unprecedented insights about individuals and societies. Used with appropriate restraint, this data has great potential for good, including immediate use in the fight against Ebola.[2]

To operate their networks, mobile phone operators collect call detail records—metadata of who called whom, at what time, and from where. After the removal of names, phone numbers, or other obvious identifiers, this data can be shared with researchers to reconstruct precise country-scale mobility patterns and social graphs. These data have already been used to study importation routes of infectious diseases,[3] migration patterns, and economic transactions.[4] Such data is now being actively sought to inform the fight against Ebola,[5] but, despite the promise, this effort appears stalled.[6]

As part of our research at MIT, we examined two operational use cases of mobile phone data for development modeled on previous research. The first case involved the use of location metadata to understand and quantify the spread of infectious diseases (e.g., malaria or Ebola) within and among countries.[6] The second case considered the use of behavioral indicators derived from mobile phone metadata to microtarget outreach or drive uptake of agricultural technologies or health seeking behavior.[7] Here, mobile phone data could be used to define subgroups based on specific traits and behaviors, which would then receive messages or other outreach from the mobile operator.[8] We also considered cases where the data could be used to select individuals to be identified and contacted directly in limited circumstances. These two scenarios are quite distinct from a regulatory and privacy perspective, as we discuss below.

These mobile phone data case studies revealed ways in which, despite the promise, regulatory barriers and privacy challenges are preventing the use of mobile phone metadata from realizing its full potential. More specifically, our analysis showed: (1) the lack of commonly accepted practices for sharing mobile phone data in privacy-conscientious ways; and (2) an uncertain and country-specific regulatory landscape for data sharing, especially for cross-border data sharing.

While some forward-looking companies have been sharing limited data with researchers in privacy-conscientious ways, these barriers and challenges are making it unnecessarily hard for carriers to share data for humanitarian purposes.[9,10] We describe these issues further and offer recommendations moving forward.

PROTECTING THE IDENTITY OF SUBJECTS

Mobile phone metadata made available to researchers should never include names, home addresses, phone numbers, or other obvious identifiers. Indeed, many regulations and data-sharing agreements rely heavily on protecting anonymity by focusing on a predefined list of personally identifiable information that should not be shared. In the United States, for example, the privacy rule issued by the Department of Health and Human Services to protect the privacy of patient health records specifies[18] different types of data about patients that must be removed from datasets for them to be considered de-identified.[11]

However, elimination of specific identifiers is not enough to prevent re-identification. The anonymity of such datasets has been compromised before, and research[12] shows that, in mobile phone datasets, knowing as few as four data points— approximate places and times where an individual was when they made a call or sent a text—is enough to re-identify 95% of people in a given dataset. In general, there will be very few people who are in the same place at the same time on four different occasions, which creates a unique "signature" for the individual making it easy to isolate them as unique in the dataset. The same research also used unicity to show that simply anonymized mobile phone datasets provide little anonymity even when coarsened or noised.

This means that removing identifying information makes isolating and identifying a specific person in the dataset only slightly more challenging because that person can be identified using available sources of data that link location with a name or another identifier (e.g., geotagged posts on social media, travel schedules, etc.). Wholesale re-identification is more difficult, however, because re-identification of a large fraction of the dataset requires access to a full list of people and the places they have been, which may not be as easy to acquire. Nevertheless, a determined attacker can still re-identify people using such data. Therefore, removing personally identifiable information is only a first step in most instances and more stringent approaches are required unless trust in the recipient of a dataset is high.

Recognizing the limits of an approach to anonymity and re-identification that focuses only on identity information like names or ID numbers, governments have sought to expand protection beyond identity to any information that can be used to identify an individual. In 2007, the federal Office of Management and Budget added to its list of identifiers "any other personal information which is linked or linkable to an individual."[13] In Europe, the Directive 95/46/EC cautions that "account should be taken of all the means likely to be used" to identify an individual,[14] and a thorough recent opinion of EU privacy regulators provided technical guidance on the challenges and risks of re-identification.[15]

The challenge of these broad definitions is that they are open-ended. No existing anonymization methods or protocols can guarantee to 100% that mobile phone metadata cannot be re-identified unless the data has been greatly modified or aggregated. Thus, open-ended requirements can be unverifiable and, taken to their logical extreme, so strict as to prohibit any sharing of data even when risk of re-identification is very limited.

We believe that this places too much emphasis on a limited risk of re-identification and unclear harm without considering the social benefits of using this data, such as better managing disease outbreaks or informing government response after a disaster.[16] Special consideration should be given to cases where the data will be used for significant public good or to avoid serious harm to people. Furthermore, data sharing should allow for greater levels of disclosure to highly trusted data recipients with strong processes, data security, audit, and access control mechanisms in place. For example, trusted third parties at research universities might warrant access to richer, less anonymized data for research purposes and be relied on not to try to re-identify individuals or to use the data inappropriately.

For both use cases, we defined data-sharing protocols that would allow for the intended analysis, while protecting privacy. We contemplate releasing anonymized data to research teams and NGOs in a form that adds technical difficulty to re-identification, limits the amount of data that would be re-identified, and further limits the risk of re-identification or abuse with a legal agreement that specifies that only specific purposes and other protocols can be applied to the data. In our analysis, we focused on a middle ground scenario of relatively open sharing of data with multiple research teams and/or NGOs, with some (but limited) accountability and auditability. We did not consider a fully public release where a very high level of anonymization would be required, nor a release to a highly trusted third party with strong data protection in place that might allow weakly anonymized data sharing.

For our first use case, we concluded that a 5% sampling of the data on a monthly basis, resampled with new identifiers every month for a year, and coarsened temporally and spatially into twelve-hour periods (7 a.m. to 7 p.m.) and by regions within countries, would be the right balance between utility and privacy.[17] It would adequately show individuals' mobility across regions under study and the number of nights spent in infected regions while providing significant—but not absolute—protection of identity and a limit to the amount of data that would be re-identified.

For our second use case, we concluded that the behavioral indicators[18] derived from metadata can be shared with the researchers safely, provided outliers have been removed. Researchers could then use this data to segment the population into specific subgroups based on traits like calling patterns, mobility, number of contacts, etc. People fitting these criteria could then be contacted by the mobile phone operators through text messages or other communications. Their phone numbers would be known only to the mobile phone operators.

We also considered cases where specific individuals could be contacted based on criteria applied to the data. To do so would require either: (1) including in the dataset pseudonymous—but unique—identifiers that make it possible to connect data showing certain traits (such as a likely exposure to disease based on travel patterns) with specific individuals; or (2) including telephone numbers in the dataset so that researchers and/or NGOs can contact the individuals identified directly. Because it enables re-identification, the former would be a departure from good privacy practices unless the data was recipient highly trusted, and the second would be a clear departure because it discloses unmodified personally identifiable information.

Nevertheless, re-identification could be vital in case of emergencies such as an earthquake.[19] These alternate use cases illustrate further the need to develop mechanisms for trusted third parties to maintain data under strong controls for use, access, security, and accountability.[20]

More generally, promising computational privacy approaches to make the re-identification of mobile phone metadata harder include sampling the data, making the antenna GPS coordinates less precise (for example, through voronoi translation),[21] or limiting the longitudinality of the data to cover shorter periods of time. These could go as far as to set up systems or collaborations where researchers could pose questions of the data, but where mobile operators would only share with researchers "answers,"[22] such as behavioral indicators or summary statistics.[23] Each of these alternatives could be employed depending on the use the data is put to, the amount and sensitivity of the data that would be uncovered, how and by whom the data will be governed and housed, and the attendant risks of harm.

ENGAGING GOVERNMENT SUPPORT

The second challenge we identified to humanitarian use of mobile phone metadata is an uncertain and country-specific regulatory landscape for data sharing. Our study focused on Africa, where data privacy regulation has been evolving along two lines. The Francophone countries—mostly located in West Africa, where current exposure to Ebola is greatest—have tended to adopt privacy frameworks modeled on the 1995 European Privacy Directive and supervised by national data protection authorities. Meanwhile English-speaking countries with common law systems either have not yet adopted comprehensive privacy laws, or have adopted country-specific laws.

This landscape presents a number of barriers to humanitarian use of mobile phone metadata.

First, legal uncertainty complicates the design of data-sharing protocols. Indeed, even in countries that have had laws and regulatory agencies in place for some time, the relevant rules have not developed in enough detail to address an issue that is often uncertain even in the most developed legal systems.

Second, as discussed above, questions about the validity of most methods of de-identification persist particularly in countries that use open-ended definitions of anonymization such as the EU one. There exists no widely accepted data-sharing standards to help various actors achieve a rational privacy/utility tradeoff in using mobile phone metadata.

Third, regardless of legal systems, compatible data-sharing protocols—including data de-identification—have to be designed and validated on a country-by-country basis. For example, data-sharing protocols have to be compatible, which includes having both the phone number and the mobile phone identifier[24] hashed with the same function and salt[25] to allow for mobile phones to be followed across borders, even if the user changes SIM cards. These issues make cross-border data sharing or intraregional tracking of population flows particularly complex and costly. Yet such cross-country sharing is essential in the fight against diseases such as malaria or an Ebola outbreak.[26]

Fourth, our second use case contemplated that, in general, only behavioral indicators derived from carriers' metadata would be shared with researchers. But in specific and limited circumstances, where these indicators show an individual would benefit from intervention, the identity could be used to enable remote intervention, such as targeted texts sent by the operator, or identification through mechanisms that carefully control the release and use of this information.

In the absence of explicit consent from users to such disclosure and use of data from their mobile phones, these forms of re-identification of data subjects presents obvious privacy challenges and may come into conflict with most privacy legal regimes absent specific exceptions. The EU Privacy Directive provides that data processing must have a lawful basis, but that such a basis may be "to protect the vital interests of the data subject," or "in the public interest, or in the exercise of official authority, and recognizes 'public health' as such a public interest."[27] Thus, it will take the support of national governments, their health ministries, and their data protection authorities to enable use of data especially in such exigent situations, but also for a range of humanitarian applications.[28]

CONCLUSION: ROADMAPS NEEDED

These privacy challenges and regulatory barriers are making humanitarian data sharing much harder than it should be for mobile phone operators and are significantly limiting greater use of mobile phone metadata in development or aid programs and in research areas like computational social science, development economics, and public health.

To realize the potential of this data for social good, we recommend the following:

1. There is a clear need for companies, NGOs, researchers, privacy experts, and governments to agree on a set of best practices for new privacy-conscientious metadata sharing models in different development use cases—a wider and higher-level discussion of the kind our MIT working group conducted. These best practices would help carriers and policymakers strike the right balance between privacy and utility in the use of metadata and could be instantiated by data protection agencies, institutional review boards, and in data protection laws and policies. This would make it easier and less risky

for carriers to support humanitarian and research uses of this data, and for researchers and NGOs to use these metadata appropriately.

2. Such best practices should accept that there are no perfect ways to de-identify data—and probably will never be.[29] There will always be some risk that must be balanced against the public good that can be achieved. While much more research is needed in computational privacy, widespread adoption of existing techniques as standards could enable this trend of sharing data in a privacy-conscientious way.

3. Standards and practices, as well as legal regulation, also need to address and incorporate trust mechanisms for humanitarian sharing of data in a more nuanced way. Protection of individual privacy includes not only protection against re-identification, but also data security and protection against unwanted uses of data. Risk of re-identification is not a purely theoretical concept nor is it binary and it should be assessed vis-à-vis the level of trust placed in the data recipient and the strength of their systems and processes. Tracking of migration patterns or analysis of behavior patterns may offer enormous benefits for disease prevention and treatment, but it is possible to envision more malignant uses by actors ranging from disgruntled employees of the data recipient to authoritarian governments. The recognition of trusted third parties and systems to manage datasets, perform detailed audits, and control the use of data could enable greater sharing of these data among multiple parties while providing a barrier against risks.

There is a need for governments to focus on adopting laws and rules that simplify the collection and use of mobile phone metadata for research and public good purposes. Governments should also seek to harmonize laws on the sharing of metadata with common identifiers across national borders. The African Union took what could be a step in this direction in June 2014, when it approved the African Convention on Cyber Security and Personal Data Protection, seeking to advance Africa's digital agenda and harmonize rules among African nations.[30] The treaty, which will not take effect until adopted by fifteen member states, commits members to adopting a legal framework that follows the template of the European Privacy Directive. Clear and consistent rules will help but only provided they take a pragmatic and privacy-conscientious approach to anonymization, cross-border transfers, and novel approaches that enable public good uses of data and allow for public health emergencies and other valuable research.

Research based on mobile phone data, computational privacy, and data protection rules all may seem secondary when confronted by the challenges of poverty, disease, and basic economic growth. But they are on the critical path to realizing the great potential of information technology to help address these critical problems.

REFERENCES

1. ITU. 2013. "ICT Facts and Figures." http://www.itu.int/en/ITU-D /Statistics/Documents/facts/ICTFacts-Figures2013-e.pdf.

2. For a longer piece on the various ways in which mobile data can be used in the development sphere see: Kendall et al. 2014. "Using Mobile Data for Development." http://www.impatientoptimists.org/Posts/2014 /07/Big-Data-and-How-it-Can-Serve-Development.

3. Wesolowski, A., N. Eagle, A. J. Tatem, D. L. Smith, A. M. Noor, R. W. Snow, and C. O. Buckee. 2012. "Quantifying the Impact of Human Mobility on Malaria." *Science* 338 (6104): 267–270. http://www.sciencemag.org /con-tent/338/6104/267.abstract.

4. Examples include: WorldPop. 2014. "Ebola." http://www.worldpop .org.uk/ebola/; Eagle, N., M. Macy, and R. Claxton. 2010. "Network Diversity and Economic Development." *Science* 328 (5981): 1029–1031.

http://www.sciencemag.org/content/328/5981/1029; or Eagle, N., Y. de Montjoye, and L. M. Bettencourt. 2009. "Community Computing: Comparisons between Rural and Urban Societies Using Mobile Phone Data." In *Proceedings of the 2009 International Conference on Computational Science and Engineering*, 144–150. Los Alamitos, CA: IEEE Computer Society. http://doi.ieeecomputersociety.org/10.1109/CSE.2009.91.

5. Wesolowski, A., C. O. Buckee, L. Bengtsson, E. Wetter, X. Lu, and A. J. Tatem. 2014. "Commentary: Containing the Ebola Outbreak—the Potential and Challenge of Mobile Network Data." *PLOS Currents Outbreaks* (Edition 1). DOI: 10.1371/currents.outbreaks.0177e7fcf52217b8b 634376e2f3efc5e.

6. "Call for Help & Waiting on Hold." 2014. *The Economist*, October 25.

7. Sundsøy, P., J. Bjelland, A. Iqbal, A. Pentland, and Y. A. de Montjoye. 2014. "Big Data-Driven Marketing: How Machine Learning Outperforms Marketers' Gut-Feeling." In *Social Computing, Behavioral-Cultural Modeling and Prediction* (LNCS 8393), edited by Ariel M. Greenberg, William G. Kennedy, and Nathan D. Bos, 367–374. Berlin: Springer. https://doi.org /10.1007/978-3-319-05579-4_45.

8. This is very similar to how some mobile marketing interfaces work where marketers will specify the criteria and identifying characteristics for the people they want to target with specific messages but would not receive actual numbers. Alternatively, anonymized data could be shared with encrypted identifiers that would be passed back to the operator to trigger outreach.

9. One example is the open Data for Development contest run by Orange: de Montjoye, Y. A., Z. Smoreda, R. Trinquart, C. Ziemlicki, and V. D. Blondel. 2014. "D4D-Senegal: The Second Mobile Phone Data for Development Challenge." arXiv:1407.4885. http://arxiv.org/abs/1407 .4885.

10. UN Global Pulse. 2014. "Data Philanthropy: Where Are We Now?" http://www.unglobalpulse.org/data-philanthropy-where-are-we-now.

11. "Department of Health and Human Services—Section 164.514: Other Requirements Relating to Uses and Disclosures of Protected Health

Information." Electronic Code of Federal Regulations (e-CFR), 45 CFR Section 164.514. Accessed March 26, 2019. https://www.law.cornell.edu /cfr/text/45/164.514.

12. de Montjoye, Y. A., C. A. Hidalgo, M. Verleysen, and V. D. Blondel. 2013. "Unique in the Crowd: The Privacy Bounds of Human Mobility." *Scientific Reports* 3. http://www.nature.com/srep/2013/130325/srep01376 /full/srep01376.html.

13. Executive Office of the President, Office of Management & Budget. 2007. "Safeguarding Against and Responding to the Loss of Personal Information." Memorandum M-07-16 (May 22).

14. European Union. General Data Protection Regulation (GDPR), Directive 95/46/EC, Recital 26.

15. Article 29 Data Protection Working Party. 2014. Opinion 05/2014 on Anonymisation Techniques. 0829/14/EN (April 10).

16. Bengtsson, L., X. Lu, A. Thorson, R. Garfield, and J. Von Schreeb. 2011. "Improved Response to Disasters and Outbreaks by Tracking Population Movements with Mobile Phone Network Data: A Post-Earthquake Geospatial Study in Haiti." *PLOS Medicine* 8 (8): e1001083. https://journals.plos.org/plosmedicine/article?id=10.1371/journal.pmed .1001083.

17. The back-of-the envelope reasoning goes as follows: We use a spatial resolution of 17 antennas on average ($v = 17$) and a temporal resolution of 12 hours ($h = 12$). This means that with 4 points in a given month, we'd have a ~20% chance ($\mathcal{E} = .20$) at re-identifying an individual in a given month (resp. $\mathcal{E} = .55$ with 10 points) (see http://www .nature.com/srep/2013/130325/srep01376/fig_tab/srep01376_F4.html). This means that in order to have between 20% to 55% chances of re-identifying an individual, we'd need 4 to 10 points every month (meaning 48 to 120 points total for a year). Even in this case, as we use a 5% sampling and we resample every month, an individual has only a 45% chance to be in at least one of the sampled months ($1 - 0.95 ^ {12}$ months).

18. Bandicoot, a python toolbox to extract behavioral indicators from metadata. http://bandicoot.mit.edu/.

19. For a discussion of the use of mobile data to direct aid delivery in the 2010 Haiti earthquake, see: Bengtsson et al., "Improved Response to Disasters and Outbreaks."

20. We assume here that the mobile operator does not have explicit permission from the data subject to disclose their information. If users were to opt-in to sharing this would then become permissible.

21. https://github.com/yvesalexandre/privacy-tools/. Accessed March 26, 2019.

22. de Montjoye, Y.-A., E. Shmueli, S. S. Wang, and A. S. Pentland. 2014. "openPDS: Protecting the Privacy of Metadata through SafeAnswers." *PLOS ONE* 9 (7): e98790. http://www.plosone.org/article/info%3Adoi %2F10.1371%2Fjournal.pone.0098790.

23. While promising, these solutions are not yet ready for primetime. Standardized software to process call detail records along with testing and reporting tools are still under development, while the use of online systems allowing researchers to ask questions that would be run against the data and only receive answers would imply architecture investments from mobile phone operators.

24. IMEI, or International Mobile Station Equipment, is a unique number that identifies a mobile phone on the network.

25. One potentially interesting solution here would be to rely on multiple hash functions that can be nested.

26. BBC News. 2014. "Ebola: Can Big Data Analytics Help Contain Its Spread?" http://www.bbc.com/news/business-29617831.

27. European Union, Directive 95/46/EC, Article 7 (d), (e). An update to this legislation, the Privacy Regulation proposed by the European Commission in 2012, http://ec.europa.eu/justice/data-protection/document /review2012/com_2012_11_en.pdf, also included an exception from certain requirements for "scientific, historical, statistical, and scientific research purposes," but this was removed from legislation as passed by the European Parliament. http://www.europarl.europa.eu/meetdocs/2009 _2014/documents/libe/pr/922/922387/922387en.pdf.

28. Under the World Health Organization's International Health Regulations, the WHO and member states undertake to conduct "surveillance" for public health purposes and member states are permitted to "disclose and process personal data where essential for purposes of assessing and managing public health risks." WHO, Fifty-eighth World Health Assembly Resolution WHA58.3: Revision of the International Health Regulations, Articles 1 (definition of surveillance), 5.4, and 45. 2005. http://www.who.int/ipcs/publications/wha/ihr_resolution.pdf.

29. Narayanan, Arvind. 2014. "No Silver Bullet: De-identification Still Doesn't Work." Freedom to Tinker, July 9. https://freedom-to-tinker.com /blog/randomwalker/no-silver-bullet-de-identification-still-doesnt-work/.

30. Draft African Union Convention on the Establishment of a Credible Legal Framework for Cyber Security in Africa. http://www.au.int/en /cyberlegislation.

9 LIVING LABS FOR TRUSTED DATA

David L. Shrier and Alex Pentland

We have discussed the imperatives for a better data and trust architecture, the methods for delivering one, and some of the privacy and private market implications associated with new methods of data governance and societal interplay. How can we be assured that the theories developed in the lab, in conferences and workshops, and in simulation systems, correlate to actual behavior in real-world settings? How do we produce quantifiable, repeatable results and systems that scale to the level of a country? What are ways we can explore the potential of these new systems to improve society?

Over decades of experimentation, we have found that "living labs" generate society-scale results that can be examined, debated, approved, and ultimately replicated across domains as diverse as health, crime prevention, and transportation. We can also guide corporate innovation and societal change, since living labs can apply equally to corporate settings as well as civic and community. We will now discuss how this platform can build scalable solutions to problems faced by people worldwide.

INTRODUCTION

Living labs are unique, new type of field research platform that translates big data analysis into action, generating new insights by quantifying real-world interactions and delivering interventions that change behavior at scale.

For each lab, we typically construct a team of twelve to sixteen researchers, leveraging new technologies and data infrastructure, to investigate and deploy interventions against societal problems. We apply unique software and hardware platforms developed at MIT for big data analysis of social patterns in real environments, in order to uncover actionable insights into human behavior. We then use our data platform to leverage these insights to effect change and provide results during the project.

Our living labs are highly collaborative efforts that typically involve regional universities, government, corporations, and nonprofit entities, in order to maximize the benefits delivered by the program by ensuring compatibility with local conditions and promoting effective knowledge transfer.

Labs currently extant or in development include: the Principality of Andorra; Trento, Italy; Luxembourg; Bogota, Colombia; and Mexico City, Mexico.

Funding can come from a combination of corporate, governmental, and private sources, to support a living lab with a duration of typically two to five years (although our lab in Trento just renewed for another three-year term). An additional, and typical greater, amount is normally invested to build local capacity, since once solution paths are uncovered, the scale-up is taken on by local partners rather than our research team.

FOCUS PARAMETERS

Living labs are typically set up in a particular city, province, or district in order to maximize impact while minimizing cost. In a corporate setting they may be established initially at a single worksite, although we currently are developing research streams around remote workers and multisite collaborative environments.

For civic living labs, we typically look at governmental regions (whether cities, districts, or states) that have the following characteristics:

- Population of two million to twenty million.
- Viable economic foundation.
- Progressive government with a desire to drive growth.
- Strong university or other local partners for us to collaborate with.

In a corporate setting, we would normally seek:

- Deployment into more than one hundred employees (although initially may start with a work group or department).
- Clear identification of a problem space (innovation, efficiency, health of the worker, intergeneration communication and knowledge transfer, etc.).
- Stakeholders in both line operating roles as well as administrative functions such as human resources.

SCOPING PROCESS

MIT engages in a scoping and design process with its stakeholders when developing a living lab. Examples of solution spaces that we can pursue in civic engagement include:

- Understanding and improving public health.
- Optimizing transportation systems.
- Financial inclusion and financial access.
- Systems to prepare for, detect, and address contingencies such as floods, epidemics (H1N1 outbreak), etc.
- Enhancing innovation to support economic development.
- Reducing crime.

Examples of corporate solutions spaces:

- Improving workflow efficiency.
- Enhancing collaboration within groups and across groups.
- Decoding behaviors of highly successful archetypes (i.e., the "ideal researcher," the "ideal sales person," etc.) and development of assessment methods to assist with recruiting and onboarding.
- Optimizing creativity and innovation.

EXAMPLES OF LIVING LABS

Below are examples that illustrate the span and scope of living labs we have deployed or are currently deploying:

Dimension	Description
Energy Consumption	We used data analytics and a unique set of social incentives, in collaboration with a private sector partner, to reduce energy utilization by over 17% in a Swiss Canton. This enabled the Canton to use all hydroelectric power instead of needing to activate diesel generators. The behavior change was equivalent to what would normally be achieved with a 100% price increase.[1]

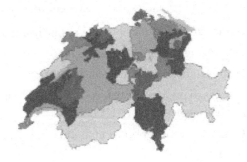

Dimension	Description
Financial Services	Employing transaction data extracted from a bank's own customers in Europe, we were able to demonstrate an improvement to credit modeling for behaviors such as late payment, over limit, or credit default that were 30% to 49% better than traditional demographic models. This holds the promise of not only helping the bank better manage its existing customer base, but even to extend credit to the unbanked or underbanked (over two billion people worldwide lack bank accounts).[2]
Health	Working with the telecom Orange, we organized the first Data Commons for the D4D Challenge in conjunction with the United Nations and the World Economic Forum. Convening eighty-six research teams from around the world, we analyzed a large phone dataset for the largest city in a West African country and determined how to reduce the spread of infectious disease by 20% through placement of health clinics and timing of vaccinations.

Crime	Using a combination of geospatial data from the telecom O2 and government statistics, we were able to build a predictive model that illustrated in London that, by redeploying existing police personnel into areas predicted to have high incidence of crime, you could substantially reduce crime rates. We were told that this technique was used in Latin America in a major city to reduce crime … by 70%.

(cont.)

Dimension	Description
Tourism	Andorra is a tiny country in the Pyrenees bordered by France to the north and Spain to the south. With approximately 80,000 citizens, the country sees as many as twelve million tourists annually. Changing dynamics of its tourism industry have prompted the government and the local businesses to form a nonprofit to collaborate with MIT around re-architecting the national economy to make it more vibrant and innovative, focused on improving the tourism experience.

Young Families	In Trento, an autonomous part of Italy, our living lab (sponsored by Telecom Italia, Telefonica, the local Cooperative, and local government) enrolled more than one hundred young families for three years, measuring social interactions, mobility routines, spending patterns, surveys, etc. From this data came practical systems that allowed these young families to improve their lives by predicting daily stress and mood, spending habits, etc., and providing relevant feedback. This living lab also developed new models for managing and sharing data, and explored the idea of personal data markets where subjects can sell their own data.

Dimension	Description

Corporate Culture Change	In two different large (more than 100,000 employee) corporations in different industries (aerospace and telecommunications), we are helping management address profound and company-wide culture change issues. Instrumenting teams of workers, we are identifying common behavioral characteristics and seeking to bridge different communications styles, workgroup organization, and shift behaviors at scale to transform their culture and create more nimble, entrepreneurial organizations.
Teamwork (and Education)	Using our online classroom into ninety-five countries, we are studying the dynamics of over one thousand teams of business people working on innovation/entrepreneurship projects, to see how distance groups of typically half a dozen people can be enhanced to perform more like in-person teams around a month-long project deliverable (creation of a business plan for a new venture). We are also exploring aspects of peer learning and mentorship in a distance learning environment.

UNIQUE DATA-DRIVEN APPROACH

MIT Connection Science benefits from having proven software, legal, and management tools for instrumenting, understanding, and changing user behavior.

Setting up a living lab begins with an initial data and systems audit conducted by MIT researchers in order to outline what capabilities are present and which will need to be created, in the given environment in which we are forming the living lab. Comprehensive data will then be fed into a pooled data common. Implementation of MIT's OPAL/ENIGMA privacy and personal data protection systems (an open source platform developed by Professor Pentland and collaborators), along with other best practices, can provide security and robustness, and protect user privacy while unleashing innovation.

Data analytics will be built, in part, around our Bandicoot library (bandicoot.mit.edu) of over one hundred tools for mobile-derived behavioral analytics and visualization, providing a high degree of efficiency for deployment of effective interventions.

Bandicoot-derived and other data are normalized, cross-linked, and integrated into a Connections Engine for deployment against select interventions.

We have recently begun the Rhythm project (http://rhythm .mit.edu), which takes social physics methodology and deploys it into remote communications platforms like video chat and

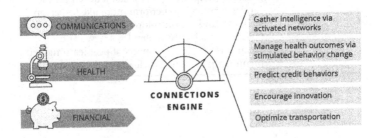

text channels, in harmony with in-person sociometric sensing from a new generation of sociometric badges. This platform holds the promise of enabling us to sense the full spectrum of communication within a typical corporate workplace, where in-person and remote meetings are everyday occurrences and sometimes blended experiences (with some participants remote and some in person).

Over time, as the OPAL/ENIGMA system is developed, we anticipate using this as the central data management platform for our living labs.

Data Privacy and Security. MIT is a world leader in protection of personal data and personal data privacy standards, and can help implement best-in-class methodologies and governance policies for personal data protection (likely with the OPAL/ENIGMA standard at the center of a solution). To further our work with data privacy and security, MIT has formed the Internet Trust Consortium (trust.mit.edu), which provides core tools for our living labs.

Telecom Data. As we discussed in chapter 4, we often use telecom data. The most essential elements are typically mobile data including call record (which number called which number, at what time) and location data, which can be abstracted inside the telecommunications company into "metadata" for subsequent analysis by MIT (i.e., no personally identifiable information leaves the telecom company).

For a given solution space, specific data sources may be needed or helpful, like economic growth data. MIT can make intelligent guesses using telecoms data even if certain other information is not available; for example, by overlaying telecoms positional signals on Google Maps, and looking at rate of change of location, it is possible to make a reasonable guess if someone is in a car or on foot.

MIT Connection Science has long-standing relationships with a number of incumbent telecommunications companies around the world who can facilitate opening discussions for living lab collaboration in a given geography. We have also we have successfully conducted living labs using other data sources, such as a bank's own payments data for our credit analytics projects. This is especially effective in countries where payments data is geolocated.

Data Commons Benefits. The use of pervasive technologies as a proxy to more expensive traditional survey methods is of a particular interest as such methods can provide quick insights and understanding of social patterns, supply, and demand. Our living labs not only cover a larger sample of the population but also are also immune to some of the biases of surveys and have much higher time and space resolutions enabling better understanding at unprecedented scales. Another key advantage of the analysis of data gathered from pervasive technologies such as mobile phones is the very short time required to conduct a study. In contrast, conducting surveys requires a period of months if not years, and is often prohibitively expensive.

ACTIVATING SOCIAL ORGANIZATIONS

Living labs have a life beyond the experimental period. Through exploration of a portfolio of societal interventions, we identify scalable solutions to critical issues. But what happens next? That's when private and public interests take over, expanding the initial interventions into repeatable, sustainable "social utilities" that scale up in domains such as health, transportation, financial, safety/crime, and economic development. The sensing platform crafted in the initial living lab can be maintained and extended for continuous innovation.

BUILDING A BETTER TOMORROW

MIT's mission is to solve humanity's greatest challenges, particularly via advancing the frontier of human knowledge and training the next generation of leaders to fulfill this promise. Living labs support both the theory and practice of innovation, and therefore are central to achieving these goals. Living lab initiatives align closely with MIT's mission by enhancing our understanding of human behavior at scale, especially with reference to social groupings, and also provide a means of having positive impact on the world.

In building living labs, we draw on interdisciplinary expertise across several of MIT's schools (Engineering, Management, Science, and Architecture & Planning / MIT Media Lab), as well as our research collaborators from dozens of universities around the world.

We are by no means the only researchers using the living lab methodology. With increasing numbers of living labs proliferating around the world, we see our role as one of providing tools and insights that can be used globally to improve the human experience.

We continue to seek out new partners who can help us on the journey of exploration of the potential of living labs. We hope to transform societies and help companies to better engage their stakeholders. To make this possible, we need the Trust::Data framework described in this book, and advocates and evangelists who raise awareness of, and enhance the capabilities of, these powerful new tools. Please join us in building this better world.

REFERENCES

1. Mani, A., C. Michelle-Loock, I. Rahwan, T. Staake, E. Fliesch, and A. Pentland. 2013. "Incentives Promote Peer Pressure in an Energy Saving Campaign." In *Proceedings of the 2013 Behavior Energy and Climate Change Conference*. Sacramento, CA: ACEEE.

2. World Bank. 2015. Global Findex Database. https://globalfindex.world bank.org.

III CURRENT

10 ACTIVE FAIRNESS IN ALGORITHMIC DECISION-MAKING

Alejandro Noriega-Campero,
Michiel Bakker, Bernardo Garcia-Bulle,
and Alex Pentland

Society increasingly relies on machine learning models for automated decision-making (ADM). Yet, efficiency gains from automation have come paired with concern for algorithmic discrimination that can systematize inequality. Consequently, research on algorithmic fairness has surged, focusing on either post-processing trained models, constraining learning processes, or pre-processing training data. Recent work has proposed optimal post-processing methods that randomize decisions of a fraction of individuals in order to achieve fairness measures related to calibration and error parity. In contrast, the present work proposes an alternative active framework, where, in deployment, a decision-maker adaptively acquires information according to the needs of different groups or individuals, in order to balance disparities in classification performance. We propose two such methods, where information collection is adapted to group- and individual-level needs, respectively. We show on real-world data sets that these can achieve: (1) calibration and single error parity (e.g., equal false-negatives); and (2) parity in both false-positive and false-negative rates (i.e., equal odds). Moreover, we show that these fairness goals can be achieved at substantially lower information costs while avoiding other limitations of randomized classifiers such as Pareto suboptimality and intragroup unfairness.

INTRODUCTION

Automated decision-making systems (ADMs) have become increasingly ubiquitous—e.g., in criminal justice,[17] medical diagnosis and treatment,[16] human resource management,[6] social work,[11] credit,[14] and insurance. For example, a bank's decision to issue a loan might depend on the predicted probability that a borrower will default or that a defendant might be released by a judge based on the predicted likelihood that the defendant will commit another crime. As the influence and scope of these ADMs increases, there is widespread concern about how these can deepen social inequalities and systematize discrimination.

Consequently, research work on defining and optimizing for algorithmic fairness has surged in recent years, where most methods fall in one of three broad categories: (1) adjustments by post-processing the output of black-box models;[13] (2) introducing constraints during the learning process of these models;[3,25] or (3) improving the collection and/or pre-processing of training data.[5,20]

Recent work has proposed optimal post-processing methods that randomize decisions of a fraction of individuals in order to achieve fairness measures related to calibration and error parity.[13,21] Yet, strong limitations of randomized approaches have been noted, such as information wastefulness, Pareto suboptimality, and intragroup unfairness.[8,13,21] In this work, we propose a complementary approach, *active fairness*, where, in deployment, an ADM adaptively collects information (features) about decision subjects, collecting more information for those harder to classify, in order to achieve equity in predictive performance. Thereby, the approach leverages a natural affordance of many real-world decision systems—adaptive information collection—and allocates an ADM's information budget among decision subjects towards group- and individual-level fairness.

Intuition and motivating contexts. Consider the medical domain, where a patient entering a hospital seeking diagnosis typically undergoes a progressive inquiry process—declaring symptoms, measuring vitals, and potentially procuring lab tests, imaging tests, specialists' opinions, etc.[31] At each step, diagnosis is attempted, and, absent sufficient certainty, the inquiry continues. Intuitively, a fair health system allocates resources to provide all patients with similar-quality diagnoses. Likewise, active inquiry under cost constraints is at the core of decision-making in many relevant contexts—from the assessment of damage of natural disasters, by means of satellite, aircraft, and UAV data to contexts such as the selection of human capital,[16] the distribution of telemedicine, eligibility determination for social benefit programs,[23] refugee status determination,[12] and credit allocation to micro-entrepreneurs in the developing world.[15]

BACKGROUND

Sources of Unfairness

There are several reasons for a machine learning based ADM to make unfair decisions. First, machine learning algorithms leverage statistical patterns in the data, and thus, if this data reflects existing biases, the trained ADM will likely incorporate these biases in its predictions. An example of this is the gender bias that is implicit in word2vec, a well-established machine learning based word embedding model that is used to pretrain numerous natural language processing systems.[28] Word2vec is trained on Google News texts that are written by journalists who are, though not intentionally, gender biased. Nonetheless, the system learns implicitly, from training on these texts, that jobs like nurse and receptionist are more female occupations while philosopher and architect are more male occupations.

The second reason is related to the sample sizes. In most cases, a machine learning model improves the accuracy of its predictions when it has access to more training data. Naturally, there are proportionally fewer data available for groups classified as "minorities," which, in turn, leads to a higher error rate for minorities. Therefore, ADMs have a tendency to perform better for those who belong to the dominant population groups. Refer to Friedman and Nissenbaum[29] for a survey of sources of unfairness in computer systems.

Notions of Fairness

A multitude of formal definitions of fairness and their corresponding mathematical formalizations have been proposed in recent years to support the design of *fair* ADMs. Most fall in three broad categories.

First, there is *anti-classification* or *fairness through unawareness*, requiring ADMs to ignore any of the protected attributes like race and gender when making its decisions. The risk is, however, that other attributes can serve as proxies for these protected attributes, and thus that the protected attributes have redundant encodings in these attributes[30]—a phenomenon that is particularly common in modern high-dimensional datasets, comprised by dozens or hundreds of attributes.

Second, there is *demographic* or *statistical parity*, which, in its most extreme version, requires that decisions are independent of group membership,[4,19,26] such that for binary classification the average outcomes are equalized across population subgroups. In other words, statistical parity requires that the proportion of individuals classified positive are the same across population subgroups, regardless of the comparative prevalence of characteristics such as skill or risk across groups.

Most recent work focuses on meritocratic notions of fairness, namely, *classification parity* or *error rate matching*,[3,13] which requires common statistical measures of classification accuracy to be equal across population subgroups. Common notions of *classification parity* require population subgroups to have equal false positive rates (FPR), equal false negative rates (FNR), or both (*equalized odds*). The false positive rate is the proportion of instances for which a given condition doesn't exist (false positive or type-I error) while the ADM yields a positive outcome. In contrast, the false negative rate is the proportion of instances for which a given condition exists while the ADM yields a negative outcome (false negative or type-II error). Refer to Žliobaite[27] for a survey on computational measures of fairness.

RELATED WORK

Achieving Equal Opportunity and Equal Odds

Hardt et al. (2016) propose parity in false negative rates and/or parity in false positive rates as a measure of unfair discrimination across population subgroups.[13] Parity in both types of error is referred to as *equal odds*, and its relaxation, equality in only FPRs, is conceptualized as *equal opportunity* (as in contexts of positive classification, it means that subjects within the positive class have an equal probability of being correctly classified positive, regardless of group membership).

A simple way to achieve *equal opportunity*, equality in only false positive rates, is to shift the decision threshold only for one group. By increasing the threshold for one group relative to the other, decision subjects in that group are less likely to be wrongly labeled as positive. At the same time, however, this increases the false negative rates, hindering the achievement of *equal odds*. Therefore, Hardt et al. (2016) propose a post-processing method of the classifier that, based on naive randomization of a fraction of individuals in the advantaged group, balances both false positive and false negative rates; and proves conditions under which decisions are both equitable and optimal with respect to accuracy.

Although effective in achieving *equal odds*, the approach has been considered discouraging for a number of reasons outlined below.

Achieving Calibration and Error Parity

In many real-world uses of algorithms for risk estimation—such as criminal justice or credit risk estimation—it is important to require that predictions are *calibrated*. A calibrated estimator is one where, if we look at the subset of people who receive any given probability estimate, a number p between 0 and 1, we find indeed p fraction of them to be positive instances of the classification problem. In the context of credit assignment, for example, we would expect a p fraction of credit applicants with estimated default risk of p to default. Moreover, in the context of algorithmic fairness across population groups, it is desired for calibration to hold for each group.[10]

Calibration is not necessary nor sufficient to achieve parity in classification errors.[8] However, it is particularly desirable in cases where the output of an algorithm is not directly a decision but used as input to the subsequent judgment of a human decision-maker. In such contexts—e.g., recidivism[9,10] and child maltreatment hotlines[7,11]—the risk estimates of an uncalibrated algorithm could carry different meaning for two different groups (e.g., African American and white defendants)—and thus its use to informing human judges' decisions would entail a disparate impact across groups.

Recently, Kleinberg et al. demonstrated that a tension exists between minimizing error disparity across different population groups and maintaining calibrated probability estimates.[17] In particular, it showed that calibration is compatible only with a single error constraint (i.e., equal FNR or equal FPR). In the same vein, Pleiss et al. (2017) showed that the results hold for even a strong relaxation of *equal odds*, named *equal cost* where FPR and FNR are allowed to compensate one another.[21] Finally, they propose a method that, using naive randomization, is able to achieve parity on one error rate or *equal cost*.

Objections to Naive Randomization

The above results, both in achieving *equal odds* as well as in jointly achieving calibration and a single error parity measure, rely on naive randomization as means to fairness and therefore have been interpreted as unintuitive, discouraging, and unsettling.[8,13,21] Several important objections have been put forth against the use of naive randomization to achieve classification parity, among them:

- *Inefficiency.* As pointed out by several authors,[8,13, 21] it is inefficient and appears unintuitive to withhold information that is already in hand but to instead randomize the classification of a subset of individuals.

- *Individual unfairness.* Moreover, classifiers based on naive randomization[8,13,21] entail intragroup unfairness. As pointed out by others,[8,21] individuals who are randomized are not necessarily those with higher uncertainty but simply the ones who were unlucky, thus breaking ordinality between the probability of classification error and the actual uncertainty in the decision.

- *Pareto domination and undesirability.* Finally, consider an unconstrained and unfair classifier that incurs higher errors on group A than group B; and consider an alternative "fair" classifier where a percentage of individuals of group B are randomized to achieve parity in errors. Considering groups A and B as the system's stakeholders, we note that the original unfair classifier Pareto dominates the fair alternative (i.e., the disadvantaged group A will be indifferent, as its classification remained unchanged, while group B will strongly prefer, the original classifier before accuracy was degraded via randomization). In summary, no group would prefer the new classifier.

ACTIVE FAIRNESS

The present work explores *active* approaches for achieving fairness—i.e., classification strategies where a decision-maker adaptively acquires information according to the needs of different groups or individuals, in order to balance disparities in classification performance. This section defines two such active strategies, one that allocates group-level information budgets, which are constant for all members of a group, and one that allocates individual-level information budgets, which are computed dynamically at test-time. The sections below, "Achieving Equal Opportunity and Calibration" and "Achieving Equal Odds," demonstrate their use and advantages in attaining fairness.

Problem Formulation

We study the context where a decision-maker can choose what information to collect about each decision subject and that seeks to maximize accuracy and fairness under an information budget constraint. This budget is the amount of information that can be collected for an individual. In this work, the information consists of features that can be collected one-by-one until the budget is used. This context is natural to many real-world decision systems, from poverty mapping to HR recruitment, and healthcare.[31] Yet, its affordances and implications to algorithmic decision systems—at the intersection of accuracy, fairness, and cost-efficiency—have not been thoroughly studied.

This paper focuses on contexts with constant costs across features. However, we note that the active fairness framework allows generalizations to common contexts with varied costs across features, as well as richer and context-specific utility functions with potential costs to decision-subjects, such as monetary, opportunity, or privacy costs. For example, in the context of poverty mapping, presented in the "Achieving Equal Opportunity" section, making a decision based on only a satellite image of a household's living environment minimizes privacy risks and is cost-effective for the decision-maker, but, at the same time, reflects only limited information on the classification problem leading to a high error rate. At the same time, a detailed questionnaire is expensive for the decision-maker and presents more privacy risks to the decision subject, but contains much more detailed information.

Information Budgets

Group-level. First, we consider the strategy with constant information budgets for all members in a group. Thus, the decision-maker can collect a different set of features for members from different groups, but collects the same features for members of the same group. The "Achieving Equal Opportunity and Calibration" and "Achieving Equal Odds" sections show how decision-makers can achieve calibration and group-level equity by allocating different budgets to each group.

Individual-level. Similar in spirit to predictors with group-level information budgets, an ADM may adaptively collect information of each decision subject until a confidence threshold is met, upon which a classification decision is made. Thereby, individual-level information budgets are set dynamically according to the needs of each decision subject, towards attaining equity.

Furthermore, to optimize performance within the budget constraint, a decision-maker can select the features in a different order for each decision subject. Depending on the value of features that are already selected, certain features will become more or less likely to decrease uncertainty and selecting those features will thus increase efficiency while still meeting the budget constraint.

Intuitively, this adaptive process resembles processes in the medical domain. If a doctor is not yet confident on the diagnosis, additional tests may be recommended or the patient is referred to a specialist for further diagnosis. Subsequently, a patient may be subjected to even more tests and doctor appointments as long a confident diagnosis cannot be yet made. At each step, depending on the insights that are generated, the additional tests or specialists at the next step will be different, making the whole process personal and adaptive.

Random Forest Implementation

Implementation of the active fairness method requires two elements: (1) a machine learning model that is able to estimate the probability of an outcome for arbitrary feature sets; and (2) a feature selection method for choosing expanding feature sets, either at the group or individual level.

Probabilistic model. We implement distribution-based classification with incomplete data based on a probabilistic random forest, extending related methods for dealing with incomplete data in trees.[22] In particular, when given the values for an arbitrary set of features for a single subject, the algorithm traverses all possible paths of each tree, thereby splitting its path into two paths when a feature is missing. We then compute classification probabilities as a weighted average of the leaf purity across all leaves landed on by the search. We extend this procedure from a single tree to a forest by computing the average probability across all trees. Similar methods can be derived more generally for a number of probabilistic graphical models and for adapting logistic regressions to admit arbitrarily incomplete feature vectors.[24]

DATASET

Social programs are challenged with the task of predicting which household qualifies for their program. It is especially tricky when a program focuses on the poorest segment of the population who typically cannot provide the necessary income and expense records to prove that they qualify. The proprietary *Mexican poverty dataset* is based on a sample of 70,305 households in Mexico with 183 categorical and continuous features, related to the family's observable household attributes like the material of their walls and ceiling, or the assets found in the home. Classification is binary with 36% of the households having the label poor. We seek to find equality first across young and old families, split by the mean (53% are young), and second across families living in urban and rural areas (64% are urban). Across all data, a random 80%/20% split was used for training and testing.

Targeted social programs—such as conditional cash transfers—are challenged with inferring household poverty levels in order to determine eligibility.[14] The Mexican poverty dataset is extracted from the Mexican household survey 2016, which contains ground-truth household poverty levels, as well as a series of visible household features on which inferences are based. Like in many other countries around the world, Mexico bases its eligibility rules on inference algorithms trained and tested on this household survey dataset. The dataset comprises a sample of 70,305 households in Mexico, with 183 categorical and continuous features, related to households' observable attributes, such as the materials of their walls and ceiling, households' access to basic services and utilities, the assets found in the home, and other sociodemographics. Classification is binary according to the country's poverty line, with 36% of the households having the label poor. We study fairness across groups defined by: (1) young and old families, split by the mean (where 53% are young), and (2) across families living in urban and rural areas (where 64% are urban).

In addition, the Mexican poverty data, we refer readers to our paper,[32] in which we study and compare methods on three additional domains, based on public datasets from the UCI Machine Learning Repository.[18]

ACHIEVING EQUAL OPPORTUNITY AND CALIBRATION

This section demonstrates how an active strategy with group-level budgets can be used to achieve calibration and single error parity, more efficiently, and without resorting to naive randomization. We follow Pleiss et al. (2017), and study predictive performance in terms of the generalized false positive (GFPR) and generalized false negative rates (GFNR), appropriate for contexts where risk scores themselves are the outputs of the algorithm (as opposed to automated classification). We aim at designing classifiers that satisfy calibration and error parity. As shown by Kleinberg et al.,[17] the GFNR and GFPR of all calibrated classifiers for a given group A fall along the straight line that connects the perfect classifier at the origin (where both GFPR and GFNR are 0) with the base rate, the probability that the outcome is positive when no features are collected.

Panel A in figure 10.1 shows the space of calibrated classifiers achievable by naive randomization (method in Pleiss),[21] for the Mexican poverty dataset described in the "Dataset" section above. These replicate results from Pleiss,[21] showing how naive randomization of individuals in the advantaged group can, by eroding prediction performance, achieve calibration as well as either parity in false positives, parity in false negatives (but not both), or an equal cost generalization.

Similarly, panel B in figure 10.1 demonstrates how calibration and one of the three parity objectives can be achieved by adjusting information budgets according to the group's needs, without resorting to naive randomization. Moreover, the right panel C in figure 10.1 shows that classifiers with group-level budgets achieve these fairness goals with much higher efficiency in terms of information cost. In particular, we set an overall information budget restriction for both types of classifiers, equal to the minimum budget required by the naive random classifier to achieve equal opportunity. It is observed in panel C that the classifiers with group-level budgets Pareto-dominate random classifiers by a wide margin, on both datasets—that is, for the same information budget, both population subgroups are better off, being exposed to substantially lower false positive and false negative errors.

ACHIEVING EQUAL ODDS

This section shows how active methods with group- and individual-level information budgets can be used to achieve parity in false positives and false negatives.

Figure 10.2 illustrates the achievable regions in the FPR-FNR space for classifiers with group-level information budgets, for two subgroups in the Mexican poverty dataset. It is observed that urban households are more predictable than rural households (achievable regions closer to the origin). The light and dark gray areas comprise the achievable regions for urban and rural groups. A substantial overlap is observed, showing a wide-ranging achievable region for equal odds.

Similarly, by varying the probability thresholds for the two groups, we obtain the achievable region for the individual-level information budget classifier described in the earlier "Active Fairness" section.

We compare the achievable *equal odds* regions for the active methods against the naive randomized classifier proposed in Hardt et al. (2016), and compare their information cost-efficiency. In particular, we introduce a fixed information budget constraint and compare solutions sets that satisfy it. Figure 10.3 shows results for the Mexican poverty dataset. Points in the FNR-FPR space were filtered to include only classifier designs that satisfied equal odds for the dataset's corresponding sensitive attribute.

It is observed that both group-level and individual-level strategies yield equal odds solutions, covering a wide range along the FNR-FPR tradeoff curve, and without resorting to naive randomization. Moreover, it is shown that both types of active classifiers are substantially more information-efficient than the randomized classifier—Pareto dominance along most of the FNR-FPR tradeoff curve—leading to lower false positive and false negative errors in budget-constrained environments.

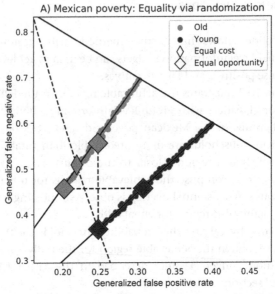

A) Mexican poverty: Equality via randomization

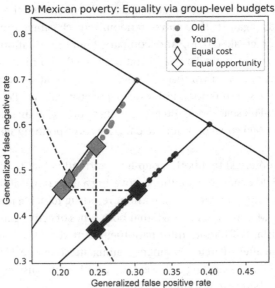

B) Mexican poverty: Equality via group-level budgets

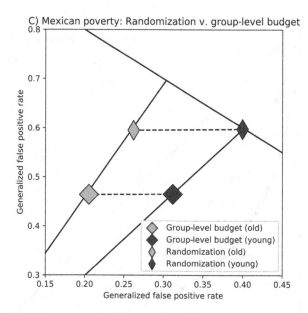

FIGURE 10.1

Achieving calibration and single error rate parity: classifiers with group-level information budgets versus naive randomization analyzed on the Mexican poverty dataset. Gray and black colors correspond to error rates of two population subgroups (old versus young households). The leftmost panel (A) shows the generalized false positive and false negative rates (GFPR and GFNR) of classifiers that randomize an increasing proportion of individuals (0% to 100%).[21] The middle panel (B) shows the same analysis for classifiers with active fairness using group-level budgets. Finally, the rightmost panel (C) compares the efficiency of both methods, by showing the best classifiers that achieve equal opportunity and calibration, under an information budget restriction.

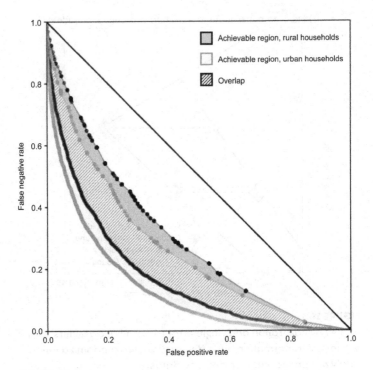

FIGURE 10.2

Achieving parity in false positives and false negatives (equal odds) via group-level information budgets. Results correspond to the Mexican poverty dataset. Achievable regions of classifiers for each population subgroup are plotted in dark and light gray. The outer and inner FPR-FNR curves of each achievable region correspond to classifiers using maximum and minimum information budgets. Points along the curve correspond to different values of the decision threshold.

CONCLUSIONS

From medicine to poverty prediction, analysts and policymakers are increasingly turning to ADMs to help guide and improve human decisions. An algorithmic approach can avoid some of the implicit and explicit biases made by human decision-makers. However, these same algorithms can also deepen social inequality and systematize discrimination if they are not developed while keeping fairness in mind. To attack this problem, researchers have developed a multitude of formal definitions and frameworks to measure bias in algorithmic systems as well as methods to mitigate this bias.

We have proposed and demonstrated methods for simultaneously achieving equal opportunity and calibration, as well as to achieve equal odds. In contrast to prior work, the active framework does not rely on naive randomization to reach these fairness notions, avoiding several known disadvantages of randomized approaches. Instead, a decision-maker acquires partial information sets according to the needs of different groups or individuals, allocating resources equitably in order to achieve balance in predictive performance. By leveraging this additional degree of freedom, the active approach can outperform randomization-based classifiers previously considered optimal.

More broadly, this work illustrates how, by jointly considering information collection, inference, and decision-making processes, we can design automated decision systems that more flexibly optimize social objectives, including fairness, accuracy, efficiency, and privacy. A natural direction for future work is to consider richer utility functions relevant to real-world decision systems. We expect future studies that generalize results here presented to contexts with varying feature costs, as well as to contexts with multi-stakeholder value functions, where the opportunity, privacy, and monetary costs that inquiry and decision-making bring to decision subjects are jointly considered as part of the adaptive inquiry process.

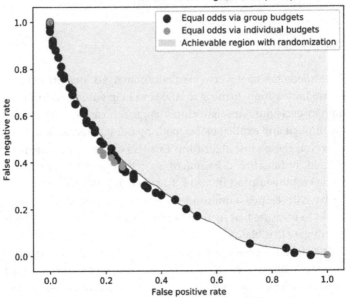

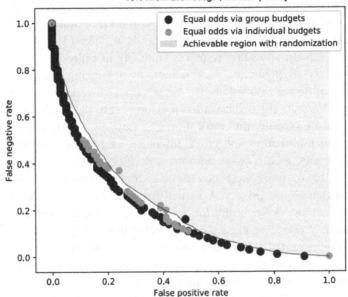

Lastly, a relevant path forward is to allow observations with partial feature sets both during training and test phases. The current implementation of this work necessitates access to full-feature observations at training time. More efficient training and further model refinement could be achieved under schemes that can learn from partial feature vectors, or proactively collect features at training time. This approach would allow the incorporation of a wider set of features tailored to increase prediction accuracy over different types of individuals.

REFERENCES

1. Agarwal, Alekh, Alina Beygelzimer, Miroslav Dudík, John Langford, and Hanna Wallach. 2018. "A Reductions Approach to Fair Classification." arXiv:1803.02453.

2. Asuncion, Arthur, and David Newman. 2007. UCI Machine Learning Repository. UCI School of Information and Computer Sciences. https://archive.ics.uci.edu/ml/index.php.

3. Bechavod, Yahav, and Katrina Ligett. 2017. "Learning Fair Classifiers: A Regularization-Inspired Approach." arXiv:1707.00044.

4. Calders, Toon, Faisal Kamiran, and Mykola Pechenizkiy. 2009. "Building Classifiers with Independency Constraints." In *Proceedings*

FIGURE 10.3
Achievable space of equal odds classifiers for the Mexican poverty dataset. Comparison of active classifiers with group- and individual-level information budgets, and naive randomization.[12] Classifiers are constrained by the same constant information budget. Panels correspond to different levels of budget constraints. It is observed that active classifiers yield equal odds solutions along the FPR-FNR tradeoff, without resorting to randomization. Moreover, these are substantially more information-efficient, and Pareto-dominate randomized classifiers in budget-constrained environments.

of the 2009 IEEE International Conference on Data Mining Workshops (ICDMW'09), 13–18. Washington, DC: IEEE Computer Society. DOI: 10.1109/ICDMW.2009.83.

5. Calmon, Flavio P., Dennis Wei, Karthikeyan Natesan Ramamurthy, and Kush R. Varshney. 2017. "Optimized Data Pre-Processing for Discrimination Prevention." arXiv:1704.03354.

6. Chalfin, Aaron, Oren Danieli, Andrew Hillis, Zubin Jelveh, Michael Luca, Jens Ludwig, and Sendhil Mullainathan. 2016. "Productivity and Selection of Human Capital with Machine Learning." *American Economic Review* 106 (5): 124–127.

7. Chouldechova, Alexandra, Diana Benavides-Prado, Oleksandr Fialko, and Rhema Vaithianathan. 2018. "A Case Study of algorithm-assisted decision making in Child Maltreatment Hotline Screening Decisions." In *Proceedings of ACM Conference on Fairness, Accountability and Transparency—Machine Learning Research* 81, 134–148. New York: ACM. http://proceedings.mlr.press/v81/.

8. Corbett-Davies, Sam, and Sharad Goel. 2018. "The Measure and Mismeasure of Fairness: A Critical Review of Fair Machine Learning." arXiv:1808.00023.

9. Corbett-Davies, Sam, Emma Pierson, Avi Feller, Sharad Goel, and Aziz Huq. 2017. "Algorithmic Decision Making and the Cost of Fairness." In *Proceedings of the 23rd ACM SIGKDD International Conference on Knowledge Discovery and Data Mining*, 797–806. New York: ACM.

10. Flores, Anthony W., Kristin Bechtel, and Christopher T. Lowenkamp. 2016. "False Positives, False Negatives, and False Analyses: A Rejoinder to Machine Bias: There's Software Used across the Country to Predict Future Criminals. And It's Biased against Blacks." *Fed. Probation* 80: 38.

11. Gillingham, Philip. 2015. "Predictive Risk Modelling to Prevent Child Maltreatment and Other Adverse Outcomes for Service Users: Inside the 'Black Box' of Machine Learning." *British Journal of Social Work* 46 (4): 1044–1058.

12. Hamlin, Rebecca. 2012. "International Law and Administrative Insulation: A Comparison of Refugee Status Determination Regimes in the United States, Canada, and Australia." *Law & Social Inquiry* 37 (4): 933–968.

13. Hardt, Moritz, Eric Price, Nati Srebro, et al. 2016. "Equality of Opportunity in Supervised Learning." In *Advances in Neural Information Processing Systems* 29, edited by D. D. Lee, M. Sugiyama, U. V. Luxburg, I. Guyon, and R. Garnett, 3315–3323. New York: Curran Associates Publishers. http://papers.nips.cc/paper/6374-equality-of-opportunity-in-supervised -learning.pdf.

14. Huang, Cheng-Lung, Mu-Chen Chen, and Chieh-Jen Wang. 2007. "Credit Scoring with a Data Mining Approach Based on Support Vector Machines." *Expert Systems with Applications* 33 (4): 847–856.

15. Karlan, Dean, and Jonathan Zinman. 2011. "Microcredit in Theory and Practice: Using Randomized Credit Scoring for Impact Evaluation." *Science* 332 (6035): 1278–1284.

16. Kleinberg, Jon, Jens Ludwig, Sendhil Mullainathan, and Ziad Obermeyer. 2015. "Prediction Policy Problems." *American Economic Review* 105 (5): 491–495.

17. Kleinberg, Jon, Sendhil Mullainathan, and Manish Raghavan. 2016. "Inherent Trade-Offs in the Fair Determination of Risk Scores." arXiv:1609.05807.

18. Lichman, Moshe et al. 2013. UCI Machine Learning Repository. UCI School of Information and Computer Sciences. https://archive.ics.uci .edu/ml/index.php.

19. Louizos, Christos, Kevin Swersky, Yujia Li, Max Welling, and Richard Zemel. 2015. "The Variational Fair Autoencoder." arXiv:1511.00830.

20. Phillips, Richard L., Kyu Hyun Chang, and Sorelle A Friedler. 2017. "Interpretable Active Learning." arXiv:1708.00049.

21. Pleiss, Geoff, Manish Raghavan, Felix Wu, Jon Kleinberg, and Kilian Q Weinberger. 2017. "On Fairness and Calibration." In *Advances in Neural Information Processing Systems* 30 (NIPS 2017), edited by I. Guyon, U. V. Luxburg, S. Bengio, H. Wallach, R. Fergus, S. Vishwanathan, and R. Garnett, 5680–5689. New York: Curran Associates Publishers. http:// papers.nips.cc/paper/7151-on-fairness-and-calibration.pdf

22. Quinlan, J. Ross. 1993. *C4.5: Programs for Machine Learning*. San Francisco: Morgan Kaufmann Publishers Inc.

23. Stampini, Marco, and Leopoldo Tornarolli. 2012. "The Growth of Conditional Cash Transfers in Latin America and the Caribbean: Did They Go Too Far?" Technical Report. IZA Policy Paper.

24. Williams, David, Xuejun Liao, Ya Xue, and Lawrence Carin. 2005. "Incomplete-Data Classification Using Logistic Regression." In *Proceedings of the 22nd ACM International Conference on Machine Learning*, 972–979. New York: ACM.

25. Bilal Zafar, Muhammad, Isabel Valera, Manuel Gomez Rodriguez, and Krishna P. Gummadi. 2017. "Fairness Constraints: Mechanisms for Fair Classification." arXiv:1507.05259.

26. Bilal Zafar, Muhammad, Isabel Valera, Manuel Gomez Rodriguez, and Krishna P. Gummadi. 2015. "Learning Fair Classifiers." arXiv:1507.05259.

27. Žliobaitė, Indrė. 2017. "Measuring Discrimination in Algorithmic Decision Making." *Data Mining and Knowledge Discovery* 31 (4): 1060–1089.

28. Bolukbasi, T., K. W. Chang, J. Y. Zou, V. Saligrama, and A. T. Kalai. 2016. "Man Is to Computer Programmer as Woman Is to Homemaker? Debiasing Word Embeddings." In *Advances in Neural Information Processing Systems 29*, edited by D. D. Lee, M. Sugiyama, U. V. Luxburg, I. Guyon, and R. Garnett, 4349–4357. New York: Curran Associates Publishers. http://papers.nips.cc/paper/6228-man-is-to-computer-programmer-as -woman-is-to-homemaker-debiasing-word-embeddings.pdf.

29. Friedman, B., and H. Nissenbaum. 1996. "Bias in Computer Systems." *ACM Transactions on Information Systems (TOIS)* 14 (3): 330–347.

30. Dwork, C., M. Hardt, T. Pitassi O. Reingold, and R. Zemel. 2012. "Fairness through Awareness." In *Proceedings of the 3rd Innovations in Theoretical Computer Science Conference* (ITCS'12), 214–226. New York: ACM.

31. Gorry, G. Anthony, and G. Octo Barnett. 1968. "Sequential Diagnosis by Computer." *JAMA* 205 (12): 849–854.

32. Noriega-Campero, A., M. Bakker, B. Garcia-Bulle, and A. Pentland. 2018. "Active Fairness in Algorithmic Decision Making." arXiv:1810.00031.

11 BEYOND GDPR: EMPLOYING AI TO MAKE PERSONAL DATA USEFUL TO CONSUMERS

David L. Shrier

INTRODUCTION

With the General Data Protection Regulation (GDPR), the European Union established a global standard for the protection of personal data and digital privacy. The ramifications of this body of law extend beyond the EU, with domiciles ranging from the United States to the United Arab Emirates and an array of others experiencing the benefits, as technology leaders such as Facebook and Google implement aspects of GDPR around the world.

Protection is only the beginning of the journey for personal data and the average citizen. The digital information traces that we leave across online platforms and in a proliferating array of distributed digital platforms (from the Internet of Things to blockchain) create a rich picture of human life that can, in turn, enable insights into personal health and financial behaviors, civic infrastructure, transportation systems, and other aspects of society. Such insights can diminish individual dignity, autonomy, and privacy, and they can also provide significant benefits both to individual data subjects and to society.

How can the average citizen harness these benefits from this new era that GDPR enables (and, on a more narrow scope, what Open Banking makes possible)? How can society explore and expand the wider benefits in ways consistent with data protection and fundamental rights?

What are the mechanisms that translate the concepts of "you control your own data" into practical reality for five hundred million Europeans?

Most people will have neither the time nor the inclination to manage their digital information streams or to deeply understand how their personal data can enable better lives. Yet, they would enjoy some of the benefits greater control over personal data can bring, such as easier access to more and better services. What is the bridge from our current state to a future state with a vibrant personal data ecology?

CORE ISSUES OF PERSONAL DATA

We see two basic issues to address:

1. The mechanism whereby *people control their personal data* and digital identity. Given individual lack of time, inclination, or capacity, this control could preferably be implemented through community information fiduciaries, which are described in detail later in this document. These fiduciaries would help promote and implement consent and provide mechanism for individuals to deal with complexities of the information environment. They would also allow startups to have access to the historical data (with user consent) needed to produce innovative services that compete with the big guys.

2. The systems to *keep track of what information was used* by which algorithm and resulted in what decision. "Algorithmic audit" capabilities allow monitoring of fairness, equity, and similar dimensions, as well as accountability of impact for government regulation. This is a key precondition for user-centric regulation and access to justice, and it is how we can couple digital processes to existing judicial and legislative processes.

Tracking of information also provides the historical database that can be used for the benefit of the data subject and can reduce barriers to entry for new applications.

The debate must go beyond a stale question that is being asked today: "Does the user own the data or is it the corporation?" Although we need a discussion on ownership, part of the answer to this question today hinges on a distinction between raw data, in which the data subject clearly retains a strong and enduring interest, and demographically aggregated information, which is the corporation's work product through the processes and algorithms used to create demographics but in which the data subject still has an affected interest. The concept of "legitimate interest" as a grounds for processing under Article 7 of the GDPR recognizes this continuum of interests in data rather than simplistic notions of mere ownership or absolute control, but properly puts the interests of the individual first.

Additionally, if we believe truly decentralized companies are possible, which is part of the promise that blockchain offers, the question of what a "corporation" *is* becomes more tenuous. A decentralized company has no headquarters, no CEO, no single decision-maker. The corporate balance sheet is ratably distributed among the nodes and potentially token holders. Decisions of the organization are undertaken by a vote of the token holders, and presumably ownership of the corporate assets (including the data assets) are attached to the tokens and not to a "corporate person." There are, of course, a plethora of uncharted legal waters to navigate when contemplating such an organization, but for the purposes of the current discussion—in such a world with a decentralized company, won't this issue of who owns the user data be more complicated to untangle?

In the realm of personal financial data, the EU Open Banking and Payment Services Directive 2 (PSD2) regulations provide for greater portability of personal data from one financial institution to another. While intended to open up competition from incumbent financial institutions to new entrants, they also create the risk for enabling the large incumbent institutions to build or solidify an oligopoly at the expense of less well-funded startups.

PRIVACY BY DESIGN

GDPR has profound implications and all of the nuances that will emerge in regulatory and business practice have yet to emerge. It seems that if control/monetization of personal data is going to shift to the individual, then this data will have to be afforded protections beyond what other forms of data are given. For example, GDPR is an effort to shift the default assumptions about data—where individuals retain the fundamental ability to control their data even after it has been shared with a corporation. Unfortunately, the interactions between customers and corporations remains locked in a disclosure/acknowledgement framework, rather than being guided by a living interaction over time. Given advances in cryptography and data architecture, it is now feasible for more operational control of individuals' data to remain in their hands; but much work still must be done to bring what is feasible into reality. This creates the potential of architecting "privacy by design" rather than hoping for "privacy by default."

THE NEED FOR TRUSTED THIRD PARTIES

What are possible solutions to the personal data conundrum?

The concept of *trusted third parties* provides a vehicle by which the technological and market sophistication needed to understand, and monetize, personal data is possible. The motivation for trusted third parties is grounded in the idea that while people want the benefits of personal data governance, the average citizen lacks both time and sophistication to acquire the level of knowledge necessary to effectuate it. Think of the complex inner workings of today's smartphone. Nobody wants, or needs, to get a PhD in electrical engineering in order to press the power button, open a social media app, and begin interacting with others. Behind that simple set of three or four gestures lie hundreds of millions of dollars of R&D and user interaction design. Simple is, in fact, difficult.

We also have a question of how to align regulators and policy-makers with industry, consumer privacy advocates, and academia in order to ensure that whatever trusted third-party solutions emerge, are acceptable to government, commercial interests, and consumers.

We draw on the model of the Windhover Principles developed four years ago by a previous working group convened by what is now the MIT Trust::Data Consortium. At the time of their formulation, cryptocurrencies such as Bitcoin were just emerging from academic experiment to commercial market deployment. Regulators around the world were beginning to consider whether intervention was required, some even considering whether, in fact, Bitcoin needed to be shut down.

The Windhover Principles articulated a mechanism that enabled the emergent cryptocurrency industry to comply with extant government regulations regarding Anti Money Laundering (AML) and Know Your Client (KYC), and were incorporated into the Terms of Service (TOS) of a number of predominant crypto wallet companies and exchanges, aligning compliance with market practice and enabling the current flourishing of a blockchain-based ecology.

CONSTRUCTING THE PERSONAL DATA ECOLOGY

How do we architect a similar process and set of market players for personal data?

In particular, there is a need to explore how the principle of self-sovereignty of digital identity and personal data can be more firmly enshrined in European law and practice. Although some may claim GDPR provides for self-sovereignty of personal data, there is no such thing as self-sovereignty in the GDPR—GDPR refers to "control" on a number of instances in its recitals. The GDPR empowers individuals indirectly by interposing protection between a controller and the data subject; self-sovereignty empowers data subjects directly.

Going one step further, we could not only argue in favor of control of personal data but in favor of ownership of the same, although we anticipate that this will be a much more complicated debate than the debate about control. The debate must however go beyond the stereotypes; the debate must, for instance, go beyond the question that is being asked today: "Does the user own the data or is it the corporation?" And—who knows—we may well end up concluding that actually no one (whether an individual or a corporation) owns a dataset, which in itself is of value, but that several sets of data owned by different parties need to be combined to create data value.

Something else we are currently seeing is that, whereas GDPR was aimed at containing the activities of the Facebooks of this world, Facebook and the like have the resources and infrastructure to comply readily with GDPR, while small- and medium-sized enterprises (SMEs) are suffering the most from this new regulation and indeed are not capable of complying.

It therefore seems to us that the framework regarding personal data in particular, and information architecture in general, needs to be reframed in such a way that SMEs or entities that are not buying or selling (or otherwise making money) with data to be largely exempted from GDPR—i.e., we need a GDPR-light for SMEs.

We propose the creation of *data fiduciaries*: entities that have the right to represent individuals in data relationships and collect and hold data about themselves (the individuals' data) on their behalf. By analogy, think of banks and money. Credit unions (of which there are nearly two thousand in Europe) are community organizations owned by their members and chartered to do pretty much exactly this (although they currently do only monetary activities). The MIT Trust::Data consortium is building a prototype of such a fiduciary as a model of how this all might work.

INCENTIVES: ENABLING POSITIVE REINFORCEMENT

There will always be inventive companies/individuals that will find a way around regulations to do what they can to benefit themselves.

Behavioral psychologists demonstrated in the 1930s that positive reinforcement has far longer lasting effects than negative reinforcement. Regulations and fines are like negative reinforcement in a lab experiment: they work as long as the subject thinks they will be administered. Firms will spend as much time to find creative ways to avoid fines as to comply with onerous (from the firm's perspective) regulations.

We observed this perverse behavior on the trading floor of one of the largest financial markets in the world, the New York Mercantile Exchange (which, in the words of one of the board members, was "half free market capitalism and half prison experiment"). People, even ethical ones, but especially unethical ones, can and will subvert ANY rules-based system. The best-run prison in the world is littered with "shanks" (illegal weapons). Ethical people subconsciously fall into subsystems that subvert rules in favor of personal gain (economic, pleasure, ease, etc.).

To be effective, any body of regulation needs not only to include deterrents, but also to provide some clear benefit to companies as well as to individuals.

Today's corporations claim proprietary rights in data, whereas individuals intuitively believe that data about them belongs to them and not the corporations. Others argue that the data only gain their full value after they have been processed through algorithms—i.e., technologies invested in and developed by those same corporations.

Moreover, these intuitions exist largely in public discussion on data, but behaviors of individual consumers suggest an overwhelming inertia to the current data architectures—where consumers freely release data in exchange for services, and corporations process and monetize those data. With the first months of GDPR compliance behind us, empirical evidence can now be reviewed to examine how consumers responded to the new data notices. The EU can and should look for the outcomes of these early interactions in order to optimize consumer-facing messaging in the future. We hypothesize that these early experiments suggest that the wave of notices precipitated by GDPR has had little impact, and stronger incentives are needed to change our culture around data.

Some efforts to create incentive markets offer cautionary tales. Take, for example, the differences between experiments in affecting carbon markets in the United States and the European Union. In the US, a legislative/private partnership had little regulatory backing, and, as such floundered domestically and became infiltrated with scam artists. Similar efforts in the European Union that received a firmer regulatory backing through stricter and more harmonized emissions and offset standards (across EU member states) did not produce a perfect result, but nevertheless led to the establishment of a modest but active carbon emissions market.

Complex issues of national law also come into play, which creates a lack of clarity around where we will end up; it may be somewhere unexpected. Decentralization is certainly an important aspect in the debate, and we see an opportunity to converge the emerging dialog around blockchain in Europe with the personal data and AI discussions.

ETHICAL APPLICATIONS OF AI

Personal data has become a fertile area for artificial intelligence systems to be deployed by companies (and governments) seeking how to optimize which messages are delivered to which people. A number of ethical questions have arisen, in particular with respect to large-scale social media platforms. As the EU contemplates applications of AI to personal data, it is critically important to bear in mind unintended consequences and ethical implications of any actions that interact with personal data. In fact, this is an opportunity for a first use case of ethically regulated AI.

NEXT STEPS

These are the initial outlines for how to go beyond GDPR into implementing a personal data ecology that leverages AI to bring more benefits and control to the individual citizen.

We recommend a series of convenings to bring together government, academic, consumer/user, and industry perspectives to help shape the next body of regulation around personal data in Europe.

PERSONAL DATA WORKING GROUP

- John D'Agostino, Managing Director, DMS Governance
- Amias Gerety, Partner, QED Investors
- Cameron Kerry, Fellow, Brookings Institution; Visiting Scholar, MIT Media Lab
- Vicki Raeburn, Independent Consultant; Board Member, Distilled Analytics
- Jean-Louis Schiltz, Honorary Professor, University of Luxembourg
- Alex Pentland, Professor, Massachusetts Institute of Technology; Visiting Professor, Saïd Business School, University of Oxford

12 SOCIAL CAPITAL ACCOUNTING

Takeo Nishikata, Thomas Hardjono,
and Alex Pentland

INTRODUCTION

In order to quantify and improve the quality of our lives, we have long been dependent upon economic metrics at a national level. The Gross Domestic Product (GDP) created in 1937 has been a major metric for our society and helped to drive our economy. In 2009, Stiglitz, Sen, and Fitoussi[1] pointed out that GDP had not accurately represented citizen well-being. They also made recommendations on measuring a society from three angles: economic capital, non-economic capital, and sustainability. Since then, new ways to measure non-economic capital, combined with an increase in digital technology, have been explored. The IEEE Global Initiative on Ethics of Autonomous and Intelligent Systems categorizes those emerging metrics into four areas: Positive Psychology Well-Being Metrics, International Governmental Well-Being Metrics, Business Well-Being Metrics, and Social Media Well-Being Metrics.[2] While these metrics have relied upon a long list of survey questions or social network data, there is another new approach that captures real-life data by utilizing various sensor devices including smartphones, wearable devices, and cameras. Mood Meter Project is one of the examples of utilizing advanced technology to quantify emotion.[3] However, the novel metrics that have been developed are not widely deployed or accepted.

In this chapter, we will propose a mechanism to digitize social capital based on solid research in computational social science, the study of human behavior by means of large-scale operational data from digital systems data and machine learning analytics methods. The reason to choose to measure social capital is that some studies have shown that social connections, among various non-economic factors, are among the most influential factors on human well-being. For instance, a study that tracks the life activities of hundreds of people for ninety years found that the primary determinant of individual well-being is the quality of their social connections with people they trust.[4] Digital non-economic capital (our "digital identities") is also an essential part of the system when it comes to improving the quality of our lives.

DESIGN PRINCIPLES

General Properties

The system needs to have the following properties.

1. *A model to quantify human interactions.*

   First, the system needs a model to quantify human interactions. The recent advances in computational social science have provided a number of methods to quantify social connections. For instance, mobile phone data, including proximity, time, and location, allows accurate inference of friendship network structure.[5] The structure, reciprocity, and directionality of friendship play an important role in the spread of new behaviors and norm enforcement.[6] Moreover, trust, a central component of social and economic interactions among humans, can be accurately predicted using passive sensing and network analysis.[7] We can combine these ideas in order to quantify the social capital created by human interactions by use of passively sensed signals.

2. *A mechanism to convert human interactions to a real asset.*

The second essential part of the system is a mechanism to convert human interactions to a useful asset. Our model considers that each time a reciprocal human interaction happens, an asset is created as a proof of her/his contribution to the relationship. This asset may be considered to be a kind of credit score, and could act as a potentiating or gating factor for economic capital in many ways. The more contributions you make to building a reciprocal relationship means the higher the social credit score you gain, which in turn may be used to help you in financial interactions requiring interpersonal trust.

3. *A total amount of asset within the network.*

Third, the system needs to have the capability of calculating an individual asset as well as the total amount of social assets in the network. If the system can measure the total amount of assets, we can then begin to quantify the social capital within a community.

4. *Diversity, transparency, and consensus concerning models to quantify human interactions.*

Human relationships are diverse and differ depending on contexts in nature. Therefore, if a single model dominates the determination of how much social capital people have, that would be catastrophic to society. To avoid this scenario, it is critical to ensure that the system has multiple and diverse models, with models selected in a democratic manner. In order to insure transparency and accountability, it is also necessary to record which model is being used each time an asset is generated, and the circumstances of that generation event.

5. *A low entry barrier.*

A practical system needs to have a low entry barrier to be able to start the system quickly and easily for individuals, thus driving wider adoption. For this study, we chose a smartphone and smartphone application to capture the data since smartphones are one of the most prevalent devices, and they can capture data passively and continuously.

6. *Privacy and security.*

With the recent increase in the number security breaches to corporate databases (e.g., Equifax breach[8]), there is the strong concern on the part of the citizen for the security and privacy of their personal data. It is with this backdrop of concern that we have adopted the Open Algorithms (OPAL) architecture[9] as the basis for our data privacy approach.

There are several key design aspects of the OPAL architecture:

- *Data remains in personal datastores.* Instead of collecting data from each Personal Data Store (PDS) of individuals, it is the algorithm that is sent to each PDS for local execution. Thus, each PDS must observe the OPAL principles, where raw data cannot be accessed directly but only through local safe execution of algorithms.

- *Vetted algorithms.* Algorithms that are sent to each PDS must be vetted by experts in the domain to ensure that the algorithms preserve personal privacy. That is, the algorithms themselves must not inadvertently "leak" private information, and must not lead to re-identification of individuals.

- *Local use of data encryption.* Encryption should be employed to protect data while it is in storage. New types of encryption schemes that allow for computations on encrypted data (homomorphic encryption, secure multi-party computation) provide a promising direction for data security.

- *Legal foundation for communities of PDS.* The group of personal datastores should collectively operate under the Open Algorithms scheme, defining legal agreements under which the system should operate. New legal constructs, such as the Personal Information Protection Company (PIPC) legislation in Vermont, US, provide a good start at such a foundation.

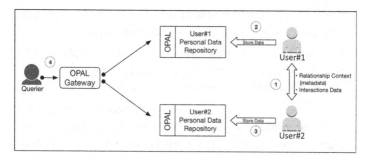

FIGURE 12.1
System architecture.

SYSTEM ARCHITECTURE

We employ the OPAL system developed by MIT.[9] Figure 12.1 summarizes the high-level architecture. Two users (User#1 and User#2) have a social relationship and an ongoing interaction, both online and face-to-face. In these interactions, both users generate data (e.g., common geolocation data points), and each user stores these interaction-generated data on their respective personal data repositories. This is shown in step 1 and steps 2 and 3 in figure 12.1. When a querier entity seeks to obtain insights from these interactions data, it employs the OPAL system to perform privacy-preserving queries to the respective user repositories.

OWNERSHIP OF METADATA AND DATA

There are several subtle points summarized in figure 12.1:

- *Joint-ownership of data.* Both User#1 and User#2 claim joint-ownership on their personal data, as generated through their interactions. This is because the two users created the relationship, and therefore own the context metadata (identifying that the relationship exists). This is akin to jointly owning an edge between two nodes in a relationship graph.

- *Data never leaves the repositories.* The OPAL principles dictate that: (1) data never leaves the repository; and (2) vetted algorithms are sent to the repository endpoints.

- *Authorization required from both users.* In order for the querier entity to request the execution of vetted algorithms (at the relevant repositories), authorization permission and consent must be obtained by both users.

SIMULATION

For the purpose of simulating how social capital is created in a real-world community, we constructed a simplified model and applied it to a real-world community of young families, as documented in the Friends and Family dataset.[10]

Friends and Family dataset was first introduced by Nadav Aharony.[11] The dataset is based on a yearlong study, and participants of the study consisted of 130 adult members within a young-family residential living community adjacent to a major research university in North America. All members of the community are couples, and at least one of the members is affiliated with the university. Among the 130+ adult members, fifty-five were added in the experiment in the spring of 2010 and the rest in the fall of 2010. Their interactions were passively sensed through mobile phones, with signals including call log, SMS log, Bluetooth devices nearby, GPS, WiFi access points, and so forth. The benefit of using this dataset is that, because of its richness and density, it is possible to utilize results from a number of previous research efforts[5,6,7] that have been conducted upon the dataset.

Our model quantifies social capital by specifying that each reciprocal interaction between two persons generates one unit of social capital for each of them, as a proof of their contribution to the relationship. Although a way to identify an interaction differs by signals, we selected call logs since operational measures of trust are most accurately predicted through call logs.[7]

The results of this measurement of social capital accumulation throughout the experimental period is shown in figure 12.2, illustrating a network graph as well as the distribution of social capital in the community. In the network graph, each node represents a participant and the size of a node shows how much social capital each participant holds. Each edge represents a connection and the width of an edge represents the volume of interactions between two participants.

In this experiment we ask each participant three "trust" questions about every other participant, where "X" is the other experiment participant:

1) Would you ask person X for help in sickness?

2) Would you ask person X for a hundred-dollar loan?

3) Would you ask person X for babysitting?

Using our social capital measure, we were able to predict answers to these trust questions with an average 94% accuracy.

DISCUSSION

The design of this system could be scalable with other devices, signals, models, etc.—that is, there are a number of possibilities to quantify human interactions. Although a smartphone was selected as a sensor device in this research, wearable devices or other media that connect people could be employed depending on the data identified to capture, as each device or media has its own advantages and disadvantages. As for signals, this study chose call logs as a signal. However, other types of signals, such as email logs, SMS logs, and application logs, are all possible

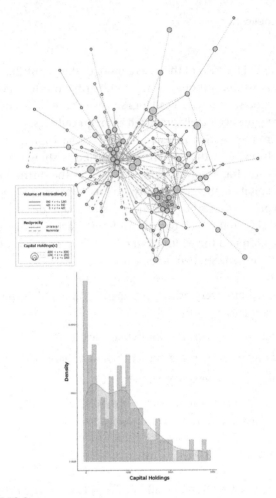

FIGURE 12.2
Social graph showing distribution of social capital in the Friends and Family community. In this network graph, each node represents a participant and the size of a node shows how much social capital each participant holds. Each edge represents a connection and the width of an edge represents the volume of interactions between two participants. The measured social capital predicted the experimental subjects' answers to trust questions concerning babysitting, loaning money, borrowing automobiles, with 94% accuracy.

predictors for trust among humans and in addition have been shown to be useful predictors of interpersonal trust.

Moreover, the idea of being able to digitize human relationships is not limited to the number of interactions, as we demonstrated in this study, but can include multiple types of models in order to better quantify human interactions. If a model includes multiple contexts, such as friends, family members, and, coworkers, it could represent more diverse human interactions, giving users the freedom to choose a model from various options depending on contexts or needs. One of the examples of other models involves measuring the extent to which people have diverse connections. It was shown that there is a strong correlation between the diversity of individual relationship and the economic development of communities,[12] which means city planners could introduce the system to stimulate the economy of a city by enhancing the diversity of individual relationships.

From the users' perspective, a number of applications can be enabled by measuring social capital. At an individual level, users can utilize their social capital in order to borrow money at lower interest rates or without collateral, gain access to better jobs, or receive a discount for purchasing goods and services. Combining such a measure of social capital with other types of noneconomic capital can also open up more opportunities.

In addition, if widely accepted, social capital can become a means of enhancing human-to-human exchanges. At a local level, managers in any organizations can monitor and improve their group's performance by referring to the total amount of social capital within the group or total social capital across organizations, without endangering individual privacy. At a national or global level, the total amount of social capital could act as a new economic indicator for factors that have never been quantified on such a wide scale.

SOCIAL NETWORKS AND DIGITAL TRUST

In human societies, the reputation of a person within a community is a function of not only the network of community interactions; it is also influenced by the degree and frequency of interactions. Networks that are "dense"—where everyone is connected—are the traditional source of local trust regarding an individual. For example, if Carol is close friends with Alice and with Bob independent of one another, it will be less risky for Alice to trust Bob even though they may have only transacted infrequently. It is in Bob's self-interest to remain honest in dealing with Alice due to their respective strong connectivity with Carol.

Similarly, a person's digital identity credentials—data about them that is used in digital transactions—becomes trusted within a human community because the reputation of the person is attested to by the human members of the community. Consequently, accurate data regarding individuals and their network of connections is crucial to the establishment of digital trust among members of a group or a community. A community with a dense, accurate digital network representation of their interpersonal interactions can potentially create a digital "trust network" consisting of assertions between community members, and this could provide a trustworthy foundation for digital exchanges between the members. The bedrock of digital trust, just like human-to-human trust, is a human community with frequent positive interactions.[13]

CONCLUSION

We have shown a system where any individual can start measuring their social capital and turning this capital into a real-world asset that improves their well-being, while preserving individual privacy and security.

REFERENCES

1. Stiglitz, J. E., A. Sen, and J. P. Fitoussi. 2010. *Mismeasuring Our Lives: Why GDP Doesn't Add Up*. New York: The New Press.

2. IEEE. "The State of Well-being Metrics (An Introduction)." The IEEE Global Initiative on Ethics of Autonomous and Intelligent Systems. Accessed September 3, 2018. https://standards.ieee.org/content/dam/ieee-standards /standards/web/documents/other/eadv2_state_wellbeing_metrics.pdf.

3. Hernandez, J., M. E. Hoque, and R. W. Picard. 2012. "Mood Meter: Counting Smiles in the Wild." In *Proceedings of the 2012 ACM Conference on Ubiquitous Computing* (Ubicomp'12), 301–310. https://doi.org/10 .1145/2370216.2370264. New York: ACM.

4. Waldinger, R. 2015. "What Makes a Good Life? Lessons from the Longest Study on Happiness." Accessed September 15, 2018. https:// www.ted.com/talks/robert_waldinger_what_makes_a_good_life_lessons _from_the_ longest_study_on_happiness.

5. Eagle, N., Alex 'Sandy' Pentland, and D. Lazer. 2009. "Inferring Friendship Network Structure by Using Mobile Phone Data." *Proceedings of the National Academy of Sciences* (PNAS) 106 (36): 15274–15278. https://doi .org/10.1073/pnas.0900282106.

6. Almaatouq, A., L. Radaelli, A. Pentland, and E. Shmueli. 2016. "Are You Your Friends' Friend? Poor Perception of Friendship Ties Limits the Ability to Promote Behavioral Change." *PLOS ONE* 11 (3): 1–13. http:// doi.org/10.1371/journal.pone.0151588.

7. Shmueli, E., V. K. Singh, B. Lepri, and A. Pentland. 2014. "Sensing, Understanding, and Shaping Social Behavior." *IEEE Transactions on Computational Social Systems* 1 (1): 22–34. http://doi.org/10.1109/TCSS.2014 .2307438.

8. Bernard, T. S., T. Hsu, N. Perlroth, and R. Lieber. 2017. "Equifax Says Cyber Attack May Have Affected 143 Million in the U.S." *New York Times*, September.

9. Hardjono, T., D. Shrier, and A. Pentland. 2016. *Trust::Data: A New Framework for Identity and Data Sharing*. Boston: Visionary Future.

10. MIT Human Dynamics Lab. "Friends and Family Dataset." http://realitycommons.media.mit.edu/friendsdataset.html. Accessed March 26, 2019

11. Aharony, Nadav, W. Pan, C. Ip, I. Khayal, and A. Pentland. 2011. "Social fMRI: Investigating and Shaping Social Mechanisms in the Real World." *Pervasive and Mobile Computing* 7 (6): 643–659.

12. Eagle, N., M. Macy, and R. Claxton. 2010. "Network Diversity and Economic Development." *Science* 328 (5981): 1029–1031. http://doi.org/10.1126/science.1186605.

13. Pentland, A., and T. Hardjono. 2018. "Digital Identity Is Broken—Here's a Way to Fix It." *Wall Street Journal*, April 3. https://blogs.wsj.com/cio/2018/04/03/digitalidentityisbrokenheresawaytofixit/.

13 TRADECOIN: TOWARDS A MORE STABLE DIGITAL CURRENCY

Alexander Lipton, Thomas Hardjono, and Alex Pentland

This chapter describes the concept of the asset-backed *Digital Trade Coins* (DTCs), currently under development at MIT.[1] It outlines an approach to building a consortium of sponsors, who contribute real assets, a narrow bank handling financial transaction, involving fiat currencies, and an administrator, who issues the corresponding digital token in exchange for fiat payments and makes fiat payments in exchange for digital tokens. In short, our proposal is to apply distributed ledger technology to give a new lease on life to the old notion of a sound asset-backed currency, and to use this currency as a transactional tool for a large pool of potential users, including small and medium enterprises (SME) and individuals. We intend to build a currency that encourages legitimate commerce, but makes illegal activities difficult. Our contribution should be viewed as a position/vision paper, since at the moment there is no working prototype for the DTC.

We wish to replace physical cash with a supranational digital token, which is insulated from adverse actions by central banks and other parties, due to the fact that it is asset-backed. We believe the DTC is ideally suited as a medium of exchange for groups of smaller nations or supranational organizations, who wish to use it as a counterweight to large reserve currencies.

Supranational currencies have been known for two millennia. For instance, Roman, and later Byzantine and Iranian, gold coins were used along the entire Silk Road; Spanish and Austrian silver coins were the prevalent medium of exchange in the Age of Sail. Closer to our time, the British Pound was used as reserve currency for the British Empire and, to a lesser degree, the rest of the world; the US Dollar and the British Pound were used as a reserve currency basket for the world economy in the twentieth century, to which the Euro and the Yen were added in late twentieth century; and now the Yuan might be used along a revived Silk Road.

Today, for the first time, there is a possibility of designing a digital currency that combines the best features of both physical cash and digital currencies, including finality of settlement, partial anonymity, and usability on the web. This currency is largely immune to policies of central banks that control the world's reserve currencies. Such a currency has enormous potential to improve the stability and competitiveness of trading and natural resource producing economies. In the DTC we propose to develop a trade-oriented asset-backed digital currency, aimed at facilitating international trade and making it as seamless as possible. This currency will be based on a proprietary framework combining the most recent advances in blockchain and distributed ledger technology, cryptography, and secure multi-party calculations, together with time-tested methods for preventing double spending. In view of the fact that our framework relies in part on our own research and in part on ideas readily available in the public domain, we don't anticipate specific intellectual property rights issues. Unlike Bitcoin, it will be fast, scalable, and environmentally friendly. It will also be transaction friendly because of its low volatility versus fiat currencies, not to mention cryptocurrencies.

Over the past decade, potential advantages and disadvantages of distributed ledgers or blockchains have been discussed by numerous researchers (see, e.g., Lipton 2018[2] and references therein). While numerous potential applications of blockchains have been entertained in the literature—including title deeds, post-trade processing, trade finance, rehypothecation, and syndicated loans, to mention but a few—the main usage of blockchains has so far been in the general area of payments, more specifically cryptocurrencies.

Worldwide interest in distributed ledgers was ignited by *Bitcoin*, which is a cryptocurrency protocol operating without a central authority. It was described first in the seminal white paper by S. Nakamoto.[3] Since then Bitcoin has inspired creation of more than a thousand of other cryptocurrencies, all with various degree of novelty and utility (if any). One of the most promising is *Ethereum*, which is significantly more versatile than Bitcoin, not least because is supports so-called smart contracts.[4] Another interesting and popular cryptocurrency protocol is *Ripple*.[5] The Ripple system departs from the Nakamoto consensus approach. It is not truly decentralized because it does not rely on the thousands of anonymous (pseudonymous) mining nodes that form the peer-to-peer network underlying Bitcoin. Instead, the Ripple system uses a small set of nodes that act more like notaries, validating transactions at a higher throughput and much lower cost in comparison with Bitcoin. Unlike Bitcoin, in Ripple most entities in the system are known and not anonymous. By their very nature, all of these currencies are native tokens, residing on a blockchain. Their transition from one economic agent to the next is controlled by the set of rules that are inherent or "hardwired" in the blockchain setup and are needed to maintain the integrity of their blockchain as a whole. However, until now, attempts to build tokens backed by real-world assets (first and foremost, fiat currencies) have been unsuccessful. Yet, until this all-important problem is solved, it is virtually impossible to make cryptocurrencies a part of the mainstream financial infrastructure, because otherwise the inherent volatility of cryptocurrencies will severely curtail their usability.

Although potential applications of distributed ledgers mentioned earlier, such as post-trade processing and trade finance, are very important, they are technical in nature and lack the revolutionary spirit. However, a distributed ledger can potentially play a truly transformative role and bring a dramatic departure from the past by making *Central Bank Digital Currency* (CBDC) and stable cryptocurrencies a reality.

In the current work we propose a stable asset-backed cryptocurrency that we refer to as DTC (Digital Trade Coin). It can be viewed as a natural extension of a fiat-backed cryptocurrency called the *Utility Settlement Coin* (USC).[6] Setting aside operational aspects of gathering and managing collateral assets, we need to design a ledger associated with value transfers. Since, by design, Nakamoto's approach is neither scalable, nor efficient, we need to use a different design. Our analysis indicates that combining blockchain with an earlier approach for issuing electronic cash (eCash), developed by Chaum,[7,8] seems to be promising. Recall that Chaum introduced a blind signature procedure for converting bank deposits into anonymous cash. On the one hand, Chaum's protocol is much cheaper, faster, and more efficient compared to Bitcoin. It also offers an avenue towards true anonymity and unlinkability (as in paper cash), as compared to the weak pseudonymity of Bitcoin. If true anonymity is not desired, there are variations on the Chaum approach on offer, for instance, anonymity for the purchaser but not for seller, and so forth. However, on the other hand, the basic Chaum model and many of its variants rely on the integrity of the issuing bank. To alleviate this issue we propose the use of blockchain technology itself to track the relevant transaction parameters, reducing the opportunity for parties to be dishonest. Payments are still direct between users as in Chaum's proposal.

In the DTC we propose a solution to the stable cryptocurrency problem, which boils down to assembling a pool of assets, contributed by *sponsors*, appointing an *administrator*, who will manage the pool, and digitizing the ownership rights on this pool. In addition, we will build a special-purpose *narrow bank*, which facilitates activities of the administrator. By construction, neither the pool itself nor the supporting bank can fail due to market and liquidity risks. Their operations are streamlined as much as possible to limit operational risks. It is worth noting that operational risks are always present; this statement is true not only for the setup we are proposing, but for ordinary cash and bank deposits too—not to mention cryptocurrencies, which are notorious for their operational risk exposures. The narrow bank receives fiat currency submitted by the users, passes it to the administrator, and ultimately, to sponsors, while the administrator issues digital tokens in return. These tokens will circulate within the group of users in a fast and efficient manner by utilizing a distributed ledger mechanism, thus creating native tokens proportionally convertible into the underlying assets at will. Their value is maintained in a relatively narrow band around the value of the underlying asset pool, with the lower bound being enforced by arbitrage, while the upper bound is enforced by the administrator assisted by sponsors.

The key insight of the paper is that the properly designed DTC can serve as an international reserve currency remaining stable in the long run and also serve as a much-needed counterbalance to fiat currencies issued by individual nations, which can be easily affected by their respective central banks.

ASSET-BACKED CURRENCIES

The idea of anchoring value of paper currency in baskets of real assets is old.[29] Gold and silver as well as bimetallic standards have been used for centuries to achieve this goal. Two approaches are common: (1) a redeemable currency backed by a basket of commodities; (2) a tabular standard currency indexed to a basket of commodities.

Lowe[30] was the first to explain how to use a tabular standard of value to the price inflation; a similar plan based on a basket of fifty commodities was developed by Scrope.[31] Jevons[32] pushed these ideas (much) further and proposed an indexation scheme based on a basket of one hundred commodities; while Marshall[33] proposed a similar tabular standard.

Inspired by developments during the Great Depression, F. Graham[34] developed an automatic countercyclical policy based on 100% backing of bank deposits by commodities and goods, while B. Graham[35] proposed backing the USD with a commodity basket at 60% and gold at 40%. Hayek[36] advocated establishing a universal basket of commodities, which every country would use to back its currency. Roughly at the same time, Keynes[37] designed an international gold-linked multilateral transaction currency, which he called the *Bancor*. Unfortunately, his ideas were discarded by the architects of the Bretton Woods system.

After the WWII, interest in commodity-based currencies has been lukewarm. Still, Kaldor[38] proposed a new commodity reserve currency, which he also called *Bancor*. More recently, Zhou[39] proposed a new international reserve currency anchored to a stable commodity basket benchmark. The choice of the actual asset basket backing DTC is not an easy one. It is partly dictated by the composition of the sponsors' pool and partly by what assets they actually possess and are willing to contribute. For instance, depending on their resources and abilities, sponsors can contribute oil, gold, base metals, and agricultural commodities. Given that storage of significant amounts of the above is difficult and costly, it is natural to use collateral, which is in storage already, thus making stored commodities economically productive.

EXISTING CRYPTOCURRENCIES

Bitcoin

Since its first announcement in 2008 Bitcoin[3] has captured the imagination of the public by proposing the first cryptographic electronic currency having no intrinsic value, issued without central authority, and capable of peer-to-peer digital transfers. Anyone can join the Bitcoin ecosystem, which is both a strength and a weakness.

Because it's currently the best-known form of cryptocurrency, it's worth exploring how Bitcoin works. Financial transactions are made directly between users, without the help of designated intermediaries. Transactions are publicly broadcast and recorded in a "blockchain ledger," which can be seen by all participants. Once a transaction is broadcast, the so-called "miners" come into play. They aggregate individual transactions into blocks (currently of about two thousand transactions each), verify them to ensure that there is no double spend by competitively providing *proof of work* (PoW), and receive mining rewards in Bitcoins (BTCs). The proof of work is based on finding a cryptographic nonce making the hash value of the candidate block of transactions lower than a given threshold. As such, the "hash power" (i.e., hardware and software processing capacity) of a node makes a difference in the likelihood of the node finding the match.

It is assumed (but not proven) that there are a sufficient number of honest miners, so that collusion among them (known as a 51% attack) is not possible. A transaction is considered to be confirmed if there are at least six new blocks built on the top on the block to which it belongs. The Bitcoin ecosystem is not without very serious issues: it can handle no more than seven transactions per second ([TpS], versus Visa which can handle more than twenty thousand); and it consumes enormous amounts of electricity used by miners (by virtue of underlying PoW computation). Thus, the immutability of Bitcoin's blockchain ledger and the prevention of double spending are achieved through mining based on PoW.

In view of the above, bitcoins themselves are just unspent transactions outputs of a long chain of transactions, which can be traced all the way back to the time when it was minted, either to the very first "genesis" block, or as part of a "coinbase" transaction included in a block by a successful miner. Bitcoin architecture is shown in figure 13.1 (a).

Since Bitcoin's inception in 2009, its price has gone up several orders of magnitude, making it the darling of speculators across the globe. However, a word of caution is in order. Since Bitcoin has no value, it can have any price; therefore, one should not be surprised if its price falls dramatically. Other than for speculative purposes, Bitcoin's uses are rather limited, because its price versus the US dollar and other fiat currencies is extremely volatile, which prevents it from becoming a medium of transaction. In addition, in spite of claims to the opposite, Bitcoin transaction costs are very high and growing. We believe that Bitcoin has contributed significantly to the area of digital money by providing the first working example of a decentralized system based on a peer-to-peer network, allowing entities to share common state (i.e., the set of confirmed transactions) without the mediation of any centralized entity. Given the tiny amounts of bitcoins being exchanged so far and with very slow transaction rates, Bitcoin and blockchain technology have garnered tremendous interest for their future potentials but they have not as yet disrupted the finance industry in the US or globally. Although Bitcoin may not be the disruptive force its supporters are claiming, its underpinning distributed ledger technology has a clear potential to transform the financial ecosystem as a whole.

Ripple

"Ripple" is a money transfer protocol; "ripples" are the underlying native currency of that protocol. Ripple is completely different from Bitcoin. For starters, ripples are pre-minted, while bitcoins are mined. In fact, Ripple is not decentralized at all. The stated purpose of the protocol is to facilitate fiat currency transfers among participating banks. However, due to the fact that there is a native token, Ripple can be used along the lines of

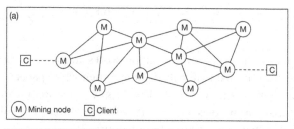

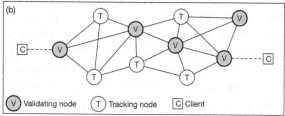

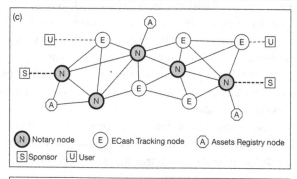

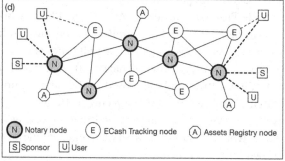

FIGURE 13.1

Comparison of different blockchain architectures: (a) Bitcoin;
(b) Ripple; (c) DTC for sponsors; (d) DTC for sponsors and users.

Bitcoin as well. Details of how Ripple works are given in various Ripple promotional materials including their white paper.[5]

The main ingredients of the Ripple ecosystem can be summarized as follows: (1) servers, which maintain the ledger; (2) clients, who can initiate transactions; (3) proposers, which can be any server; and (4) the unique nodes list (UNL), indicating parties that can be trusted by the participants in the protocol.

The lifecycle of a single transaction consists of several steps. First, a transaction is created and signed by an account owner. Second, this transaction is submitted to the network. If it is badly formed, this transaction may be rejected immediately; otherwise, it is provisionally included in the ledger. Validating nodes propose a new ledger. Transmitting nodes broadcast it to the network. Consensus is achieved by voting of the validators. The result of a successful consensus round is a validated ledger. If a consensus round fails, the consensus process repeats until it succeeds. The validated ledger includes the transaction and its effects on the ledger state.

Ripple consensus assumptions are: (1) every non-faulty server makes a decision in finite time; (2) all non-faulty servers arrive at the same decision; and (3) both true and false decision regarding a given transaction are possible.

The Ripple Protocol Consensus Algorithm (RPCA) works in rounds: (1) initially, every server compiles a list of valid candidate transactions; (2) each server amalgamates all candidates coming from its UNL and votes on their veracity; (3) transactions passing the minimum threshold are passed to the next round; and (4) the final round requires 80% agreement. In general, RPCA works well; however, it can fail provided that validating nodes form cliques, which cannot agree with each other. Ripple architecture is shown in figure 13.1 (b).

CBDC AND USC

CBDC

Could and should central banks issue *Central Bank Digital Currency*? Recently, a previously academic question of the feasibility and desirability of CBDC came to the fore.[9,20] By issuing CBDC, states can abandon physical cash in favor of its electronic equivalent and replace a large chunk of government debt with it. The impact on society at large will be huge.[21] CBDC can obviate the need for fractional banking and dramatically improve the stability of the financial system as a whole. On the other hand, the ability of the banking sector to create money "out of thin air" by making loans will be significantly curtailed and transferred to central banks. It is clear that developments in this direction are inevitable, but their timing and magnitude are uncertain.

Interest in CBDC has been ignited by two unrelated factors—the introduction of Bitcoin, and a persistence of negative interest rates in some developed countries. In Medieval Europe negative interests existed in the form of demurrage for centuries. Recall that demurrage is a tax on monetary wealth. In principle, demurrage encourages spending money, rather than hoarding it, thus accelerating economic activity. The idea of demurrage was reborn shortly after World War I in the form of scrip money, which requires paying of periodic tax to stay in circulation. Scrip money was proposed by the German-Argentinian entrepreneur and economist S. Gesell,[22] whose idea was restated by Irving Fisher during the Great Depression.[23] Demurrage was thought to be a suitable replacement for mild inflation. Since in the modern economy demurrage is hard to orchestrate due to the presence of paper currency, its conversion into the electronic form is necessary for making seriously negative rates a reality.[15]

Currently, there are three approaches to creating CBDC on a large scale:

1. Economic agents, from enterprises to private individuals, can be given accounts with central banks. However, in this case, central banks would have to execute *know your customer* (KYC) and *anti-money laundering* (AML) functions, tasks they are not equipped to perform. Besides, under duress, rational economic agents might abandon their commercial bank accounts and move their funds to central bank accounts, thus massively destabilizing the entire financial system.

2. Inspired by Bitcoin,[3] CBDC can be issued as a token on an unpermissioned distributed ledger, whose integrity is maintained by designated notaries receiving payments for their services.[24] Given that notary efforts do not require mining and thus are significantly cheaper and faster than that of Bitcoin miners, this construct is scalable and can satisfy needs of the whole economy. Users are pseudo-anonymous, since they are represented by their public keys. Because at any moment there is an immutable record showing the balance of every public key, it is possible to deanonymize transactions by using various inversion techniques applied to their recorded transactions[25] thus maintaining AML requirements.

3. A central bank can follow the Chaumian scheme,[7,8] and issue numbered and blind signed currency units onto a distributed ledger, whose trust is maintained either by designated notaries or by the bank itself. In this case it would have to rely on commercial banks, directly or indirectly, for satisfying the KYC/AML requirements.

To summarize, by using modern technology it is possible to abolish paper currency and introduce CBDC. On the positive side, CBDC can be used to alleviate some of the societal ills and eliminate costs of handling physical cash, which are of order of 1% of the country's GDP. It can help the unbanked to participate in the digital economy, thus positively affecting the society at large. On the negative side, it can give central authorities too much power over the economy and privacy, which can potentially be misused.

While CBDC is absolutely stable with respect to the underlying fiat currency, it does not make the fiat currency stable in itself. For that we need a carefully constructed DTC.

USC

CBDC is technically possible but politically complicated. Therefore, several alternatives have been proposed. One promising venue is USC, which is developed by a consortium of banks and a fintech startup called *Clearmatics*. Initially, USC can be an internal token for a consortium of participating banks. These coins have to be fully collateralized by electronic cash balances of these banks, which are held by the Central Bank itself. Eventually, these coins can be circulated among a larger group of participants. However, in this case, issuance of USCs has to be outsourced to a narrow bank, which can perform the all-important KYC and AML functions.

Recall that a narrow bank has assets, which include solely marketable low-risk securities and central bank cash in an amount exceeding its deposit base as per the regulatory prescribed capital cushion,[26] among many others. As a result, such a bank is impervious against credit and liquidity shocks. However, as any other firm, it can be affected by operational failures, including fraud, computer hacking, inability to solve the KYC/AML problem, etc. These failures can be minimized, but not eliminated, by virtue of using proper modern technology. Accordingly, narrow bank deposits would be as close to the fiat currency, as technically possible. ("Neither a borrower nor a lender be, for loan oft loses both itself and friend, and borrowing dulls the edges of husbandry." *Hamlet*, Act 1, Scene 3.) Ideally, one narrow bank per fiat currency is required. Further details are given in Lipton et al. (2018).[6]

USC is helpful from a technical perspective, but it does not solve issues of monetary policy. We wish to address this issue by building a counterweight for fiat currencies by backing the DTC with a pool of real assets.

Survivability of CBDC and USC

The idea that a blockchain system can withstand a concerted attack simply because it consists of physically distributed nodes is an untested and unproven proposition. The possible types of attacks to a blockchain system have been discussed else-where, and consist of a broad spectrum. These range from classic network-level attacks (e.g., network partitions, distributed denial of service, etc.) to more sophisticated attacks targeting the particular blockchain-specific constructs (e.g., consensus implementations), to targeting specific implementations of mining nodes or notaries (e.g., code vulnerabilities, viruses; etc.). An attack on a blockchain system may not need to cripple it entirely—a degradation in its overall service quality (e.g., slower transaction throughput) may be sufficient to disincline users to use the system.

The notion of *interoperability* across blockchain systems is an important one in the light of survivability[42,43]. The Internet was able to expand and allowed *autonomous systems* (i.e., routing domains) to interconnect with one another due to good design principles. The design philosophy of the Internet is based on three fundamental goals, namely: (1) network survivability (Internet communications must continue despite loss of networks or gateways); (2) variety of service types (the Internet must support multiple types of communications service); and (3) a variety of networks (the Internet must accommodate a variety of networks). We believe the same fundamental goals must be adopted for the current development of blockchain technology—and more specifically they must drive the technological selection for the implementations of the DTC architecture.

DTC DESIGN PRINCIPLES AND REQUIREMENTS

DTC: Motivations

Bitcoin and Ripple protocols can be used as a prototype for a distributed ledger-based cryptocurrency more suitable for transactional financial purposes. Several issues, some technical and some economical, have to be addressed before this goal can be achieved:

1. The KYC problem has to be formulated and articulated and a suitable framework for solving it has to be designed.

2. An AML mechanism has to be developed.

3. A highly efficient method for maintaining consensus on the ledger, with the industrial strength TpS capabilities, has to be built.

4. A transparent and economically meaningful system for issuing new DTCs and retiring the existing ones has to be implemented.

5. And, most importantly, a satisfactory mechanism for making DTC a stable cryptocurrency has to be designed.

Although public ledgers are not truly anonymous, but rather pseudonymous, it is difficult to use them in the KYC/AML compliant fashion. Accordingly, the DTC ledger has to be made semi-private (but probably not private) in order to solve the KYC/AML problem. At the same time, a right balance has to be struck between privacy and accountability, so that excessive restrictions should not impede the flow of legitimate commerce.

In order to achieve the level of speed and efficiency we are aspiring to, including TpS of order several thousand, the Ripple-style consensus protocol has to be used. Following Ripple's approach, we choose a group of notaries, who are known in advance and properly licensed. These notaries are responsible for performing ledger updates and maintaining its integrity by ensuring Byzantine fault tolerance.[27,28] For their services, notaries are paid a small fee, say a percentage of the transaction amount they approve, which is naturally denominated in DTC, so that their commercial interests are aligned with their functions. If notaries stay inactive, or systematically approve invalid transactions, they are financially penalized. In each round, validators create their own versions of the ledger, and propose these to the rest of the group. Several rounds of voting take place until a super-majority candidate ledger is selected. This approach is similar in spirit to the well-known Paxos algorithm. In order to increase the TpS number, we use the idea of *sharding* and assign individual notaries to particular sets of addresses. In this setup, a quorum verifies its own shard, while the full ledger is assembled out of the corresponding shards.

The DTC architecture recognizes that there are two or three types of application-level transactions commonly found in many blockchain implementations. The first is the one-party recording of assets to the ledger. Logically the DTC represents this on an assets-ledger. The second type is the two-party transferal transaction, exemplified by the transferal of coins from one party to another. The DTC captures these logically on the coins-ledger. The third type of transaction is the off-chain transferal of value (i.e., eCash) in a privacy-preserving manner. Here the goal is to allow a limited amount of coin-backed anonymous eCash to be transferred from one user to another, following the classic Chaum approach. Relevant parameters of the eCash flow are recorded on the DTC tracking-ledger in order to reduce the opportunity of fraud by entities involved in the eCash flows.

This design decision of recognizing the three types of application-level transactions provides the broadest flexibility for the DTC architecture to be tailored for specific use cases, and for different implementations of the three ledgers to be chosen according to the requirements of the use case.

Creation and Annihilation of DTC

For now, we shall consider this pool and its associated narrow bank as given, and describe the creation and annihilation mechanisms for the DTC. New coins are injected in the distributed ledger by virtue of the following mechanism. During the initial stage, participants who wish to acquire a freshly minted DTC have to proceed as follows. First, they have to have a conventional fiat account, which can be held either directly with the narrow bank or with their commercial bank. Second, they have to open an initially empty wallet ready to accept DTCs. Third, participants transfer the desired amount of fiat currency to the narrow bank. Fourth, the narrow bank transfers these funds to sponsors, who, in turn, release some of the DTCs created when the asset pool is built to the pool administrator. Fifth, the administrator transfers the corresponding DTCs from its public key address to the public key address provided by the participant. Thus, in effect, the participant becomes a shareholder in the pool administrator. Subsequently, participants can acquire DTCs from other participants in exchange for goods and services, so that a newly born DTC starts its journey from one address represented by a public key to the next, until it is annihilated by a participant sending it to the administrator in exchange for cash. When a participant in the ledger wishes to receive fiat currency for their DTC, they transfer DTCs from their public key to the public key of the administrator, who, in turn, sells an appropriate proportion of the assets, deposits proceeds with the associated narrow bank, which, in turn, credits fiat currency either to the account on its own ledger or to a designated account in a different bank. The corresponding DTCs are destroyed by sending them to the "terminal" public key without a private key.

As a result, the administrator is in possession of real assets, sponsors with fiat currency, and the general public with DTCs, which can always be converted into fiat at the current market price.

Mechanisms of Stabilization of DTC

Finally, the value of the DTC is kept relatively stable by virtue of the independent actions of participants and the administrator. If the value of a DTC goes below the value of the fraction of the asset pool it represents, which we call its intrinsic value, then rational economic agents will turn it back to the administrator in exchange for cash. If, on the other hand, the market value starts to deviate upward compared to the intrinsic, then, after a certain threshold is breached, the sponsors will contribute more assets to the pool, which can come from their own sources or be purchased on the open market, in exchange for DTCs, which they will sell on the open market, thus pushing the market price of DTCs down. These two complementary mechanisms can keep the market price of the DTC in a bank around the market price of the underlying basket.

More precisely, the price P_{DTC} of DTC will be close to (but not exactly at) the market price of the corresponding asset pool, P_M. Indeed, if P_{DT} falls significantly below P_M economic agents will put DTC back to the administrator, who will have to sell a fraction of the pool's assets for cash and pass the proceeds to these agents. If P_{DT} increases significantly above P_M, sponsors will supply more assets to the administrator, who will issue additional DTCs and pass them to sponsors, who will sell them for cash, just pushing the price down. This mechanism ensures that $|P_{DTC} - P_M|/P_M \ll 1$, a very desirable feature, especially compared for conventional cryptocurrencies, habitually exhibiting extreme volatility. At the same time, outright manipulation by central banks is not possible either.

Note that the notion of economic agents (e.g., sponsors with assets) is distinct from system entities (e.g., notaries) in the DTC architecture (see below).

System Design Principles

In order for DTC to be a stable and durable digital currency that can store value as well as provide utility, there are a number of principles driving its architecture. The DTC architecture seeks to be a "blueprint" that allows the DTC to be implementable for various use cases. Some uses cases that have been identified are: (1) a reserve digital currency shared by a number of geopolitically diverse small countries, as a means to provide local financial stability; and (2) a digital currency operating for a narrow-bank that can provide relative stability during financially volatile periods. A number of system design principles are as follows:

- *Unambiguous identifiability and ownership.* Assets (represented digitally), coins, and eCash must be uniquely identifiable, and have unambiguous ownership at any given time. A corollary of true ownership is that each of these must be transferrable (portable) by its owner.

- *Visibility into shared state.* Entities in the ecosystem should have visibility into the state of the DTC system and network, and have equal access to such information. More specifically, this means visibility into the assets that back the issuance of coins, and visibility into the circulation of coins and eCash.

- *Mechanisms implementing monetary policies and governance.* In order for the DTC ecosystem to operate according to the desired community behavior, there must be technical mechanisms that allow agreed governance policies to be carried out in the system as a whole. Such mechanisms can be controlled centrally (e.g.. by a single entity), in a group-oriented manner (e.g., by a consensus of entities), or a combination of both (e.g., using leader election protocols).

- *Unambiguous authenticable identification of entities.* Entities and system components must be unambiguously identifiable and authenticable. This means that human participants, user-driven devices, and network machines/nodes must each be authentically identifiable.

- *Correct, accurate and unhindered system-wide reporting.* System components that implement DTC must each be unhindered in the reporting of its internal state. Furthermore, there must be ways to validate reported state, so that misbehavior can be detected and acted upon. Such misbehaviors can be the result of human or system error, degradation in system components over time (hardware and software), or the result of active or passive compromises (i.e., attacks).

The above system design principles borrow from a number of key design principles underlying the Internet.[42] The need for unambiguous ownership of an asset is an obvious one. The DTC seeks to use standard object identification solutions (e.g., GUID standard) for digital assets. The legal ownership of assets is a construct that is external to the DTC system, and as such must be established prior to assets being introduced by its legal owner (e.g., sponsor) into a given DTC deployment.

The principle of visibility is driven by the need for entities in a DTC implementation to have equal access to data, and is implemented through the *assets-ledger* and *coins-ledger*. The Consortium Administration (see below) must have full visibility into all operational aspects of a given DTC implementation. Certain DTC implementations may restrict visibility of parts of the systems (e.g., assets-ledger) to entities that have "skin in the game" (e.g., sponsors who have actual assets on the DTC assets-ledger).

A key aspect of the success of a DTC implementation is the ability of the Consortium to carry out monetary policies and other governance rules in the system as a whole. Technical mechanism can be implemented as "hooks" or control-points through which policy decisions are executed. For example, a DTC implementation may require that each sponsor have assets (in the assets-ledger) above a given threshold (i.e., reserve ratio) at all times. The actual value of the threshold should be dynamically adjustable according to the Consortium-agreed policies and be carried out by the Consortium Administration as the appointed authority. In this case, the Consortium Administration can transmit a special "policy implementation" transaction (to the assets-ledger and coins-ledger) setting the new threshold value. Notaries observe such policy decisions by declining an asset-to-coin conversion transaction from a sponsor if it causes the sponsor's asset reserves to dip below the new threshold value.

Key to the operation of a DTC implementation is the ability of entities to identify and authenticate each other. We believe this is closely related to the principle of system-wide reporting. Some DTC implementations may choose to deploy advanced cryptographic techniques that provide anonymity and untraceability of entities. However, such features must still satisfy the principle of unambiguous identifiably and mutual authentication.

Sponsors, Consortium, and Users

There are a number of active (human-driven) entities in the DTC ecosystem (figure 13.2):

- *Sponsor.* A sponsor is an entity who supplies assets to the DTC ecosystem in return for coins. The community of sponsors forms a consortium (see below) tasked with the various management aspects of coins and eCash in the ecosystem.

- *Consortium.* A community of sponsors forms a consortium, operating under an agreed governance model that specifies the legal, business, and technical operational rules of members of the consortium. In essence, the consortium is a network of sponsors who are participating in the DTC ecosystem. Additionally, a *Consortium Administration* carries out the monetary policies of the membership of the consortium. The consortium administration is legally empowered by the consortium membership to implement (centralized) control over certain system functions.

- *Users.* A user is an entity that obtains eCash from the consortium for the purpose of payments for goods and services from other users.

The DTC architecture is shown in figure 13.1 (c).

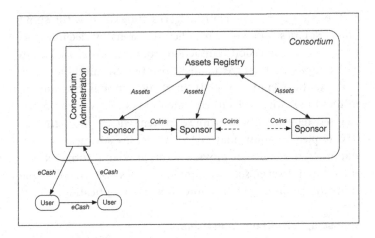

FIGURE 13.2
The Tradecoin entities.

Logical Functions

The DTC architecture logically separates functions into those pertaining to assets, coins, and eCash. Here we use the term ledger generically without calling out specific realizations, to allow focus on logical functions that meet the system design principles stated above.

Specific technical implementations of the ledger may include a distributed database system, a peer-to-peer network of nodes, a fully distributed blockchain system, or even an append-only single database system.

- *Assets management.* Visibility into the assets that sponsors contribute in exchange for coins represents a foundational requirement in DTC. DTC employs an *assets registry* and an *assets-ledger* (figure 13.3). The registry records verified real-world assets that are associated with a sponsor who forwards those assets to the consortium. The assets-ledger captures the binding between real-world assets (put forward by a sponsor) and the amount of coins equivalent to (proportional to) those assets. The assets-ledger also records the proportion of coins that are in the consortium's reserves and those that are in a sponsor's reserve. These coin-equivalents are considered to be non-circulation.

- *Coin circulation.* Allowing sponsors to exchange (i.e., sell or lend) with each other their asset-backed coins represents a cornerstone of DTC. The *coins-ledger* records the coin movements and transactions in the DTC ecosystem (figure 13.4). The coins-ledger is used by sponsors and the consortium administration. Sponsors exchange or "trade" coins with each other on this ledger.

- *eCash circulation.* Providing stable digital currency to users also represents a cornerstone of DTC. The eCash *tracking-ledger* (figure 13.5) records the movement of eCash (i.e., cryptographic keys and parameters) between users.

Each of the three ledgers in DTC are independent, but are connected in the sense that transaction in one ledger may refer to (point to) recorded transactions in other ledgers. This independence of ledgers is important not only from the perspective of technological choice (i.e., adoption of new ledger technologies), but also crucial to the operational resilience of the system as a whole.

An example of the connection of the ledgers is the "pushing" (or pulling) of coins into (out of) circulation by a sponsor following the policies of a given DTC implementation. When a sponsor seeks to have its assets (on the assets-ledger) be converted to coins and for the resulting coins to be accessible by the sponsor on the coins-ledger, the sponsor must transmit a push-transaction. This results in a transaction occurring on the assets-ledger and a corresponding transaction occurring on the coins-ledger. These two transactions—albeit on different ledgers—are related in that one refers to (i.e., carries a hash of)

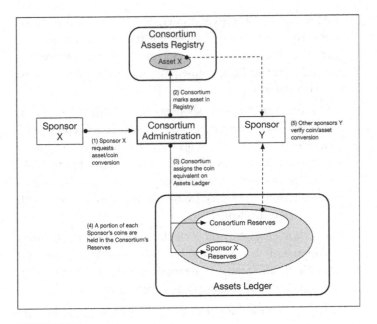

FIGURE 13.3
Converting assets to coins

another. In the push case, the transaction on the coins-ledger
points to a completed transaction on the assets-ledger.

Converting Assets to Coins

The purpose of the assets-ledger, together with the assets registry,
is to satisfy the design principles with regards to the conversion
of real-world assets into its coin equivalent. A key requirement
here is the validation of the legal ownership of assets as claimed
by a given sponsor. The sponsor must provide legal evidence in
such a way that a digital representation of the evidence can be
captured and presented within the assets-ledger.

Examples of such evidence include a paper certificate and its
digital representation that has been digitally signed by the issuer

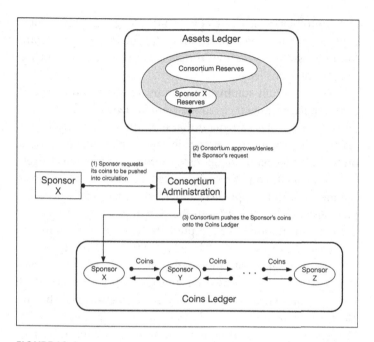

FIGURE 13.4
The coins-ledger.

using legally acceptable digital signature technology (e.g., Digital Signature Act of 2000); for example, a digital version of a gold certificate (e.g., unallocated gold) could be signed by an authority and presented by a sponsor as evidence. It is the responsibility of the consortium administration to validate the evidence.

Coins for Sponsors

The medium for sponsors to exchange coins with each other is the coins-ledger. The notion here is that coins are to be bought, lent, and returned among sponsors on the ledger, providing transparency and visibility into the trading behavior of all sponsors in the DTC network.

Prior to having access to coins on this ledger, a sponsor must explicitly request the consortium to "push" the sponsor's coins from the assets-ledger (from the sponsor's reserves) into circulation on the coins-ledger.

The consortium administration must respond to this request in an explicit manner (i.e., request granted, denied, or postponed) on the assets-ledger. A request that is granted is followed by the consortium administration transferring coins from its account on the coins-ledger to the sponsor's account on the same ledger.

This explicit request-response paradigm is a manifestation of the mechanism to implement monetary policies (as mentioned previously). It is a "hook" into the system in which the consortium administration—as the representative of the community of sponsors—enforces policies agreed to by the community.

A simple example of a monetary policy decision is the reserve ratio that must be met by each sponsor on the assets-ledger. A sponsor that exhausts its reserves on the assets-ledger, thereby violating the policy of sponsors maintaining a minimum reserve, should not be granted a request to push further coins into circulation onto the coins-ledger.

A symmetric operation to pushing coins to the coins-ledger is that of "pulling" coins from circulation. This may occur when a sponsor wishes to enlarge its reserves on the assets-ledger by moving coins from the coins-ledger to the assets-ledger.

eCash for Users

A third important aspect of DTC is its use of eCash for users in the ecosystem. In general, a user is distinguished from a sponsor in that a user does not possess assets in the consortium. The user obtains eCash in exchange for fiat currencies that are acceptable by the consortium. The goal of the user is to utilize a convenient and low-cost (zero-cost) eCash payment method, one that is stable on a day-to-day basis and that can store value over a reasonably long period of time.

In DTC the entity that issues and redeems is the consortium itself. This ensures that the stability of eCash is directly related to the stability of coins and assets in the consortium, all three of which are under the monetary control of the consortium as a community.

The consortium as the issuer of eCash to a user enacts monetary policies that govern how much eCash a user can request specifically at any one time. More generally, the consortium can govern how much eCash is permitted to be in circulation at any given moment in time, as a function of the total assets at the consortium.

The eCash tracking-ledger (figure 13.5) is used for the purposes of fraud-prevention, and does not hinder the flow of eCash as understood in the classical Chaum sense. Electronic cash—first defined in 1981 by David Chaum[7]—employs a direct transfer paradigm between users, involving the delivery of a number of cryptographic parameters. Different variants or schemes of eCash[7,8,40] deploy differing cryptographic parameters. As such, the purpose of the tracking-ledger is to record the cryptographic

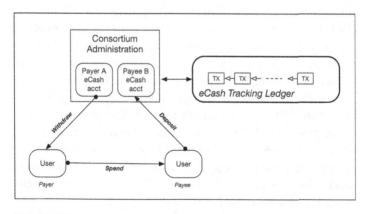

FIGURE 13.5
The Tradecoin eCash tracking-ledger.

hash of these parameters with the goal of reducing fraud and error, and providing postevent audit and accountability.

CONCLUSIONS

In this chapter, we have discussed conceptual underpinnings and technical approaches to building DTCs. We have shown that DTCs have several decisive advantages as compared to more established cryptocurrencies, such as Bitcoin and Ripple. In addition to being a convenient transactional cryptocurrency for the Internet era, DTCs can serve as important counterbalance to fiat currencies, and, when fully developed, can play the role of a supranational currency facilitating international commerce and allowing groups of small countries to create their own viable currencies.

As Dr. Zhou Xiaochan, Governor of the Peoples Bank of China stated,[39] "The desirable goal of reforming the international monetary system, therefore, is to create an international reserve currency that is independent from individual nations and is able to remain stable in the long run, thus removing the inherent deficiencies caused by using credit-based national currencies." We believe that DTC has the potential to provide such an international reserve currency for the following reasons: (1) DTC has real value, because its price is pinned to a representative basket of commodities; (2) the price of the DTC versus a fiat currency has very low volatility compared to other cryptocurrencies; (3) as a result, DTC can be used as a transaction currency (think of a mortgage taken in DTC in a country that is naturally aligned with some of the major constituent commodities); and (4) DTC can also be used as a unit of account and a store of value (as much as gold or oil can). To conclude, DTC can serve as a much-needed counterpoint for fiat currencies.

REFERENCES

1. Lipton, A., and A. Pentland. 2018. "Breaking the Bank." *Scientific American* 318 (1): 26–31.

2. Lipton, A. 2018. "Blockchains and Distributed Ledgers in Retrospective and Perspective." *Journal of Risk Finance* 19 (1): 4–25. https://doi.org /10.1108/JRF-02-2017-0035.

3. Nakamoto, S. 2008. "Bitcoin: A Peer-to-Peer Electronic Cash System." www.bitcoin.org.

4. Buterin, V. 2014. "Ethereum: A Next-Generation Smart Contract and Decentralized Application Platform." http://blockchainlab.com/pdf /Ethereum_white_paper-a_next_generation_smart_contract_and_decen tralized_application_platform-vitalik-buterin.pdf.

5. Schwartz, D., N. Youngs, and A. Britto, 2014. "The Ripple Protocol Consensus Algorithm." Ripple Labs Inc. White Paper 5.

6. Lipton, A., T. Hardjono, and A. Pentland. 2018. "Digital Trade Coin: Towards a More Stable Digital Currency." *Royal Society Open Science* 5: 180155. http://dx.doi.org/10.1098/rsos.180155.

7. Chaum, D. L. 1981. "Untraceable Electronic Mail, Return Addresses, and Digital Pseudonyms." *Communications of the ACM* 24 (2): 84–88.

8. Chaum, D., A. Fiat, and M. Naor. 1990 [1988]. "Untraceable Electronic Cash." In *Proceedings on Advances in Cryptology*, ser. CRYPTO '88, 319–327. New York: Springer-Verlag.

9. Ali, R., J. Barrdear, R. Clews, and J. Southgate. 2014. "The Economics of Digital Currencies." https://papers.ssrn.com/sol3/papers.cfm?abstract _id=2499418.

10. Andolfatto, D. 2015. "Fedcoin: On the Desirability of a Government Cryptocurrency." http://andolfatto.blogspot.com/2015/02/fedcoin-on -desirability-of-government.html.

11. Barrdear, J., and M. Kumhof. 2016. "The Macroeconomics of Central Bank Issued Digital Currencies." https://papers.ssrn.com/sol3/papers .cfm?abstract_id=2811208.

12. Broadbent, B. 2016. "Central Banks and Digital Currencies." Speech at London School of Economics.

13. Dyson, B., and G. Hodgson. 2016. "Digital Cash. Why Central Banks Should Start Issuing Electronic Money." London: Positive Money. http:// positivemoney.org/publications-old/digital-cash-why-central-banks -should-startissuing-electronic-money-new-report.

14. Fung, B. S., and H. Halaburda. 2016. "Central Bank Digital Currencies: A Framework for Assessing Why and How." Bank of Canada Staff Discussion Paper 22.

15. Lipton, A. 2016. "The Decline of the Cash Empire." *Risk Magazine* 29 (11): 53.

16. Bordo, M. D., and A. T. Levin. 2017. "Central Bank Digital Currency and the Future of Monetary Policy." Working paper number 23711. National Bureau of Economic Research. https://www.nber.org/papers /w23711.

17. He, M.D., M. R. B. Leckow, M. V. Haksar, M. T. M. Griffoli, N. Jenkinson, M. M. Kashima, T. Khiaonarong, M. C. Rochon, and H. Tourpe. 2017. "Fintech and Financial Services: Initial Considerations." International Monetary Fund.

18. Mersch, Y. 2017. "Digital Base Money: An Assessment from the ECB's Perspective." Speech at the Farewell ceremony for Pentti Hakkarainen, Deputy Governor of Suomen Pankki–Finlands Bank, Helsinki.

19. Powell, J. 2017. "Innovation, Technology, and the Payments System." Speech. Blockchain: The Future of Finance and Capital Markets.

20. Scorer, S. 2017. "Central Bank Digital Currency: DLT or Not DLT? That Is the Question." https://bankunderground.co.uk/2017/06/05/central -bank-digital-currency-dlt-or-not-dlt-that-is-the-question/.

21. Rogoff, K. 2016. *The Curse of Cash*. Princeton, NJ: Princeton University Press.

22. Ilgmann, C. 2015. "Silvio Gesell: 'A Strange, Unduly Neglected' Monetary Theorist." *Journal of Post Keynesian Economics* 38 (4): 532–564.

23. Fisher, I. 1933. *Stamp Scrip*. New York: Adelphi Company.

24. Danezis, G., and S. Meiklejohn. 2015. "Centrally Banked Cryptocurrencies." arXiv:1505.06895.

25. Reid, F., and M. Harrigan. 2013. "An Analysis of Anonymity in the Bitcoin System." In *Security and Privacy in Social Networks*, edited by Y. Altshuler et al., 197–223. New York: Springer.

26. Pennacchi, G. 2012. "Narrow Banking." *Annual Review of Financial Economics* 4 (1): 141–159.

27. Lamport, L., R. Shostak, and M. Pease. 1982. "The Byzantine Generals Problem." *ACM Transactions on Programming Languages and Systems (TOPLAS)* 4 (3): 382–401.

28. Castro, M., and B. Liskov. 1999. "Practical Byzantine Fault Tolerance." *OSDI* 99: 173–186.

29. Haas, A., L. J. Ussher, K. T¨opfer, and C. C. Jaeger. 2014. "Currencies, Commodities, and Keynes." Unpublished manuscript. http://www.sandelman.ca/tmp/earthreserve.pdf.

30. Lowe, J. 1823. *The Present State of England in Regard to Agriculture, Trade and Finance: With a Comparison of the Prospects of England and France*. London: Longman, Hurst, Rees, Orme, and Brown.

31. Scrope, G. P. 1833. *An Examination of the Bank Charter Question: With an Inquiry into the Nature of a Just Standard of Value, and Suggestions for the Improvement of Our Monetary System*. London: J. Murray.

32. Jevons, W. S. 1875. *Money and the Mechanism of Exchange, Vol. 17*. London: Henry S. King.

33. Marshall, A. 1887. *Remedies for Fluctuations of General Prices*. London.

34. Graham, F. D. 1940. "The Primary Functions of Money and Their Consummation in Monetary Policy." *The American Economic Review* 30 (1): 1–16.

35. Graham, B. 1933. "Stabilized Reflation." *The Economic Forum* 1 (2): 186–193.

36. Hayek, F. A. 1943. "A Commodity Reserve Currency." *The Economic Journal*: 53 (210/211): 176–184.

37. Keynes. 1943. "The Objective of International Price Stability." *The Economic Journal*: 185–187.

38. Kaldor, N. 2007. *Causes of Growth and Stagnation in the World Economy*. New York: Cambridge University Press.

39. Zhou, X. 2009. "Reform the International Monetary System." Bank of International Settlements, Basel.

40. Camenisch, J., S. Hohenberger, and A. Lysyanskaya. 2005. "Compact e-Cash." In *Proceedings of the 24th Annual International Conference on Theory and Applications of Cryptographic Techniques*, ser. EUROCRYPT'05, 302–321. Berlin, Heidelberg: Springer-Verlag.

41. Grothoff, C. 2016. "GNU Taler—a Privacy-Preserving Online Payment System for Libre Societies." https://grothoff.org/christian/fsfe2016 .pdf.

42. Hardjono, T., A. Lipton, and A. Pentland. 2018. "Towards a Design Philosophy for Interoperable Blockchain Systems." Presented at the IEEE Global Blockchain Summit @ NIST, September 17–19. Gaithersburg, Maryland. arXiv:1805.05934.

43. Hardjono, T. and N. Smith. Forthcoming. "Decentralized Trusted Computing Base for Blockchain Infrastructure Security."

APPENDIX A PERSONAL DATA: THE EMERGENCE OF A NEW ASSET CLASS

World Economic Forum

ACKNOWLEDGEMENTS

This document was prepared by the World Economic Forum, in partnership with the individuals and organisations listed below.

WORLD ECONOMIC FORUM

Professor Klaus Schwab	Executive Chairman
Alan Marcus	Senior Director, IT & Telecommunications Industries
Justin Rico Oyola	Associate Director and Project Lead, Telecommunications Industry
William Hoffman	Head, Telecommunications Industry

BAIN & COMPANY, INC.

Michele Luzi	Director

The following experts contributed substantial research and interviews throughout the "Rethinking Personal Data" project. We extend our sincere gratitude to all of them.

Julius Akinyemi	MIT
Alberto Calero	France Telecom

Ron Carpinella	Equifax
Douglas Dabérius	Nokia Siemens Networks
Timothy Edgar	Office of the Director of National Intelligence, USA
Jamie Ferguson	Kaiser Permanente
Michael Fertik	ReputationDefender
Tal Givoly	Amdocs
Kaliya Hamlin	Personal Data Ecosystem
William Heath	Mydex
Trevor Hughes	International Association of Privacy Professionals
Betsy Masiello	Google
Mita Mitra	BT Group
Drummond Reed	Information Card Foundation
Nasrin Rezai	Cisco
Natsuhiko Sakimura	OpenID Foundation
Kevin Stanton	MasterCard Advisors
Pamela Warren	McAfee
Von Wright	AT&T

PROJECT STEERING BOARD

This work would also not have been possible without the commitment of:

John Clippinger	Berkman Center for Internet and Society, Harvard University
Scott David	K&L Gates
Marc Davis	Microsoft
Robert Fabricant	frog design
Philip Laidler	STL Partners
Alex Pentland	MIT
Fabio Sergio	frog design
Simon Torrance	STL Partners

INTRODUCTION

We are moving towards a "Web of the world" in which mobile communications, social technologies and sensors are connecting people, the Internet and the physical world into one interconnected network[1]. Data records are collected on who we are, who we know, where we are, where we have been and where we plan to go. Mining and analysing this data give us the ability to understand and even predict where humans focus their attention and activity at the individual, group and global level.

> **"Personal data is the new oil of the Internet and the new currency of the digital world."**
>
> —Meglena Kuneva, European Consumer Commissioner, March 2009

This personal data—digital data created by and about people—is generating a new wave of opportunity for economic and societal value creation. The types, quantity and value of personal data being collected are vast: our profiles and demographic data from bank accounts to medical records to employment data. Our Web searches and sites visited, including our likes and dislikes and purchase histories. Our tweets, texts, emails, phone calls, photos and videos as well as the coordinates of our real-world locations. The list continues to grow. Firms collect and use this data to support individualized service-delivery business models that can be monetised. Governments employ personal data to provide critical public services more efficiently and effectively. Researchers accelerate the development of new drugs and treatment protocols. End users benefit from free, personalised consumer experiences such as Internet search, social networking or buying recommendations.

And that is just the beginning. Increasing the control that individuals have over the manner in which their personal data is collected, managed and shared will spur a host of new services and applications. As some put it, personal data will be the new "oil"—a valuable resource of the 21st century. It will emerge as a new asset class touching all aspects of society.

At its core, personal data represents a post-industrial opportunity. It has unprecedented complexity, velocity and global reach. Utilising a ubiquitous communications infrastructure, the personal data opportunity will emerge in a world where nearly everyone and everything are connected in real time. That will require a highly reliable, secure and available infrastructure at its core and robust innovation at the edge. Stakeholders will need to embrace the uncertainty, ambiguity and risk of an emerging ecosystem. In many ways, this opportunity will resemble a living entity and will require new ways of adapting and responding. Most importantly, it will demand a new way of thinking about individuals.

Indeed, rethinking the central importance of the individual is fundamental to the transformational nature of this opportunity because that will spur solutions and insights.

As personal data increasingly becomes a critical source of innovation and value, business boundaries are being redrawn. Profit pools, too, are shifting towards companies that automate and mine the vast amounts of data we continue to generate.[2] Far from certain, however, is how much value will ultimately be created, and who will gain from it. The underlying regulatory, business and technological issues are highly complex, interdependent and ever changing.

But further advances are at risk. The rapid rate of technological change and commercialisation in using personal data is undermining end user confidence and trust. Tensions are rising. Concerns about the misuse of personal data continue to grow. Also mounting is a general public unease about what "they" know about us.[3] Fundamental questions about privacy, property, global governance, human rights—essentially around who should benefit from the products and services built upon personal data—are major uncertainties shaping the opportunity.

Yet, we can't just hit the "pause button" and let these issues sort themselves out. Building the legal, cultural, technological and economic infrastructure to enable the development of a balanced personal data ecosystem is vitally important to improving the state of the world.

It is in this context that the World Economic Forum launched a project entitled "Rethinking Personal Data" in 2010. The intent of this multiyear project is to bring together a diverse set of stakeholders—private companies, public sector representatives, end user privacy and rights groups, academics and topic experts. The aim is to deepen the collective understanding of how a principled, collaborative and balanced personal data ecosystem can evolve. In particular, this initiative aims to:

- Establish a user-centric framework for identifying the opportunities, risks and collaborative responses in the use of personal data;
- Foster a rich and collaborative exchange of knowledge in the development of cases and pilot studies;
- Develop a guiding set of global principles to help in the evolution of a balanced personal data ecosystem.

EXECUTIVE SUMMARY

**PERSONAL DATA: UNTAPPED OPPORTUNITIES
FOR SOCIOECONOMIC GROWTH**

The rate of increase in the amount of data generated by today's digital society is astounding. According to one estimate, by 2020 the global volume of digital data will increase more than 40-fold.[4] Beyond its sheer volume, data is becoming a new type of raw material that's on par with capital and labour.[5] As this data revolution era begins, the impact on all aspects of society—business, science, government and entertainment—will be profound.

Personal Data—a Definition

For this report personal data is defined as data (and metadata) created by and about people, encompassing:

- **Volunteered data**—created and explicitly shared by individuals, e.g., social network profiles.
- **Observed data**—captured by recording the actions of individuals, e.g., location data when using cell phones.
- **Inferred data**—data about individuals based on analysis of volunteered or observed information, e.g., credit scores.

Source: World Economic Forum, June 2010.

From a private sector perspective, some of the largest Internet companies such as Google, Facebook and Twitter clearly show the importance of collecting, aggregating, analysing and monetising personal data. These rapidly growing enterprises are built on the economics of personal data.

Governments and public sector institutions are also transforming themselves to use data as a public utility. Many governments have successfully launched e-governance initiatives to improve the efficiency and effectiveness of communication among various public organisations—and with citizens.

But some of the most profound insights are coming from understanding how individuals themselves are creating, sharing and using personal data. On an average day, users globally send around 47 billion (non-spam) emails[6] and submit 95 million "tweets" on Twitter. Each month, users share about 30 billion pieces of content on Facebook.[7] The impact of this "empowered individual" is just beginning to be felt.

However, the potential of personal data goes well beyond these promising beginnings to vast untapped wealth creation opportunities. But unlocking this value depends on several contingencies. The underlying regulatory, business and technological issues are highly complex, interdependent and ever changing.

THE PERSONAL DATA ECOSYSTEM—WHERE WE STAND TODAY

The current personal data ecosystem is fragmented and inefficient. For many participants, the risks and liabilities exceed the economic returns. Personal privacy concerns are inadequately addressed. Regulators, advocates and corporations all grapple with complex and outdated regulations.

Current technologies and laws fall short of providing the legal and technical infrastructure needed to support a well-functioning digital economy. Instead, they represent a patchwork of solutions for collecting and using personal data in support of different institutional aims, and subject to different jurisdictional rules and regulatory contexts (e.g., personal data systems related to banking have different purposes and applicable laws than those developed for the telecom and healthcare sectors).

Consider some of the needs and interests of stakeholders:

Private Sector
Private enterprises use personal data to create new efficiencies, stimulate demand, build relationships and generate revenue and profit from their services. But in this drive to develop the "attention economy," enterprises run the risk of violating customer trust. Overstepping the boundary of what users consider fair use can unleash a huge backlash with significant brand implications.

Public Sector
Governments and regulators play a vital role in influencing the size and shape of the personal data ecosystem as well as the value created by it. On the one hand, regulators have the mandate to

protect the data security and privacy rights of citizens. Therefore, they seek to protect consumers from the potential misuse
of their identity. On the other hand, regulators balance this
mandate with the need to foster economic growth and promote
public well-being. Policy makers around the world are engaged
in discussions to enhance legal and regulatory frameworks that
will increase disclosure rules, maximise end user control over
personal data and penalise non-appropriate usage. Finally, government agencies are using personal data to deliver an array of
services for health, education, welfare and law enforcement.
The public sector is therefore not just an active player in the
personal data universe, but also a stimulator and shaper of the
ecosystem—and potentially, the creator of tremendous value for
individuals, businesses and economies.

Individuals

Behaviours and attitudes towards personal data are highly fragmented. Demographically, individuals differ in their need for
transparency, control and the ability to extract value from the
various types of personal data (see Figure A.1). According to the
research firm International Data Corporation (IDC), individuals'
direct or indirect actions generated about 70 per cent of the digital
data created in 2010. Activities such as sending an email, taking
a digital picture, turning on a mobile phone or posting content
online made up this huge volume of data. Younger individuals are
more comfortable sharing their data with third parties and social
networks—though it remains to be seen whether their behaviours will remain the same or become more risk averse as they
age. Older consumers appear to be more sceptical, and demand
demonstrably higher security levels from service providers.[8]

Individuals are also becoming more aware of the consequences of not having control over their digital identity and personal data. In 2010 the number of reported incidents of identity
theft skyrocketed by 12 per cent.[9]

Common Needs for All Users

- Reliability
- Predictability
- Interoperability
- Security
- Ease of use
- Cost-effectiveness
- Risk and liability reduction
- Transparency
- Simplicity

A Way Forward: The Personal Data Ecosystem

One viable response to this fragmentation is to align key stakeholders (people, private firms and the public sector) in support of one another. Indeed, "win-win-win" outcomes will come from creating mutually supportive incentives, reducing collective inefficiencies and innovating in such a way that collective risks are reduced.

This vision includes a future where:

- Individuals can have greater control over their personal data, digital identity and online privacy, and they would be better compensated for providing others with access to their personal data;

- Disparate silos of personal data held in corporations and government agencies will more easily be exchanged to increase utility and trust among people, private firms and the public sector;

- Government's need to maintain stability, security and individual rights will be met in a more flexible, holistic and adaptive manner.

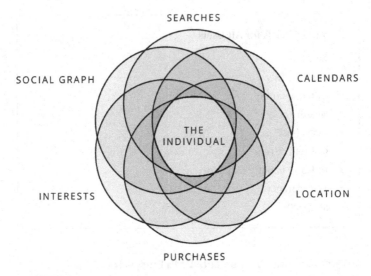

FIGURE A.1
Individual End Users Are At The Center Of Diverse Types Of
Personal Data
Source: Davis, Marc, Ron Martinez and Chris Kalaboukis. "Rethinking
Personal Information—Workshop Preread." Invention Arts and
World Economic Forum, June 2010.

In practical terms, a person's data would be equivalent to
their "money." It would reside in an account where it would
be controlled, managed, exchanged and accounted for just like
personal banking services operate today. These services would
be interoperable so that the data could be exchanged with other
institutions and individuals globally. As an essential requirement, the services would operate over a technical and legal infrastructure that is highly trusted. Maintaining confidence in the
integrity, confidentiality, transparency and security of the entire
system would require high levels of monitoring.

END USER–CENTRICITY: A CRITICAL DETERMINANT
IN BUILDING THE PERSONAL DATA ECOSYSTEM

A key element for aligning stakeholder interests and realising the vision of the personal data ecosystem is the concept of end user–centricity. This is a holistic approach that recognises that end users are vital and independent stakeholders in the co-creation and value exchange of services and experiences. A construct designed for the information economy, it breaks from the industrial-age model of the "consumer"—where relationships are captured, developed and owned.

Instead, end user-centricity represents a transformational opportunity. It seeks to integrate diverse types of personal data in a way that was never possible before. This can only be done by putting the end user at the centre of four key principles:

- *Transparency:* Individuals expect to know what data is being captured about them, the manner in which such data is captured or inferred, the uses it will be put to and the parties that have access to it;

- *Trust:* Individuals' confidence that the attributes of availability, reliability, integrity and security are embraced in the applications, systems and providers that have access to their personal data;

- *Control:* The ability of individuals to effectively manage the extent to which their personal data is shared;

- *Value:* Individuals' understanding of the value created by the use of their data and the way in which they are compensated for it.

**COMPLEX BUSINESS, POLICY AND TECHNOLOGICAL ISSUES
PERSIST AND REQUIRE COORDINATED LEADERSHIP FROM
FIRMS AND THE PUBLIC SECTOR**

A user-centric ecosystem faces challenges almost as big as its
promise, however. Firms, policy makers and governments must
resolve a series of critical questions.

For private firms, what are the concrete economic incentives
to "empower" individuals with greater choice and control over
how their data are used? What are the incentives for greater
collaboration within and across industry sectors? How can the
returns from using personal data begin to outweigh the risks
from a technical, legal and brand-trust perspective?

Policy makers are unique in their mandate to collect, manage
and store personal data for purposes such as national defence,
security and public safety. They face the issue of finding the right
balance between competing priorities: How can they ensure the
stability and security of government even as they create incentives for economic investment and innovation? How should
they define end users' rights and permissions concerning personal data? How can they more effectively clarify the liabilities?
How can they scale globally the concepts of accountability and
due process?

FIVE AREAS OF COLLECTIVE ACTION

The issues surrounding personal data—political, technological
and commercial alike—are numerous and complex. The choices
stakeholders make today will influence the personal data ecosystem for years to come. Five key imperatives require action:

1. **Innovate around user-centricity and trust.** The personal data
   ecosystem will be built on the trust and control individuals
   have in sharing their data. From a technological, policy and

sociological sense all stakeholders need to embrace this construct. One particular area of focus is the continued testing and promoting of "trust frameworks" that explore innovative approaches for identity assurance at Internet scale.

2. **Define global principles for using and sharing personal data.** Given the lack of globally accepted policies governing the use and exchange of personal data, an international community of stakeholders should articulate and advance core principles of a user-centric personal data ecosystem. These pilots should invite real-world input from a diverse group of individuals who can not only articulate the values, needs and desires of end users, but also the complex and contextual nuances involved in revealing one's digital identity.

3. **Strengthen the dialog between regulators and the private sector.** Building on a collective sense of fundamental principles for creating a balanced ecosystem, public and private stakeholders should actively collaborate as the ecosystem begins to take shape. Those responsible for building and deploying the tools (the technologists) should more closely align with those making the rules (regulators).[10] Establishing the processes to enable stakeholders to formulate, adopt and update a standardised set of rules will serve to create a basic legal infrastructure. Additionally, collaborating with policy makers as they update legislation to address key questions related to identity and personal data will be essential.[11]

4. **Focus on interoperability and open standards.** With the appropriate user controls and legal infrastructure in place, innovations in how personal data moves throughout the value chain will be a key driver for societal and economic value creation. Enabling a secure, trusted, reliable and open infrastructure (both legal and technical) will be vital. Participants should identify best practises and engage with standards bodies, advocacy groups, think tanks and various consortia

on the user-centric approaches required to scale the value of personal data.

5. **Continually share knowledge.** It's a huge challenge for entities to keep up with new research, policies and commercial developments. To stay current, stakeholders should share insights and learnings on their relevant activities, from both successes as well as failures. After all, the ecosystem's promise is about the tremendous value created when individuals share information about who they are and what they know. Clearly, this principle should also apply to practitioners within the development community.

SECTION 1: PERSONAL DATA ECOSYSTEM: OVERVIEW

PERSONAL DATA IS AN EVOLVING AND MULTIFACETED OPPORTUNITY

In the era of "anywhere, anytime" connectivity, more people connect to the Internet now in more ways than ever before. One recent estimate projects that in the next 10 years, more than 50 billion devices may connect to the Internet, global devices connected to the Internet many wirelessly (see Figure A.2).[12] Global traffic on mobile networks is expected to double each year through 2014.[13]

The variety and volume of digital records that can be created, processed and analysed will continue to increase dramatically. By 2020, IDC estimates that the global amount of digital records will increase more than 40-fold (see Figure A.3).[14]

As these devices and software continue to come online, they will generate an increasing amount of personal data. The term personal data has several meanings, but we broadly define it as data relating to an identified or identifiable person or persons.[15]

Think of personal data as the digital record of "everything a person makes and does online and in the world."[16] The wide

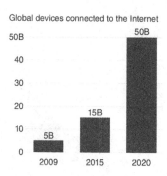

FIGURE A.2

By 2020, more than 50 billion devices will be connected to the internet

Source: Ericsson, Intel

variety of forms that such data assumes for storage and communication evolves constantly, but an initial list of categories includes:

- Digital identity (for example, names, email addresses, phone numbers, physical addresses, demographic information, social network profile information and the like);
- Relationships to other people and organisations (online profiles and contact lists);
- Real-world and online context, activity, interests and behaviour (records of location, time, clicks, searches, browser histories and calendar data);
- Communications data and logs (emails, SMS, phone calls, IM and social network posts);
- Media produced, consumed and shared (in-text, audio, photo, video and other forms of media);
- Financial data (transactions, accounts, credit scores, physical assets and virtual goods);

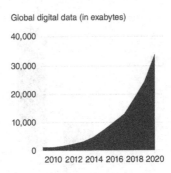

FIGURE A.3
By 2020, digital records will be 44 times larger than in 2009
Source: IDC

- Health data (medical history, medical device logs, prescriptions and health insurance coverage);
- Institutional data (governmental, academic and employer data).

Further, organisations can capture these different personal data in a variety of ways:[17]

- Data can be "volunteered" by individuals when they explicitly share information about themselves through electronic media, for example, when someone creates a social network profile or enters credit card information for online purchases;
- "Observed" data is captured by recording activities of users (in contrast to data they volunteer). Examples include Internet browsing preferences, location data when using cell phones or telephone usage behaviour;
- Organisations can also discern "inferred" data from individuals, based on the analysis of personal data. For instance, credit scores can be calculated based on a number of factors relevant to an individual's financial history.

Each type of personal data (see Figure A.4), volunteered, observed or inferred, can be created by multiple sources (devices,

Regulatory environment				
Communication standards				
Personal data	**Personal data creation**		**Storage, aggregation**	**Analysis, productisation**	**Consumption**
	Devices	**Software**			
Volunteered	Mobile phones/ smart phones	Apps, OS for PCs	Web retailers	Market research data exchanges	End users
Declared interests	Desktop PCs, laptops		Internet tracking companies	Ad exchanges	
Preferences		Apps, OS for mobile phones	Internet search engines		Government agencies and public organisations
...	Communication networks		Electronic medical records providers	Medical records exchanges	
Observed	Electronic notepads, readers	Apps for medical devices	Identity providers	Business intelligence systems	Small enterprises
Browser history	Smart appliances	Apps for consumer devices/ appliances	Mobile operators, Internet service providers		
Location				Credit bureaus	Medium enterprises
...	Sensors	Network management software	Financial institutions		
Inferred	Smart grids		Utility companies	Public administration	
Credit score					Large enterprises
Future consumption					
...	...	...	...	...	

FIGURE A.4

The personal data ecosystem: a complex web from data creation to data consumption.

Source: Bain & Company

software applications), stored and aggregated by various providers (Web retailers, Internet search engines or utility companies) and analysed for a variety of purposes for many different users (end users, businesses, public organisations).

These stakeholders range from the individual end users, who are the sources and subjects of personal data, to the various entities with which they interact. The latter encompass businesses and corporations in different industries to public sector entities like government bodies, NGOs and academia. Personal data flows through this ecosystem, within the boundaries of regulation, to result ultimately in exchanges of monetary and other value.

POINTS OF TENSION AND UNCERTAINTY

While tremendous value resides in the data generated by different sources, it often remains untapped. Unlocking the full potential of data will require addressing current uncertainties and points of tension:

- Privacy: Individual needs for privacy vary. Policy makers face a complex challenge while developing legislation and regulations;

- Global governance: There is a lack of global legal interoperability, with each country evolving its own legal and regulatory frameworks;

- Personal data ownership: The concept of property rights is not easily extended to data, creating challenges in establishing usage rights;

- Transparency: Too much transparency too soon presents as much a risk to destabilising the personal data ecosystem as too little transparency;

- Value distribution: Even before value can be shared more equitably, much more clarity will be required on what truly constitutes value for each stakeholder.

Privacy

Privacy continues to be a highly publicised, complex and sensitive issue with multiple perspectives. The complexity surrounding how privacy is conceived and defined creates challenges for policy makers as they seek to address a myriad of issues related to context, culture and personal preference.[18] Adding to the complexity is the pace of technological change and a general lack of guidance on how to accommodate and support various perspectives on "privacy" robustly, flexibly and at global scale (for multiple jurisdictions, cultures and commercial and social settings).[19] Given that many governments are drafting laws and regulations to address privacy concerns, the ambiguity and uncertainty on multiple dimensions heighten the risks that could stall investment and innovation.

> "We need to arrive at an acceptable reasonable expectation of privacy … a procedural due process that has the flexibility to address any question of privacy and institutionalise learnings into the ecosystem to prevent that grievance from happening again."
> —Interviewee, "Rethinking Personal Data" project

Global Governance

Not only are policies and legislation in flux within national borders, there is wide variation across different countries and regions. Indeed, there is no global consensus on two major questions: Which issues related to personal data should be covered by legal and regulatory frameworks? And how should those issues be addressed? While some cross-national agreements exist, for example, the Safe Harbor agreement between the US and the EU,[20] the development of a globally acceptable view of the personal data ecosystem may be years away. This fragmentation stands in the way of fully realising the global impact of the personal data opportunity.

Personal Data Ownership

"Who owns the data" and "What rights does ownership imply" are two of the most complex issues related to personal data. At first blush, these questions seem simple. Most people would intuitively assert that they own data about themselves and that therefore, they should control who can access, use, aggregate, edit and share it. However, even a cursory look at the issue quickly reveals that the answers are much less clear. Individuals do not "own" their criminal records or credit history. Medical providers are required to keep certain records about patients, even as those patients are allowed to access and share that information with others. Do companies such as Google and Amazon, which aggregate search and purchase histories across millions of users, own the proprietary algorithms they've built upon those click streams?

Given the fluid nature of data and the early stages of the personal data ecosystem, many assert that focusing on the issues of rights management, accountability, due process and the formation of "interoperable" legal frameworks is more productive. It is unlikely that there is a one-size-fits-all approach. A more likely scenario is that different classes of information (financial, health, government records, social, etc.) will get varying degrees of protection—as already is the case in the "pre-digital" world. All such solutions will need to balance individuals' rights to privacy with practical concerns about legitimate needs for critical participants (for example, law enforcement and medical personnel) to access key information when necessary. In addition, practical solutions for issues related to data portability, interoperability and easy-to-implement dashboards for consumers to set and monitor access rights will also need to be developed to overcome the growing friction in the current environment.

Transparency

Most end users still remain unaware of just how much they are tagged, tracked and followed on the Internet. Few individuals realise how much data they implicitly give away, how that data might be used or even what is known about them. Some businesses believe the solution lies in "fessing up": simply increasing the transparency on how personal data is used. But that approach not only fails to address the privacy and trust concerns end users have; for many organisations, it often poses a risk to their business model. When customers suddenly find out how their trusted brand of product or service was gathering and using their personal data, they tend to react with outrage, rather than reward the business for its transparency. Similarly, citizens fear Big Brother control and manipulation in the way government uses their personal information. As long as the risk of transparency outweighs the rewards, the personal data ecosystem will remain vulnerable to periodic seismic shocks.

Value Distribution

The notion that individuals are producers, creators and owners of their digital activities raises the question: How can value be equitably exchanged? The answer depends on variables like the structure of personal data markets; the amount of public education required; globally governed regulations needed to ensure fair compensation; and the legal frameworks that would ensure accountability and due process.

Uncertainty and tension also exist around the evolution of personal data exchanges and the degree of political empowerment they could create. Some governments can perceive empowered citizens as a disruptive threat to their agenda. Understanding the concept of user-centricity in the context of differing social, cultural and political norms is clearly needed.

Incumbents and Disrupters

During the last few decades, a regulatory patchwork has arisen that does not adequately reflect the needs of a competitive global market or the pace of technology. The personal data ecosystem

---

Personal Data and Developing Economies

As with many innovations related to mobile applications, the development of personal data exchanges could achieve scale in developing economies. The data and analytics from the increasing use of mobile devices—in particular, location data, images from cell phone cameras and mobile finance—can help countries address significant economic and health challenges with greater precision and adaptability. As the mobile platform brings the unbanked into the formal economy, real-time insights into local economies could be gained. Utilising the analytics of m-Health applications could also help improve public health.

consists of established and new participants; often the regulatory framework covers established business models, but regulation takes time to catch up with emerging, disruptive models. From a regulatory perspective, this can create a fundamentally uneven competitive playing field for creating new personal data services. Companies with established business models—those with large customer bases, legacy investments and trusted brands—typically possess vast amounts of customer data but are legally constrained on its use for commercial purposes. Given those legal constraints, established players are generally conservative in their approach to the market and deeply concerned about unclear liabilities and legal inconsistencies.

On the other hand, many new services and applications are more innovative in their approach and typically use personal data as a central component in their business models. By definition, they tend to fall outside the purview of legacy legal restrictions and typically innovate at the edges of what can be legally done with personal data. A growing concern is the widening chasm between the regulatory oversight on established business models versus new business ideas. Additionally, there are concerns on how current legal and regulatory stakeholders can systemically adapt to the velocity of innovation, the complexity of the ecosystem and the scale of personal impact. Given that a single operational or technical change to a networked communications service can immediately impact hundreds of millions of individuals (if not billions), the capability of policy makers and regulators to understand a given risk and adapt in real time is uncertain. Over time, perceptions of over-regulation and inequity on who can use certain forms of personal data for commercial purposes may create an imbalance among private sector actors.

THE RISKS OF AN IMBALANCED ECOSYSTEM

The key to unlocking the full potential of data lies in creating equilibrium among the various stakeholders influencing the personal data ecosystem. A lack of balance between stakeholder interests—business, government and individuals—can destabilise the personal data ecosystem in a way that erodes rather than creates value. What follows are just a few possible outcomes that could emerge if any one set of stakeholders gained too strong a role in the ecosystem.

The Risk of Private Sector Imbalance

As personal data becomes a primary currency of the digital economy, its use as a means to create competitive advantage will increase. If little regard is paid to the needs of other stakeholders, businesses searching for innovative ways to collect, aggregate and use data could end up engaging in a "race to the bottom," building out ever more sophisticated "tricks and traps" to capture personal data.[21] This unfettered mining of personal data would alienate end users and possibly create a backlash.[22]

The Risk of Public Sector Imbalance

As countries revise their legal frameworks, policies and regulations to catch up with the unprecedented surge in data, they could inadvertently stifle value creation by over-regulating. Additionally, individual countries may seek to act unilaterally to protect their own citizens from potential harm. The resulting lack of clarity and consistency in policy across countries could slow down innovation and investment.

The Risk of End User Imbalance

In the absence of engagement with both governments and business, end users could self-organise and create non-commercial alternatives for how their personal data is used. While small groups of dedicated individuals could collaborate on non-commercial products that have the same impact as Wikipedia and Linux, the issues of limited funding, security and lack of governance would remain. Over time, the challenges of managing personal data at a global scale could become overwhelming.

Aligning the different interests to create a true "win-win-win" state for all stakeholders represents a challenge—but it can be done. The solution lies in developing policies, incentives and rewards that motivate all stakeholders—private firms, policy makers, end users—to participate in the creation, protection, sharing and value generation from personal data. The private and public sectors can bring their interests closer by creating an infrastructure that enables the secure and efficient sharing of data across organisations and technologies. End users can be gathered into the fold of the private-public partnership by developing mechanisms that safeguard personal data, validate their content and integrity, and protect ownership. When end users begin to get a share of the value created from their personal data, they will gain more confidence in sharing it.

For such a virtuous cycle to evolve, stakeholders in the personal data ecosystem will need to define new roles and opportunities for the private and public sectors. Greater mutual trust can lead to increased information flows, value creation, and reduced litigation and regulatory costs.

Over time, all stakeholders should hopefully recognise that the collective metric of success is the overall growth of the ecosystem rather than the success of one specific participant. A defining characteristic of such a balanced ecosystem would be end user choice. With the ability to switch easily between vendors, competitive pressures would strengthen the control of the end users and help them differentiate between different trust frameworks and service providers.

Future Potential: Scenarios of a Balanced Personal Data Ecosystem

What Would the Personal Data Ecosystem Offer If the Needs of Government, Private Industry and Individuals Were Appropriately Balanced?

What Follows Are Some Possibilities for the Year 2018.

Dianne is a mother of two teenage daughters and a remote caregiver for her father. She's not terribly sophisticated with technology but she uses some social networks to keep up with her friends and family. But as the hub of family care, Dianne is tied to several services that keep her family safe, healthy and informed.

Putting a New Spring in Her Step

Dianne recently upgraded her exercise footwear to a wirelessly networked sports shoe, a product that transforms all of her daily walking into valuable data points. Her health insurance provider encourages exercise through a certified, earned credit system. With minimal data breach risk, walking translates directly into discounts on medications, food and other expenses for not only herself but also her father and daughters linked to her health savings account. This lets Dianne take better care of her loved ones, which is a more powerful motivator than her own health and wellness. The initial savings helped convert her children to regular walking as well. What was routine is now a game as the family competes in active walking challenges with one another, all the while providing better healthcare for everyone.

   Transparency—data usage disclosure

   Control—opt-in participation with immediate feedback in
      rewards balance

   Trust—certified by identity consortium across health, finance
      and other service providers

   Value—discounts powered by data collection that can be
      applied to many different needs

Source: frog design research, 2010

At Ease and Secure

Dianne's old anxiety over identity theft has been less of a worry since the Personal Data Protection and Portability Act went into effect, legislation the government passed in 2014 granting citizens greater control and transparency over their digital information. Her employer provides a private, certified Data-Plus Integrity Plan that monitors and ensures the personal data of her whole family and is portable across jobs. Dianne feels more at ease about her daughters' social habits online with the Parent Teachers Association-endorsed TeenSecure. A comprehensive activity summary and alert system means Dianne no longer feels like a spy, monitoring her kids and investigating every new social site. Her daughters' access is managed, tracked and protected by a trusted socially acceptable source. Dianne receives simple, convenient monthly statements that highlight both the activity and stored value of her data. As an added benefit, various retailers offer coupons and discounts during the holidays, in exchange for Dianne allowing them to use some of this activity data as a second currency.

Transparency—single view of all activity

Control—monitoring of dependents

Trust—government and consumer advocacy backed

Value—peace of mind and stored value

Transforming Concern into Ease

When Dianne's father moved into managed care with early-stage symptoms of Alzheimer's disease, her insurance carrier provided her with control of her father's medications and recommended an online dashboard-like tool adapted to his condition. The service is offered in a partnership with the Alzheimer's Research Foundation, as well as the Department of Public Health, which have connected her father's information and medical health records to her Data-Plus Integrity Plan. This provides Dianne with on-demand monitoring services, medication compliance tracking and feedback on how he is feeling. She is also able to keep tabs on his finances. Dianne hopes that through the sharing of her father's medical condition, they may one day find a cure. In the meantime, her in-person visits are less about evaluating his condition and much more about spending time together.

Transparency—permission of data access

Control—progression of need increases access

Trust—family-centric data safeguards

Value—transferable control

Source: frog design research, 2010

KEY ENABLERS OF A BALANCED ECOSYSTEM

While building a balanced ecosystem around personal data will require significant commitment from all stakeholders, four critical enablers are apparent:

- An easy-to-understand user-centric approach to the design of systems, tools and policies, with an emphasis on transparency, trust, control and value distribution;
- Mechanisms for enhancing trust among all parties in digital transactions;
- Greater interoperability among existing data silos;
- An expanded role for government, such that governments can use their purchasing power to help shape commercially available products and solutions that the private sector can then leverage.

User-Centricity

The concept of user-centricity is the central pivot point of the personal data ecosystem. With greater control placed in the hands of individuals, new efficiencies and capabilities can emerge.

Many perceive this shift in power as highly disruptive. It creates a diversity of perspectives on if, how and when the "pivot for the people" might occur. In short, the transition to user-centricity is anything but simple. It's hard collectively to frame and act upon it due to the significant differences in cultural, geopolitical and institutional norms.

Globally, there is a growing consensus that there is an urgent need for greater trust associated with online identities. People find the increasing complexity of managing multiple user names and passwords across different organisations a major inconvenience. Additionally, as online fraud and identity theft continue to skyrocket, people demand greater assurances about who they are interacting with. As secure and trusted online relationships are established with individuals and various institutions, silos of information that were previously unavailable can also become easier to incorporate into personalised solutions.

A market is now taking shape to address these concerns on personal identity. In fact, an ecosystem of interoperable identity service providers offering solutions that are secure, easy to use and market based is in its early stages of development.[23] As more services move online (in particular, health and financial services), the infrastructure costs of ensuring the identity of who can use a given online offering will continue to escalate. The value of paying a third party for trusted digital identities will most likely continue to increase as these services reduce both the cost of fraud as well as the risk of offering additional value-added services[24] (see sidebar, "End user principles").

Trust Enablers

Interviews and discussions with leading privacy advocates, regulatory experts and business leaders lead to an overwhelming consensus: trust is another key ingredient required for creating value from today's oceans of disparate personal data. Without the establishment of trust, particularly the trust of the end user, a personal data ecosystem that benefits all stakeholders will never coalesce.

End User Principles

Transparency	Trust

What is a meaningful way to understand transparency, and who provides the lens to the user?

People naturally expect the right to see, and thus know, the data that is being captured about them. If that right is not respected, they feel deceived and exploited. Upon seeing this reflection of themselves through their personal data, people start to feel a sense of personal connection and ownership, leading to the desire for control. However, people struggle to form a mental model of something that is fragmented and abstract in nature. This creates a challenge: what is invisible must be revealed, made tangible and ultimately be connected across different points of access.

Which investments in building trust will help users feel comfortable allowing others to access their data?

Personal data is difficult, if not impossible, to un-share. Once shared, it gains a life of its own. Given the risk of unintended consequences, people rely heavily on trust to guide their decisions. But how is trust formed? Different thresholds of trust exist for different types of data. While a majority of people accept a certain level of risk, viewing it as an opportunity cost for gaining something, the benefits are often coupled with feelings of anxiety and fear. Such concerns will continue to limit the potential value of personal data until a comprehensible model for creating and certifying trust relationships is adopted on a large scale.

Control	Value

What are the primary parameters that influence how users will want to control their data, and how are they adapted to different contexts?

People naturally want control over data that is both about them and often created by them. Control can be exercised in three ways:

(a) directly through explicit choices;
(b) indirectly by defining rules;
(c) by proxy.

People's perception of a given situation will determine whether they choose to exercise control. The more subtle qualities of an experience (such as feedback, convenience and understanding) will determine how they choose to exercise that control.

What measures must be taken to ensure that data created today is a mutually beneficial asset in the future?

The value of personal data is wildly subjective. Many business models have emerged that encourage and capitalise on the flow of that data. Consumers are becoming increasingly aware of the value of the data they generate even in mundane interactions like a Google search. While direct personal data has an inherent value, secondary inferred data can often be mined and interpreted to produce new information of equal or greater value. The long-term impact of the aggregation and unchecked dissemination of this information is unknown. Digital behaviour today may yield positive distributed value across the ecosystem in the near term, but can have detrimental consequences for the end user in the future.

To use a metaphor, trust is the lubricant that enables a virtuous cycle for the ecosystem: it engenders stakeholder participation, which, in turn, drives the value creation process. For such a virtuous cycle to evolve, mutual trust needs to be at the foundation of all relationships. Increased trust leads to increased information flows, sharing and value creation and reduces litigation and regulatory costs.

> "A collective metric of success could emerge where the overall growth of the ecosystem was the goal—rather than the success of one particular institution."
>
> —"Rethinking Personal Data" project

Increasing Interoperability and the Sharing of Personal Data

Promoting solutions that drive the exchange and "movement" of personal data in a secure, trusted and authenticated manner is also essential. Today, it is difficult to share personal data across private and public organisations and jurisdictions. This is due to a combination of technological, regulatory and business factors. Decades-old privacy laws and policies could not have fore seen the emergence of digital personal data as a valuable asset. Inadequate legislation has thus made standards surrounding the use of personal data inconsistent.

> "We do not have the data-sharing equivalent of SMTP, but as we develop or achieve real data portability we will have a standardised infrastructure for data sharing that does not require centralisation."
>
> — Interviewee, "Rethinking Personal Data" project

Furthermore, many organisations employ legacy technology systems and databases that were created in proprietary, closed environments. As a result, personal data today is often isolated in silos—bound by organisational, data type, regional or service borders—each focusing on a limited set of data types and services.

To achieve global scale, technical, semantic and legal infrastructures will need to be established that are both resilient and interoperable. The US National Strategy for Trusted Identities in Cyberspace notes three types of interoperability for identity solutions:[25]

- Technical interoperability—The ability for different technologies to communicate and exchange data based upon well-defined and widely adopted interface standards;

- Semantic interoperability—The ability of each end point to communicate data and have the receiving party understand the message in the sense intended by the sending party;

- Legal interoperability—Common business policies and processes (e.g., identity proofing and vetting) related to the transmission, receipt and acceptance of data between systems, which a legal framework supports.

It is important to stress that the call for interoperability does not equate to working exclusively with standards bodies. In many cases standards take too long. By leveraging open protocols, de facto standards, existing pilots and collaboration with industry and advocacy groups, a functional degree of interoperability can be achieved in a shorter time frame.

Despite this "need for speed," the levels of reliability, integrity and security for both the individual and the computing infrastructure cannot be understated. The broad private sector support to cooperate in the sharing of personal data will bring with it extremely high technical, legal and performance requirements.

Government as Enabler

Governments have a vital role to play in accelerating the growth of a balanced personal data ecosystem. Their influence manifests itself along three primary dimensions.

First, they play a dominant role in crafting the legal and regulatory environments that shape what is possible in the ecosystem. This is a challenging role in many respects. Within the national context, regulators are being asked to balance consumer

US Department of Health & Human Services:
"Blue Button" Initiative[26]

Personal data also has clear opportunities to create value for the
public sector. In October 2010, the US Department of Health's Medi-
care arm launched its "Blue Button" application. It's a Web-based
feature that allows patients easily to download all their historical
health information from one secure location and then share it with
healthcare providers, caregivers and others they trust—something
that wasn't possible before.

The service is innovative in many ways. First, it allows Medi-
care beneficiaries to access their medical histories from various
databases and compile sources into one place (e.g., test results,
emergency contact information, family health history, military
health history and other health-related information). Second, the
service provides the information in a very convenient and trans-
portable format (ASCII text file). That allows it to be shared seam-
lessly with virtually any healthcare or insurance provider. Finally,
Blue Button fully empowers the end user: patients are given control over how their information is shared and distributed. That
allows them to be more proactive about—and have more insight
into—the medical treatments that they need.

protection with the need to create a business environment con-
ducive to innovation, growth and job creation. On top of that,
many global industry participants are turning to national and
regional regulatory bodies to harmonise guidelines to facilitate
global platforms.

Second, governments are active participants in ongoing
experiments regarding how the personal data ecosystem can be
harnessed to achieve important social goals such as providing
more efficient and cost-effective services to citizens, stopping
epidemics before they become pandemics and using data-mining
techniques to enhance national security.

"We must have empowered users, but no one is suggesting the user should be able to edit his or her criminal records. We're looking at a collaborative model with users who are as empowered as we can make them."

— Interviewee, "Rethinking Personal Data" project

Third, and perhaps most importantly, given their purchasing power, governments are in a position to influence significantly commercially available solutions. In crafting requests for proposals to help modernise service delivery, governments can write specifications for everything from security protocols to end user interfaces and data portability options. Successful projects can serve as proof points and major references for innovative solutions.

Hands-on experience gained in leveraging personal data for government services and objectives, combined with insights gleaned from negotiations with vendors, can give regulatory deliberations a very practical bent, which should be beneficial to all parties.

SECTION 2: STAKEHOLDER TRUST AND TRUST FRAMEWORKS

Achieving a high level of stakeholder trust requires a set of legal and technical structures to govern the interactions of participants within the ecosystem. The concept of trust frameworks is emerging as an increasingly attractive means for the personal data ecosystem to scale in a balanced manner. Trust frameworks consist of documented specifications selected by a particular group (a "trust community"). These govern the laws, contracts and policies undergirding the technologies selected to build the identity system. The specifications ensure the system reliability that is crucial for creating trust within the ecosystem.

THE TRUST FRAMEWORK MODEL

The Open Identity Trust Framework model (OITF) is a working example. Built to Internet scale, it offers a single sign-on environment for trust between relying parties and end users. The model addresses two problems with the way end users and relying parties interact with the Internet today:

- The proliferation of user names and passwords;
- The inability of relying parties to verify the identity of other entities.

Most people can relate to the first problem. Almost every website requires visitors to establish a user name and password, and invariably requires the sharing of such personal data as name, address and credit card information. Not only is this inconvenient, it's unsafe. It puts our personal data onto every server with which we interact, increasing the odds that our data may be compromised.

The second problem trust frameworks address is the lack of certainty about online identities. In most of today's Internet transactions, neither the user nor the relying party is completely sure of the other's identity. That creates a huge opening for identity theft and fraud. In 2009, more than $3 billion in online revenue was lost due to fraud in North America.[27] Some $550 million of that was money lost by individual US consumers.[28] The hope is that with a richer, scalable and more flexible identity management system, these losses can be reduced.

The Magnitude of Data Breaches

The Privacy Rights Clearinghouse estimates that in the US alone, more than 2,000 publicly announced data breaches have occurred since 2005. These include instances of unintended disclosure of sensitive information, hacks and payment card fraud, all of which resulted in a staggering 500-million-plus records of data being compromised.

Source: Privacy Rights Clearinghouse

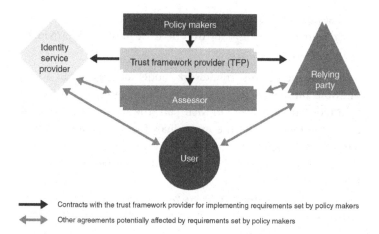

FIGURE A.5
The open identity trust framework model
Source: OITF

The model defines the following roles (see Figure A.5) to support Internet-scale identity management:

- Policy makers decide the technical, operational and legal requirements for exchanges of identity information among the group they govern;

- Trust framework providers translate these requirements into the building blocks of a trust framework. They then certify identity verification providers that provide identity management services in accordance with the specifications of the trust framework. Finally, the trust framework provider recruits assessors responsible for auditing and ensuring that framework participants adhere to the specifications;

- Identity providers (IdPs) issue, verify and maintain online credentials for an individual user. Relying parties accept these credentials and have firm assurances that the IdP has analysed and validated the individual user;

- Assessors evaluate IdPs and relying parties, and certify that they are capable of following the trust framework provider's blueprint.

Within such a trust framework model, end users can access multiple sites (relying parties) using a single credential issued by an identity provider. On their part, the sites can rest assured about the identities of the individuals they are doing business with. This screening is similar to how a car rental agent trusts that a driver can legally operate an automobile because he or she has a valid driver's licence.

With such a framework, users would need only to share less sensitive personal data with relying parties. No longer would they have to enter their name, address and credit card information in order to purchase a Web service. Using the trust framework, they would share the minimum amount of data to complete the transaction. In some cases, that may simply amount to verification of the availability of the funds being transmitted to the relying party.

PERSONAL DATA SERVICES

The trust framework model will bring benefits to end users in the form of increased privacy and a more seamless and convenient Web experience. But such advantages can be extended through the related concepts of personal data services and vendor relationship management (VRM).

Personal data services provide the safe means by which an end user can store, manage, share and gain benefit from his or her personal data. These data can range from such self-asserted attributes as the individual's likes, preferences and interests to such managed and verified attributes as a person's age, credit score or affiliations, and histories with external entities like firms, government agencies and the like (see Figure A.6).

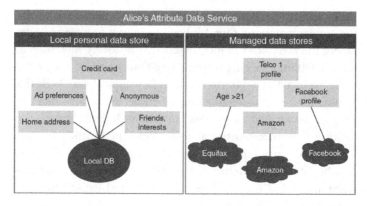

FIGURE A.6

Personal data services store end users' data and provide applications that enable them to manage, share and gain benefit from their personal data[29]

Source: The Eclipse Foundation

Personal data services consolidate end users' digital identity, allowing them to control which third parties are entitled to access—along with how, when and at what price. VRM extends this control to the realm of realising direct value—monetary or in kind—from the personal data stored and managed by personal data services providers.

These emerging concepts will help build stakeholder trust and herald additional benefits for end users and relying parties alike. Indeed, some promising trials are already under way. Yet more testing will be needed to resolve some open questions about the viability of these concepts.

KEY UNCERTAINTIES OF TRUST FRAMEWORKS

Trust frameworks and personal data services are concepts in their infancy. Despite encouraging pilots in the US and the UK, they need further refinement and testing to fulfil their promise. Implementations thus far have primarily been at websites where the level of assurance required is relatively low, such as those enabling blogging or providing news content. They need to be deployed in environments that encompass more high-risk transactions, such as logging into a bank account. Only then will proponents know if these ideas can achieve Internet scale.

Risks and uncertainties also surround the business models for both identity providers and relying parties. While a large number of private enterprises have begun working in this space (Acxiom, AOL, Citibank, Equifax, Google and PayPal) the economics are unclear.[30]

From the perspective of relying parties, the benefits of transitioning to a user-centric model are still emerging. In this new approach, relying parties will be constrained on collecting data for free and will need to start paying for end user data. While some believe that an aggregated and holistic view of an individual would be more valuable, the balance of trade between what relying parties would be willing to share versus the new insights and efficiencies they would gain from a holistic user-centric view are unclear.

However, the cost of online fraud and risk mitigation could be enough to make relying parties seriously consider participating in a more collaborative model. On average, online fraud represented 1.2 per cent of a Web retailer's revenue in 2009.[31]

Finally, building end user awareness is another uncertainty. How can firms communicate to individuals the advantages of managing their personal data? For a start, companies must themselves fully understand the convenience, value proposition, contextual nuances and usability of personal data dashboards. Further investigation is therefore needed into applications and services that provide end users with convenient, contextually relevant and simplified control over their data.

SECTION 3: CONCLUSIONS

Personal data will continue to increase dramatically in both quantity and diversity, and has the potential to unlock significant economic and societal value for end users, private firms and public organisations alike.

The business, technology and policy trends shaping the nascent personal ecosystem are complex, interrelated and constantly changing. Yet a future ecosystem that both maximises economic and societal value—and spreads its wealth across all stakeholders—is not only desirable but distinctly possible. To achieve that promise, industries and public bodies must take coordinated actions today. Leaders should consider taking steps in the following five areas:

1. INNOVATE AROUND USER-CENTRICITY AND TRUST

Where We Stand Today

Innovative concepts already exist on how personal data can be shared in a way that allows all stakeholders to trust the integrity and safety of this data. Examples of such trust frameworks include the Open Identity Trust Framework and Kantara's Identity Assurance Framework. However, no truly large-scale application of a trust framework has yet been rolled out. As a consequence, we remain uncertain about how to take advantage of personal data while still aligning stakeholder interests. Also unanswered are questions such as: What are the incentives for stakeholders to participate in trust frameworks? What are the business model mechanics? Who will pay for identity provider services?

What Is Required and Why

Complex blueprints for Internet business models typically come to life in iterative steps. For example, the retail banking sector evolved online through successive phases of change. Trust frameworks need similar pressure testing in large-scale applications to prove these concepts can be instrumental in unlocking economic and societal value. Additionally, end user participation in testing and developing these trust frameworks is crucial. Offering more transparency on how personal data is used and educating end users on the benefits they can extract from such applications—two areas lacking in the ecosystem today—will significantly strengthen trust among all stakeholders.

Recommended Next Steps

Private firms and policy makers should consider the following next steps:

- Invest in open and collaborative trials orchestrated by end user privacy groups or academics;

- Integrate principles surrounding end user trust and data protection into the development of new services and platforms (the concept of "privacy by design"), particularly when designing new "e-government" platforms;

- Engage with leading innovators and end user advocacy groups to explore the further applications for, and development of trust frameworks.

2. DEFINE GLOBAL PRINCIPLES FOR USING AND SHARING PERSONAL DATA

Where We Stand Today

Privacy-related laws and police enforcement differ significantly across jurisdictions, often based on cultural, political and historical contexts. Attempts to align such policies have largely failed.[32] But the need is growing. Many Internet services, in particular those based upon cloud computing delivery models, require the cross-jurisdictional exchange of personal data to function at optimal levels.

What Is Required and Why

The downside of the current divergence in regulatory frameworks manifests itself in several ways. First, companies striving to provide products and services based upon personal data see significant complexity costs associated with compliance. As a result of these costs, they may choose not to offer their product and services in certain smaller markets, where the cost of doing business may outweigh incremental profits. That decision to opt out obviously hurts the users who cannot access the services. Less obvious is the fact that users with access are also hurt, as the value of many of these services increases with the number of users.

A truly global and seamless exchange of personal data will not emerge without a set of internationally accepted, user-centric principles. Additionally, a set of commonly accepted terms and definitions—a taxonomy—surrounding personal data concepts must be created to allow unencumbered dialog. Although it is unrealistic to hope to develop globally accepted standards and frameworks while national and regional versions are still in significant flux, establishing a standing, cross-regional dialog will allow for more rapid harmonisation once regulatory environments do begin to stabilise.

> "Digital bill of rights have been introduced a half dozen times... If they are introduced in conjunction with a way for them to be actionable by large populations of people then it may have more success."
> — Interviewee, "Rethinking Personal Data" project

It is imperative for private sector firms to participate in at least some of these dialogs, as they can share real-world perspectives on the cost and challenges of dealing with divergent regulations and can help public sector officials adapt pragmatic and consistent policies.

Recommended Next Steps

- Policy makers and private firms should launch an international dialog to stay informed about proposed laws and policies that would have a global bearing on their markets. This dialog should encompass governments, international bodies such as the World Trade Organization, end user privacy rights groups and representation from the private sector. It should include not only US and European Union members, but interested parties from the Asia-Pacific region and emerging countries;

- Among the outputs of this body would be an agreed-upon benchmark measuring the effectiveness of national regulations and their impact on free markets. This could prove vital in unearthing and spreading best practises that could ultimately guide the development of consistent national policies.

3. STRENGTHEN THE DIALOG BETWEEN REGULATORS AND THE PRIVATE SECTOR

Where We Stand Today

The roots of today's data privacy laws grew from the aspirational principles of the early 1980s, which reflected a consensus about the need for standards to ensure both individual privacy and information flows.[33] But over the last two decades, these principles have been translated very differently into national policies in the US, the European Union and the Asia-Pacific. Although most of these laws aim to maximise data protection and individual control, many experts question their practical effectiveness given technological advances. Some governments, such as in the US and European Union, are therefore revising their policies.

What Is Required and Why

Topic experts and executives involved in the "Rethinking Personal Data" project agree that self-regulation of markets related to personal data is not a desirable outcome for all stakeholders. Instead, national and regional agencies must adopt 21st-century digital policies that promote and accelerate favourable behaviour from all market participants.

Recommended Next Steps

- In the United States: Private firms should closely watch developments of the National Strategy for Trusted Identities in Cyberspace programme and the privacy bill—and seek ways to contribute to them. Private firms and advocacy groups need to be in constant dialog with the US Department of Commerce, the Federal Trade Commission and other bodies to help shape future legislation and policies;

- In the European Union: Private firms should collaborate with the European Commission in its move to revise the EU privacy directive and to synchronise legislation across its member states. A revised EU privacy directive is scheduled to go into effect in 2011, after a period of public consultation through the European Commission's website during January;[34]

- In other countries: In other regions that differ from the US or the EU in cultural or social norms, very different paths in adopting policy frameworks will be required. However, given the global relevance of many such markets in the future digital economy, private firms and policy makers should not just wait and see. One initial step in making progress could be to seek ways to harmonise fragmented national privacy policies. For example, a starting point in Asia could be the Asia Pacific Privacy Charter Initiative, which, since 2003, aims to align privacy policies and to promote best practises in regulatory and legislative frameworks in the region.

4. FOCUS ON INTEROPERABILITY AND OPEN STANDARDS

Where We Stand Today

A large variety of syntax and semantic standards exist to describe and share personal data. Most of those standards are proprietary and were often invented in an ad hoc manner without broader consultation with industry peers. While some open standards are emerging—for example, in the realm of digital identities, standards include ISO/IEEE, Mozilla and OIX—no standards are in place for many other data types, particularly new ones. The history of the Internet shows that open standards can improve data portability significantly. One example from the 1980s was the advent of the simple mail transfer protocol (SMTP), which superseded various proprietary email standards.[35]

What Is Required and Why

If we posit that the highest potential for economic and societal value creation lies in the aggregation of different personal data types, the implication is clear: To enable the seamless sharing of personal data across organisational borders, private firms and the public sector will require common communication standards, system architectures, accepted personal data terms and definitions, and standard interface design specifications.

Recommended Next Steps

- Private firms, in particular those from the information communication technologies sector, should participate in initiatives that aim to align today's jumble of standards. The Open Web Foundation is one such example: it has helped companies define commonly accepted standards and avoid competitive deadlocks;[36]

- Private firms and public bodies should use the knowledge gained from ongoing pilot tests of trust frameworks and related services to inform standardisation bodies, such as the IEEE;

- To build momentum, firms and public organisations should monitor the ongoing dialog to identify the most valuable types of personal data and focus standardisation efforts on those first.

5. CONTINUALLY SHARE KNOWLEDGE

Where We Stand Today

Interested sponsors continually hold a large number of conferences, events, websites, private-public discussions and blogs on
the different aspects of the personal data ecosystem. Even for
active dialog participants, it's challenging to keep up with the
latest developments and research. Some platforms are aiming to
synthesise this ongoing dialog, yet none has yet reached a critical mass with private and public stakeholders.

What Is Required and Why

The goal is to aggregate the key insights—from both successful
and unsuccessful initiatives—in a timely and unbiased manner.
This would enable the sharing of lessons learned, right from the
introduction of new personal data services to the development
of further research activities.

Recommended Next Steps

- Private firms should nominate a central gatekeeper in the
  organisation who actively contributes to the personal data
  dialog. That person's purview would not only include privacy
  but also encompass a business development and strategic
  perspective;

- Private and public sector representatives should invest in a
  jointly run organisation that facilitates a truly global dialog
  about personal data—one that stretches across industries and
  regions. Given private companies' increasing propensity to be
  multinational, the onus is on them to pressure their respective governments to think on a global scale.

GLOSSARY OF TERMS

End User This term refers to individual consumers, citizens or persons
about and from whom personal data is created. End users are also able to

participate in the use and proliferation of personal data via related services, applications and technology. End users are typically represented on a broad, public scale by consumer advocacy groups, such as the American Civil Liberties Union (ACLU) in the United States.

End User-Centricity End user-centricity refers to the concept of organising the rules and policies of the personal data ecosystem around the key principles that end users value: transparency into what data is captured, control over how it is shared, trust in how others use it and value attributable because of it.

Identity Provider Identity providers (IdPs) issue, verify and maintain online credentials for an individual user. Relying parties accept these credentials and have solid assurances that the IdP has analysed and validated the individual user in accordance with specifications.

Person[37] A person can be defined as a natural person, a legal person or a digital persona. A natural person refers to a specific human being with an individual physical body (e.g., john Smith). A legal person refers to a body of persons or an entity (as a corporation) considered as having many of the rights and responsibilities of a natural person and in particular the capacity to sue and be sued (e.g., john Smith and Associates, LLC). Legal persons encompass a wide range of legal entities, including corporations, partnerships, limited liability companies, cooperatives, municipalities, sovereign states, intergovernmental organisations and some international organisations. A digital persona (or identity) can be understood as a digital representation of a set of claims made about a person, either by themselves or by another person (e.g., johnSmith@gmail.com or johnSmith@facebook.com). Note that a natural person may have multiple digital personae.

Personal Data We broadly define personal data as data and metadata (i.e., data about data) relating to an identified or identifiable person or persons. Our definition is based upon European Union Directive 95/46/EC. Personal data can be created in multiple ways, including: (1) volunteered data, which is created and explicitly shared by individuals (e.g., social network profiles); (2) observed data, which is captured by recording the actions of individuals (e.g., location data when using cell phones); and (3) inferred data, which is data about individuals based on analysis of volunteered or observed information (e.g., credit scores).

Privacy[38] The term privacy has two separate meanings. The public use of the term privacy is very broad, and it is used to reference nearly anything that has to do with personal data and more generally the perceived rights of an individual in relationship to a group. The legal meaning is much narrower. In US domestic law, it refers to a constitutional right (as interpreted by the courts) and several specific tort rights. Privacy tort rights, which are based mostly in common law (i.e., cases as opposed to statutes), are generally categorised to include the protection of solitude and has developed to include protection of "personality." Privacy tort "causes of action" are generally recognised to protect against four kinds of wrongs against the invasion of privacy. That includes (1) the appropriation of a person's picture or name by another for their commercial advantage (generally the promotion of goods), (2) the intrusion on a person's affairs or seclusion (if objectionable to a reasonable person), (3) the publication of facts that place a person in a false light (for example, publicly attributing an action or statement to a person that he or she did not make), and (4) public disclosures of private facts about the person. Both the public and legal meanings have one thing in common; they are both associated with "protection from harm" of the affected person.

Private Sector (or Companies) Within the context of the personal data ecosystem, the "private sector" refers to for-profit companies and private organisations involved in the capture, storage, analysis and sharing of personal data for the purposes of developing—and monetising—related services and applications. Private sector participants are not limited by size or industry group: they are any private entity that directly manipulates personal data for explicit financial gain.

Public Sector (or Agencies) Within the context of the personal data ecosystem, the public sector refers to governments (and their agencies) and nonprofit public organisations that are involved in the passing of legislation and policies that regulate the capture and use of personal data within their respective jurisdictions. Public sector entities also participate in capturing and storing personal data (e.g., social security information), as well as the development of related services and applications.

Relying Party In the context of trust frameworks, relying parties are typically businesses or organisations that rely on personal data as a means to verify the identities of their customers or partners. Without reliable and verifiable information, these transactions can be fraught with risks, including fraud.

Trust Frameworks Within the context of online and digital transactions, a trust framework is a formalised specification of policies and rules to which a participant (e.g., an end user, relying party or identity provider) must conform in order to be trusted. These policies include requirements around identity, security, privacy, data protection, technical profiles and assessor qualifications. This trust may be subject to different levels of assurance or protection, which are explicitly made clear to all parties.[39]

The World Economic Forum is an independent international organisation committed to improving the state of the world by engaging business, political, academic and other leaders of society to shape global, regional and industry agendas.

Incorporated as a foundation in 1971, and based in Geneva, Switzerland, the World Economic Forum is impartial and not-for-profit; it is tied to no political, partisan or national interests.

World Economic Forum
91–93 route de la Capite
CH—1223 Cologny/Geneva
Switzerland
Tel.: +41 (0) 22 869 1212
Fax: +41 (0) 22 786 2744
email: contact@weforum.org
www.weforum.org

NOTES

1. Many of these concepts and background information have been introduced in: Davis, Marc, Ron Martinez and Chris Kalaboukis. "Rethinking Personal Information—Workshop Pre-read." Invention Arts and World Economic Forum, June 2010.

2. Bain & Company Industry Brief. "Using Data as a Hidden Asset." August 16, 2010.

3. Angwin, Julia. "The Web's New Gold Mine: Your Secrets." *Wall Street Journal*. July 30, 2010. http://online.wsj.com/article/SB10001424052748 7039409045753950735129899404.html

4. IDC. "The Digital Universe Decade—Are You Ready?" May 2010.

5. *The Economist*. "Data, Data Everywhere." February 25, 2010.

6. The Radicati Group. "Email Statistics Report, 2009–2013." May 2009.

7. "Twitter + Ping = Discovering More Music." Twitter Blog. November 11, 2010; "Statistics." Facebook Press Room. January 11, 2011. http://www.facebook.com/press/info.php?statistics

8. Nokia Siemens Networks. "Digital Safety, Putting Trust into the Customer Experience." *Unite Magazine*. Issue 7. http://www.nokiasiemensnetworks.com/news-events/publications/unite-magazine-february-2010/digital-safety-putting-trust-into-the-customer

9. Javelin Strategy & Research. "The 2010 Identity Fraud Survey Report." February 10, 2010.

10. David, Scott. K&L Gates and Open Identity Exchange ABA Document. October 20, 2010.

11. In the US, recent developments emerging from the NSTIC, the Federal Trade Commission and the Department of Commerce warrant attention. In the EU, companies should work with the European Commission's efforts to revise the EU privacy directive and to synchronise legislation across its member states.

12. Ericsson [press release]. "CEO to Shareholders: 50 Billion Connections 2020." April 13, 2010.

13. Cisco. "Cisco Visual Networking Index: Global Mobile Data; Traffic Forecast Update, 2009–2014." February 9, 2010.

14. IDC. "The Digital Universe Decade—Are You Ready?" May 2010.

15. Definition based on Directive 95/46/EC of the European Parliament and the Council of 24, October 1995.

16. Davis, Marc, Ron Martinez and Chris Kalaboukis. "Rethinking Personal Information—Workshop Pre-read." Invention Arts and World Economic Forum, June 2010.

17. Ibid.

18. "Fair Information Practice Principles (FIPP) Comparison Tool, Draft." Discussion and Development Materials of the OIX Advisory Board and the OIX Legal Policy Group. October 7, 2010.

19. Ibid.

20. In 2000, the US and the European Commission agreed upon a framework that would act as a bridge for sharing data between the US and EU, while preserving the basic policy principles of both. See, for example, Thompson, Mozelle W., Peder van Wagonen Magee. "US/EU Safe Harbor Agreement: What It Is and What It Says About the Future of Cross Border Data Protection." Privacy Regulation. Federal Trade Commission, Spring 2003. http://www.ftc.gov/speeches/thompson/thompsonsafeharbor.pdf

21. Clippinger, John. Berkman Center for Internet & Society at Harvard University.

22. To learn more about how companies are using new and intrusive Internet-tracking technologies, see "What They Know" (series). *Wall Street Journal.* 2010. http://online.wsj.com/public/page/what-they-knowdigital -privacy.html

23. National Strategy for Trusted Identities in Cyberspace. Draft. June 25, 2010.

24. Reed, Drummond. "Person Data Ecosystem." Podcast Episode 2, December 2010.

25. "National Strategy for Trusted Identities." Draft pages 8–9. June 25, 2010.

26. "'Blue Button' Provides Access to Downloadable Personal Health Data." Office of Science and Technology Policy, the White House website. http://www.whitehouse.gov/blog/2010/10/07/blue-button-provides -accessdownloadable-personal-health-data

27. CyberSource. 11th Annual "Online Fraud Report." 2010.

28. 2009 "Internet Crime Report." Internet Crime Complaint Center. US Department of Justice, 2010.

29. Higgins Open Source Identity Framework is a project of The Eclipse Foundation. Ottawa, Ontario, Canada. http://www.eclipse.org/higgins /faq.php

30. Kreizman, Gregg, Ray Wagner and Earl Perkins. "Open Identity Pilot Advances the Maturity of User-Centric Identity, but Business Models Are Still Needed." Gartner, November 9, 2009. http://www.gartner.com /DisplayDocument?id=1223830

31. Cybersource. "11th Annual Online Fraud Report." 2010.

32. See, for example, Connolly, Chris. "The US Safe Harbor—Fact or Fiction?" Galexia, 2008.

33. See, for example, Cate, Fred H. "The Failure of Fair Information Practice Principles." Consumer Protection in the Age of the Informa- tion Economy, 2006. http://papers.ssrn.com/sol3/papers.cfm?abstract _id=1156972

34. Ashford, Warwick. "Revised EU Privacy Laws to Demand Greater Transparency on the Web." Computer-Weekly.com, November 5, 2010.

35. Strauser, Kirk. "The History and Future of SMTP." FSM, March 4, 2005.

36. Taft, Darryl K. "Microsoft Specs Support Open Web Foundation Agreement." eWEEK, November 25, 2009. http://www.eweek.com/c /a/Application-Development/Microsoft-Specs-Support-Open-Web -Foundation-Agreement-632362

37. Sourced from Davis, Marc, Ron Martinez and Chris Kalaboukis. "Rethinking Personal Information—Workshop Pre-read." Invention Arts and World Economic Forum, June 2010.

38. Ibid.

39. Ibid.

APPENDIX B   A WORLD THAT COUNTS: MOBILISING THE DATA REVOLUTION FOR SUSTAINABLE DEVELOPMENT

Report Prepared at the Request of the United Nations Secretary-General, by the Independent Expert Advisory Group on a Data Revolution for Sustainable Development.

November 2014

ACKNOWLEDGEMENTS

The United Nations Secretary-General's Independent Expert Advisory Group on a Data Revolution for Sustainable Development (IEAG) thanks the hundreds of individuals and organisations that contributed online and during the face-to-face meetings organised in New York and in Geneva, as well as other meetings attended by IEAG members.

Contributions, including in-kind, are gratefully acknowledged, including those from UNDP, DfID, UN Global Pulse, ECE, UN Secretariat—including DESA, DGACM, DM, and EOSG—UN Millennium Campaign, UN NGLS, Microsoft and UN Foundation.

We gratefully acknowledge help and advice from many others, especially Muhammad Abdullahi, Youlia Antonova, René Clausen Nielsen, Joe Colombano, Marie-Ange Diegue, Jaspreet Doung, Tala Dowlatshahi, Eleonore Fournier-Tombs, Caya Johnson, Eva Kaplan, Kate Krukiel, Paul Ladd, Yongyi Min, Keiko Osaki-Tomita, Anna Ortubia, Paul Pacheco, Matthias Reister, Stefan Schweinfest, Frances Simpson-Allen, Corinne Woods and Wailan Wu.

Independent Expert Advisory Group Secretary: Claire Melamed

Research team: Luis Gonzalez Morales, Yu-Chieh Hsu, Jennifer Poole, Benjamin Rae, Ian Rutherford.

Publication management: Admir Jahic

Design & layout: Green Communication Design Inc.

Produced by: Independent Expert Advisory Group Secretariat Copyright Independent Expert Advisory Group Secretariat 2014 © For more information please visit: www .undatarevolution.org

EXECUTIVE SUMMARY

MOBILISING THE DATA REVOLUTION FOR SUSTAINABLE DEVELOPMENT

Data are the lifeblood of decision-making and the raw material for accountability. Without high-quality data providing the right information on the right things at the right time; designing, monitoring and evaluating effective policies becomes almost impossible.

New technologies are leading to an exponential increase in the volume and types of data available, creating unprecedented possibilities for informing and transforming society and protecting the environment. Governments, companies, researchers and citizen groups are in a ferment of experimentation, innovation and adaptation to the new world of data, a world in which data are bigger, faster and more detailed than ever before. This is the data revolution.

Some are already living in this new world. But too many people, organisations and governments are excluded because of lack of resources, knowledge, capacity or opportunity. There are huge and growing inequalities in access to data and information and in the ability to use it.

Data needs improving. Despite considerable progress in recent years, whole groups of people are not being counted and important aspects of people's lives and environmental conditions are still not measured. For people, this can lead to the denial of basic rights, and for the planet, to continued environmental degradation. Too often, existing data remain unused because they are released too late or not at all, not well-documented and harmonized, or not available at the level of detail needed for decision-making.

As the world embarks on an ambitious project to meet new Sustainable Development Goals (SDGs), there is an urgent need to mobilise the data revolution for all people and the whole planet in order to monitor progress, hold governments accountable and foster sustainable development. More diverse, integrated, timely and trustworthy information can lead to better decision-making and real-time citizen feedback. This in turn enables individuals, public and private institutions, and companies to make choices that are good for them and for the world they live in.

This report sets out the main opportunities and risks presented by the data revolution for sustainable development. Seizing these opportunities and mitigating these risks requires active choices, especially by governments and international institutions. Without immediate action, gaps between developed and developing countries, between information-rich and information-poor people, and between the private and public sectors will widen, and risks of harm and abuses of human rights will grow.

AN URGENT CALL FOR ACTION: KEY RECOMMENDATIONS

The strong leadership of the United Nations (UN) is vital for the success of this process. The Independent Expert Advisory Group (IEAG), established in August 2014, offers the UN Secretary-General several key recommendations for actions to be taken in the near future, summarised below:

1. **Develop a global consensus on principles and standards:** The disparate worlds of public, private and civil society data and statistics providers need to be urgently brought together to build trust and confidence among data users. We propose that the UN establish a process whereby key stakeholders create a "Global Consensus on Data," to adopt principles concerning legal, technical, privacy, geospatial and statistical standards which, among other things, will facilitate openness and information exchange and promote and protect human rights.

2. **Share technology and innovations for the common good:** To create mechanisms through which technology and innovation can be shared and used for the common good, we propose to create a global "Network of Data Innovation Networks," to bring together the organisations and experts in the field. This would: contribute to the adoption of best practices for improving the monitoring of SDGs, identify areas where common data-related infrastructures could address capacity problems and improve efficiency, encourage collaborations, identify critical research gaps and create incentives to innovate.

3. **New resources for capacity development:** Improving data is a development agenda in its own right, and can improve the targeting of existing resources and spur new economic opportunities. Existing gaps can only be overcome through new investments and the strengthening of capacities. A new funding stream to support the data revolution for sustainable development should be endorsed at the "Third International Conference on Financing for Development," in Addis

Ababa in July 2015. An assessment will be needed of the scale of investments, capacity development and technology transfer that is required, especially for low income countries; and proposals developed for mechanisms to leverage the creativity and resources of the private sector. Funding will also be needed to implement an education program aimed at improving people's, infomediaries' and public servants' capacity and data literacy to break down barriers between people and data.

4. **Leadership for coordination and mobilisation:** A UN-led "Global Partnership for Sustainable Development Data" is proposed, to mobilise and coordinate the actions and institutions required to make the data revolution serve sustainable development, promoting several initiatives, such as:

   - A "World Forum on Sustainable Development Data" to bring together the whole data ecosystem to share ideas and experiences for data improvements, innovation, advocacy and technology transfer. The first Forum should take place at the end of 2015, once the SDGs are agreed;

   - A "Global Users Forum for Data for SDGs," to ensure feedback loops between data producers and users, help the international community to set priorities and assess results;

   - Brokering key global public-private partnerships for data sharing.

5. **Exploit some quick wins on SDG data:** Establishing a "SDGs data lab" to support the development of a first wave of SDG indicators, developing an SDG analysis and visualisation platform using the most advanced tools and features for exploring data, and building a dashboard from diverse data sources on "the state of the world."

Never again should it be possible to say "we didn't know." No one should be invisible. This is the world we want—a world that counts.

For more information on the composition, terms of reference and work of the IEAG, see www.undatarevolution.org

1. WHAT IS THE DATA REVOLUTION FOR SUSTAINABLE DEVELOPMENT?

Data are the lifeblood of decision-making. Without data, we cannot know how many people are born and at what age they die; how many men, women and children still live in poverty; how many children need educating; how many doctors to train or schools to build; how public money is being spent and to what effect; whether greenhouse gas emissions are increasing or the fish stocks in the ocean are dangerously low; how many people are in what kinds of work, what companies are trading and whether economic activity is expanding.

To know all this and more involves a systematic effort of finding out. It means seeking out high-quality data that can be used to compare outcomes and changes over time and between and within countries, and continuing to do so, year after year. It means careful planning, spending money on technical expertise, robust systems, and ever-changing technologies. It means making data available, building public trust in the data, and expanding people's ability to use it, so that their needs are at the heart of these processes.

Since 2000, the effort involved in monitoring the Millennium Development Goals (MDGs) has spurred increased investment to improve data for monitoring and accountability. As a result, more is known now about the state of the world and, particularly, the poorest people in it. But despite this significant progress, huge data and knowledge gaps remain about some of the biggest challenges we face, and many people and groups still go uncounted. These gaps limit governments' ability to act and to communicate honestly with the public. Months into the Ebola outbreak, for example, it is still hard to know how many people have died, or where.

And now the stakes are rising. In 2015, the world will embark on an even more ambitious initiative, a new development agenda underpinned by the Sustainable Development Goals (SDGs). Achieving these goals will require integrated action on social, environmental and economic challenges, with a focus on inclusive, participatory development that leaves no one behind. This in turn will require another significant increase in the data and information that is available to individuals, governments, civil society, companies and international organisations to plan, monitor and be held accountable for their actions. A huge increase in the capacity of many governments, institutions and individuals will be needed to deliver and use this data.

Fortunately, this challenge comes together with a huge opportunity. The volume of data in the world is increasing exponentially: one estimate has it that 90% of the data in the world has been created in the last two years.[1] As the graph above demonstrates, the volumes of both traditional sources of data (represented by the number of household surveys registered) and new sources (mobile subscriptions per 100 people) have been rising, and openness is increasing (numbers of surveys placed online). Thanks to new technologies, the volume, level of detail, and speed of data available on societies, the economy and the environment is without precedent. Governments, companies, researchers and citizens groups are in a ferment of experimentation, innovation and adaptation to the new world of data. People, economies and societies are adjusting to a world of faster, more networked and more comprehensive data—and all the fears and dangers, as well as opportunities, that brings.

This is the "data revolution": the opportunity to improve the data that is essential for decision-making, accountability and solving development challenges. This report calls on governments and the UN to act to *enable data to play its full role in the realisation of sustainable development by closing key gaps in access and use of data*: between developed and developing countries,

THE GROWTH OF DATA : TRENDS IN DATA AVAILABILITY, DATA OPENNESS AND MOBILE PHONE USE

Number of surveys registered by the International Household Survey Network, by year in which data collection was finished

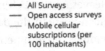

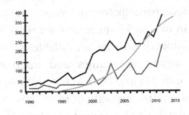

* International Household Survey Network (http://catalog.ihsn. org/index.php/catalog). For a detailed analysis of global trends in survey data availability, see, e.g., Demombynes and Sandefur (2014), "Costing a Data Revolution," Center for Global Development, Working paper 383.
** World Bank (http://data.worldbank.org/indicator/it.cel.sets.p2). Based on data from the International Telecommunication Union (ITU), World Telecommunication/ICT Indicators Database

between information-rich and information-poor people, and between the private and public sectors.

This report has been prepared in response to a request by the Secretary-General of the United Nations. We hope it will also be helpful to Member States, the UN System as a whole, and to the large constituencies that support the three pillars of the UN: peace, human rights and development.

Revolutions begin with people, not with reports, and the data revolution is no different. This report is not about how to create a data revolution—it is already happening—but how to mobilise it for sustainable development. It is an urgent call for action to support the aspiration for sustainable development and avert risks, stop and reverse growing inequalities in access to data and information, and ensure that the promise of the data revolution is realised for all.

Defining the Data Revolution

Since the phrase was coined in May 2013 in the report of the high-level panel of eminent persons on the post-2015 development agenda, the "data revolution" has come to mean many things to many people. Here, we take it to mean the following:

The Data Revolution Is:

- an explosion in the volume of data, the speed with which data are produced, the number of producers of data, the dissemination of data, and the range of things on which there is data, coming from new technologies such as mobile phones and the "internet of things," and from other sources, such as qualitative data, citizen-generated data and perceptions data;
- a growing demand for data from all parts of society.

The Data Revolution for Sustainable Development Is:

- the integration of these new data with traditional data to produce high-quality information that is more detailed, timely and relevant for many purposes and users, especially to foster and monitor sustainable development;
- the increase in the usefulness of data through a much greater degree of openness and transparency, avoiding invasion of privacy and abuse of human rights from misuse of data on individuals and groups, and minimising inequality in production, access to and use of data;
- ultimately, more empowered people, better policies, better decisions and greater participation and accountability, leading to better outcomes for people and the planet.

MINIMISING THE RISKS AND MAXIMISING THE OPPORTUNITIES OF THE DATA REVOLUTION

As with any change, the *data revolution comes with a range of new risks*, posing questions and challenges concerning the access to and use of data, and threatening a growing inequality in access to and use of information. These risks must be addressed.

Fundamental elements of human rights have to be safe-guarded: privacy, respect for minorities or data sovereignty requires us to balance the rights of individuals with the benefits of the collective. Much of the new data is collected passively, from the 'digital footprints' people leave behind, from sensor-enabled objects or is inferred via algorithms.

The growing gap between the data people actively offer and the amounts of "massive and passive" data being generated and mediated by third parties fuels anxiety among individuals and communities.

Some of this is well-founded. As more is known about people and the environment, there is a correspondingly greater risk that the data could be used to harm, rather than to help. People could be harmed in material ways, if the huge amount that can be known about people's movements, their likes and dislikes, their social interactions and relationships is used with malicious intent, such as hacking into bank accounts or discriminating in access to services. People and societies can be harmed in less mate-rial, but nonetheless real ways if individuals are embarrassed or suffer social isolation as a result of information becoming public.

There is a longer-term cost if a breakdown in trust between people and the institutions that have access to their data means that people do not feel confident giving consent to uses of their data for the social good, such as to track patterns of disease or assess inequalities.

People and the planet could also be harmed inadvertently, if data that have not been checked for quality are used for policy or decision-making and turn out to be wrong.

There is also a risk of growing inequality. Major gaps are already opening up between the data haves and have-nots. Without action, a whole new inequality frontier will open up, splitting the world between those who know, and those who do not. Many people are excluded from the new world of data and information by language, poverty, lack of education, lack of technology infrastructure, remoteness or prejudice and discrimination. While the use of new technologies has exploded everywhere in the last ten years, the costs are still prohibitive for many. In Nicaragua, Bolivia and Honduras, for example, the price of a mobile broadband subscription exceeds 10% of average monthly GDP per capita, compared to France and the Republic of Korea where it is less than 0.1%.[2] The information society should not force a choice between food and knowledge.

In several countries, the public sector is not keeping up with companies, which are increasingly able to collect, analyse and respond to real-time data as quickly as it is generated. Richer countries are benefitting more from the new possibilities than poorer countries that lack the resources for investment, training and experimentation. According to McKinsey, African countries spend about 1.1% of GDP on investment in and use of internet services, less than a third of what, on average, is spent by richer

---

This Is the Revolution

As part of a project to engage young people in disaster risk reduction, teenagers in Rio de Janeiro have used cameras attached to kites to gather aerial images, helping to identify the presence or absence of drainage systems, the availability of sanitation facilities, and potential impediments to evacuation. In Rio, this has already led to the removal of piled-up garbage and the repair of a bridge.

Source: UNICEF (http://www.unicef.org/statistics/brazil_62043.html)

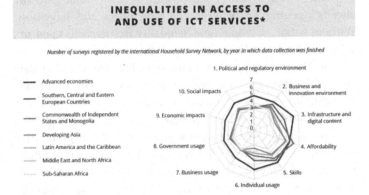

**INEQUALITIES IN ACCESS TO
AND USE OF ICT SERVICES***

Number of surveys registered by the International Household Survey Network, by year in which data collection was finished

Advanced economies

Southern, Central and Eastern
European Countries

Commonwealth of Independent
States and Mongolia

Developing Asia

Latin America and the Caribbean

Middle East and North Africa

Sub-Saharan Africa

1. Political and regulatory environment
2. Business and innovation environment
3. Infrastructure and digital content
4. Affordability
5. Skills
6. Individual usage
7. Business usage
8. Government usage
9. Economic impacts
10. Social impacts

* Regional score averages based on the Global Information
Technology Report 2013, by the World Economic Forum

© UNICEF/RWAA2011-00484/Noorani

countries—meaning that the gap in internet availability and use
is growing every year, as some regions accelerate ahead.[3] The
graph below shows how advanced economies are ahead of the
rest of the world on almost every indicator of access to, use of,
and impact of the use of digital technologies.

We believe that the data revolution can be a revolution
for equality. More, and more open, data can help ensure that

knowledge is shared, creating a world of informed and empowered citizens, capable of holding decision-makers accountable
for their actions. There are huge opportunities before us and
change is already happening.

But if our vision is of a world where data and information
reduce rather than increase inequalities, we are still a long way
from realising that ambition. Without deliberate actions, the
opportunities will be slower in coming and more unequally distributed when they arrive, and the risks will be greater.

It is up to governments to put in place the rules and systems
to realise this vision, working with domestic stakeholders and in
the multilateral system, at regional and global levels. Governments, through the legal systems they enforce, are the ultimate
guarantors of the public good. If the new world of data is to
be based on public trust and public consent, there has to be a
confidence that governments can and will play this role, at least
in part through the creation and enforcement of new rules. It
is governments—ideally working in collaboration with forward
looking and socially responsible private institutions, civil society and academia—that can set and enforce legal frameworks
to guarantee data privacy and security of data for individuals,
and ensure its quality and independence. It is governments that
can balance public and private interests and create systems that
foster incentives without creating unacceptable inequalities,
adopt frameworks for safe and responsible use and manage the
international system that can transfer finance and technical
expertise to bring the least informed people and institutions up
to the level of the most informed. And it is governments that
are elected to respond to citizens on their choices and priorities.

We believe that the data revolution can be a revolution for equality

New institutions, new actors, new ideas and new partnerships
are needed, and all have something to offer the data revolution.
National statistical offices, the traditional guardians of public

This Is the Revolution

Indonesian authorities estimated that 50,000 people in Sumatra suffered from respiratory illness as a result of forest fires in March 2014. Several major cities were effectively closed for weeks. The environmental impacts were equally severe, with valuable forest and peat land burned, contributing significantly to Indonesia's greenhouse gas emissions. The immediate availability of free forest fire data on the World Resources Institute (WRI)'s Global Forest Watch site (GFW) enabled companies—Asia Pulp and Paper (APP) and Asia Pacific Resources Limited (APRIL), Indonesia's two largest pulp and paper producers—to evaluate daily where their limited resources are best deployed to respond to fires on lands they are responsible for the governments of Singapore and Indonesia also used GFW-fires' ultra–high resolution imagery, available through a partnership with Digital Globe, to crack down on illegal burning by companies. And GFW-fires, combined with the Indonesian government's Karhutla (Land and Forest Fires) Monitoring system, enabled firefighters to reduce response time from 36 hours to 4 hours.

Source: World Resources Institute (http://www.wri.org/our-work/project /global-forest-watch)

data for the public good, will remain central to the whole of government efforts to harness the data revolution for sustainable development. To fill this role, however, they will need to change, and more quickly than in the past, and continue to adapt, abandoning expensive and cumbersome production processes, incorporating new data sources, including administrative data from other government departments, and focusing on providing data that is human and machine-readable, compatible with geospatial information systems and available quickly enough to ensure that the data cycle matches the decision cycle. In many cases, technical and financial investments will be needed to enable those changes to happen, and strong collaboration between public institutions and the private sector can help official agencies to jump straight to new technologies and ways of doing things.

New Data, Health Services and Malaria

Malaria is one of the biggest killers in several developing countries and imposes a huge strain on health systems. Using new data sources to inform planning and policy can improve services and reduce deaths.

The Mtrac programme in Uganda[4] supported by UNICEF, the WHO and USAID, uses SMS surveys completed by health workers to alert public health officials to outbreaks of malaria, and lets them know how much medicine is on hand at health facilities, so they can anticipate and resolve any shortages. Before Mtrac, the Ministry of Health had very little health facility-level data, either paper or electronic. By March 2014, thanks to this programme, about 1,200 district health officials, 18,700 health facility workers, and 7,400 village health team workers were using the system. Now the Ugandan government is collecting data from thousands of health facilities, capturing and analysing results within 48 hours at a total cost of less than US$150 per poll. The anonymous hotline receives on average more than 350 actionable reports per month, and approximately 70% of these reports are successfully followed up at the district level within 2 weeks. The number of facilities that are out of stock of Artemisinin-based Combination therapies (ACTs) to treat malaria at any given time has fallen from 80% to 15%.

Research in Cote d'Ivoire shows how, in the longer term, new sources of data might also have a role in tracking and predicting epidemics of malaria or other diseases. Combining strongly anonymised data on communication patterns from the Orange mobile telephone network with information on the spread of malaria from the WHO, the University of Minnesota School of Public Health produced epidemiological models that are more detailed than any currently in use. This knowledge could be used to create services to notify doctors, field hospitals and the general public ahead of epidemics, using mobile networks or local radio. Similar work has been done on the spread of AIDS, cholera and meningitis, and could, if the data is made available, be used for rapid response and planning for new epidemics.[5]

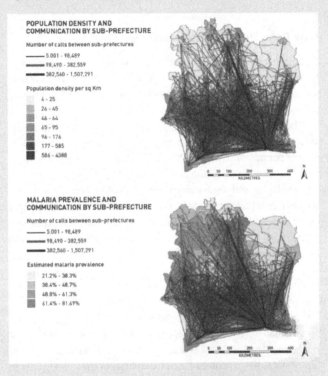

Communication patterns of mobile phone users in Côte d'Ivoire between sub-prefectures are shown, weighted by the number of calls that were made between December 2010 and April 2011, superimposed on (a) the 1998 population density and (b) the prevalence of malaria, as estimated by Raso et al. [25]. For clarity, only edges representing more than 5,000 calls over the 5-month observational period are shown.

2. THE DATA REVOLUTION FOR SUSTAINABLE DEVELOPMENT

In September 2015, the UN member states are expected to commit to an ambitious new set of global goals for a new era of sustainable development. Achieving them will require an unprecedented joint effort on the part of governments at every level, civil society and the private sector, and millions of individual choices and actions. To be realised, the SDGs will require a monitoring and accountability framework and a plan for implementation. A commitment to realise the opportunities of the data revolution should be firmly embedded into the action plan for the SDGs, to support those countries most in need of resources, and to set the world on track for an unprecedented push towards a new world of data for change.

There is much to be done, and this is the moment to do it.

WHY A DATA REVOLUTION FOR SUSTAINABLE DEVELOPMENT?

Although there have been steady and dramatic improvements in recent decades, there is still work to do to create a clearer and more up-to-date picture of the world, to use in planning, monitoring and evaluation of the policies and programmes that will together achieve the SDGs, and in holding to account those in positions of power over resources and other decisions that affect people's lives.

There are two main problems to address:

- **Not enough high-quality data.** In a world increasingly awash with data, it is shocking how little is known about some people and some parts of our environment.

    The world has made huge strides in recent years in tracking specific aspects of human development such as poverty, nutrition, child and maternal health and access to water and sanitation. However, *too many countries still have poor data,*

data arrives too late and too many issues are still barely covered by existing data. For example, in several countries data on employment are notoriously unreliable, data on age and disability are routinely not collected and a great deal of data is difficult to access to citizens or is not available until several years have passed since the time of collection.

The figure above presents a summary snapshot of current data availability in the MDG database (as of October 2014), covering 55 core indicators for 157 developing countries or areas. There, a country is counted as having data for an indicator if it has at least one observation over the reference period, and availability is broken down by whether the data comes from country or international data sources, and whether it is estimated, adjusted or modelled.[6] Overall, the picture is improving though still poor, so there is no five-year period when the availability of data is more than 70% of what

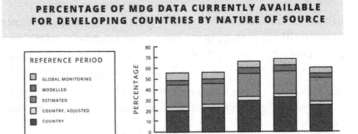

PERCENTAGE OF MDG DATA CURRENTLY AVAILABLE FOR DEVELOPING COUNTRIES BY NATURE OF SOURCE

* Availability is defined as the proportion of country-indicator combinations that have at least one data observation within the reference period. Figures are based on 55 MDG core indicators, as of October 2014.
Source: MDG database, maintained by the United Nations Statistics Division

is required. The drop in data availability after 2010 demonstrates the extent of the time lags that persist between collection and release of data.

There is considerable variation in data availability between indicators, where, for example, data on malaria indicators is very scarce, while for the ratio of girls to boys enrolled in primary, secondary and tertiary education there is relatively good country level data available for most countries and years (though much remains to be done in tracking other indicators essential to monitoring educational outcomes).

If data availability is still low for some individual indicators and/ or countries, the graph below highlights how, when looked at from a country level, there has been a tremendous improvement in the ability of national statistical systems to

---

This Is the Revolution

As part of the development of their National Strategy for the Development Of Statistics (NSDS) completed in partnership with the partnership in statistics for development in the 21st century (PARIS21), Rwanda identified some simple, yet systematic, improvements that could dramatically help make better use of evidence for policy making. One innovation included moving up the publishing date of the Consumer Price Index by five days each month in response to needs from both policy makers and businesses. The release date of the demographic and health survey and living conditions survey was changed so that the information could be used in measuring Rwanda's first poverty reduction strategy and so the information could inform planning for the next one. These changes in data scheduling increased the usefulness of the data and allowed for better evidence-based decisions to be made.

Source: PARIS21 (http://www.cgdev.org/blog/better-data-rwanda)

provide data directly over the past ten years. This has been one of the greatest achievements of MDG monitoring, and is testament to the tremendous efforts of many national and international organisations.

Beyond the MDG indicators, other disturbing gaps exist. *Entire groups of people and key issues remain invisible.* Indigenous populations and slum dwellers for instance, are consistently left out of most data sets. It is still impossible to know with certainty how many disabled children are in school.

Globally, the fact of birth has not been recorded for nearly 230 million children under age five. In 2012 alone, 57 million infants—four out of every ten babies delivered worldwide that year—were not registered with civil authorities.[7] Violence against children is often under-reported, leading to failures to protect vulnerable children.

Data is often insufficiently disaggregated at sub-national level, making it hard for policy makers or communities to

---

This Is the Revolution

Indonesia is one of the most social-media dense countries in the world today. Indonesians tweet about a range of topics, including the cost of living. A project by UN Global Pulse, the Indonesian Ministry of National Development Planning and the World Food Programme found public tweets mentioning food prices closely approximate official figures, leading to the development of a technology that extracts daily food prices from public tweets to generate a near real-time food price index. This data mining approach could be adapted to other food items and locations, not just leveraging Twitter but other crowd-sourced and social data sources.

Source: UN Global Pulse (http://www.unglobalpulse.org/nowcasting-food-prices)

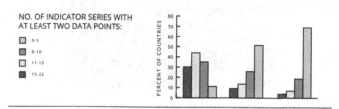

INCREASE OVER TIME IN NUMBER OF MDG INDICATOR SERIES FOR WHICH TREND ANALYSIS WAS POSSIBLE FOR DEVELOPING COUNTRIES

* Figures are based on a subset of 22 MDG indicators.
Source: Updated figures based on United Nations, "Indicators for monitoring the Millennium Development Goals," Report of the Secretary-General, 45th. Session of the United Nations Statistical Commission, 4-7 Mar, 2014. (E/CN.3/2014/29).

compare their progress with that of other communities or the country as a whole. In water supply, for example, the analysis of many household surveys produces a single national estimate of access to clean and safe water in rural areas, but does not show how it varies between districts.

Gender inequality and the undervaluing of women's activities and priorities in every sphere has been replicated in the statistical record. Many of the issues of most concern to women are poorly served by existing data; just over half of all countries report data on intimate partner violence, and where it is reported quality is not consistent, data is rarely collected from women over 49, and data are not comparable.[8] Very little data is available on the distribution of money or the division of labour within households. Much more data are needed on the economic roles of women of all ages as caregivers to children, older persons and the disabled in the household and in the labour force. Of the 42.9 million persons of concern to the

© UNICEF/NYHQ2014-1094/Nesbitt

United Nations High Commissioner for Refugees (UNHCR) globally at the end of 2013, sex composition was known for only 56 percent of the population, and sex-age composition was available for just 35 percent. A lack of demographic and location information frequently hinders needs assessment and monitoring of the global response to emergencies.[9]

The new goals will cover a wider range of environmental issues than the existing MDGs. Data on many environmental issues is particularly sparse. There is almost no useful data on chemical pollutants, despite toxic waste dumping being a serious environmental and health issue in some countries. Likewise, we lack sound and agreed-upon metrics for tracking excessive flows of reactive nitrogen.

It is quite clear that *the monitoring of the SDGs will require substantial additional investment* in order to consolidate gains made during the MDG era and to develop reliable, high-quality data on a range of new subjects, such as climate risk mitigation or inequality, ensuring that no groups are excluded, and with an unprecedented level of detail.

- **Data that are not used or not usable.** To be useful, data must be of high quality, at a level of disaggregation that is appropriate to the issue at hand, and must be made accessible to those who want or need to use them. Too many countries still have data that are of insufficient quality to be useful in making decisions, holding governments to account or fostering innovation. Good data are relevant, accurate, timely, accessible, comparable and produced free of political interferences.

Comparability and standardisation are crucial, as they allow data from different sources or time periods to be combined, and the more data can be combined, the more useful they are. Combining data allows for changes of scale—e.g., aggregating data from different countries to produce regional or global figures. It allows for comparison over time, if data on the same thing collected at different moments can be brought together to reveal trends. But too much data is still produced using different standards—household surveys that ask slightly different questions or geospatial data that uses different geographical definitions. There is, for example, no standard definition of an "urban" area. And too little data are available at a level of disaggregation that is appropriate to policy makers trying to make decisions about local-level allocation or monitoring equitable outcomes across regions. This prevents researchers, policy makers, companies or NGOs from realising the full value of the data produced.

Access, too, is often restricted behind technical and/or legal barriers, or restricted by governments or companies that fear too much transparency, all of which prevent or limit effective use of data. Data buried in pdf documents, for example, are much harder for potential users to work with; administrative data that are not transferred to statistical offices; data generated by the private sector or by academic researchers that are never released or data released too late to be useful; data that cannot be translated into action because of lack of operational tools to leverage them. This is a huge loss in terms of the benefits that could be gained from more open data and from being able to link data across different sectors.

Data needs to be generated with users in mind. Too often data providers underinvest in identifying and engaging those in a position to use data to drive action. Agencies with a mandate to collect public information are not always well-suited to ensuring their information is used by stakeholders, while civil society and the private sector could play a critical role in translating data into a form that is more readily useable.

THE DATA WE WANT FOR SUSTAINABLE DEVELOPMENT

Too much that needs to be known remains unknown. Data could be used better to improve lives and increase the power and control that citizens have over their destinies. Data is a resource, an endless source of fuel for innovation that will power sustainable development, of which we must learn to become effective and responsible stewards. Like any resource, it must be managed for the public good, and to ensure that the benefits flow to all people and not just the few. Data must be available, and must be turned

---

This Is the Revolution

In Mexico, a budget research and advocacy group called Fundar developed an online database of government farm subsidies. One of the problems brought to light was the way in which billions of dollars of the funds were distributed. Though many farm subsidy programs claim to target the neediest farmers, the database revealed that a small group of wealthy farmers had captured the vast majority of subsidy funds over time (the top 10 percent of recipients had received over 50 percent of the funds). The studies contributed to the government decision to review and change the distribution of the subsidies.

Source: Fundar (http://fundar.org.mx)

This Is the Revolution

Household survey data can be of enormous value in identifying patterns of progress among different groups and using this to inform policy. For example, the Indian government's Total Sanitation Campaign, launched in 1999, has a budget of $3.9 billion to improve access to sanitation in the country. However, data from household surveys showed that between 1995 and 2008, the outcomes were far from satisfactory. In this period, the percentage of households from the poorest 20% of Indian society practicing open defecation fell from 99% to 95%, while among the second-richest quintile it fell from 56% to 20%. Analysis of household data by UNICEF and others has helped to inform the government's efforts to improve the targeting of subsidies, in the hope of helping a larger number of the poorest people.

Source: UNICEF (http://www.unicef.org/wash/)

---

into the information that can be confidently used by people to understand and improve their lives and the world around them.

The world we need, if the data we have is to be used to the fullest to achieve sustainable development, is a world of data that is transformed in the following ways:

- **Data for everyone.** The rules, systems and investments that underpin how official data is collected and managed should be focused on the needs of people, while protecting their rights as the producers of that information. These data, and the information produced from them, should reflect what is important to people and the constraints and opportunities that affect their lives. This process should include all people— leaving no one out, and disaggregating in ways that allow the relevant differences and similarities between people and groups to be reflected in analysis and policy.

Rules and standards should be aimed at reducing information inequalities and providing the highest-quality information for all, in the most easily understood format. The priority should always be to use data and information to improve outcomes, experiences and possibilities for people in the short and long term.[10]

When the data is not confidential, it should be available and useable as open data. There must be respect for privacy and personal ownership of personal data, and mechanisms in place so that people themselves have access to the information and are able to make choices accordingly. Crucially, people must have means for redress if they feel that they are being harmed or their rights infringed by the use of their data.

• **Data for now.** If data is to be useful and support good decision-making, it has to be ready at the time when decisions are being made or where the opportunity for influencing the outcomes is there. Trade-offs between timeliness and other quality dimensions depend on the purpose to which data is being put. New technologies and innovations provide the opportunity for the public sector, citizens groups, individuals and companies to have access to data that, with due regard for privacy, security and human rights, is aligned with their own decision-making cycles and information needs— available when and how they want it—and strengthen policy planning, crisis early warning, programme operations, service delivery, impact evaluation, and disaster response.[11]

• **Data for the future.** Data are a key resource not just for decision-making now but for future modelling and problem solving. It is almost impossible to precisely predict future needs, or know how current data could be re-used in the service of complex and interconnected problems as yet unknown or unsolved. Data at different timescales will be most useful for solving future problems if they are part of a flexible and connected system, not tied to one project or research question. Data that can be re-used at different scales, and combined with other data, can better reflect the complex and dynamic interactions between people and the planet. We need to begin investing in data today as a shared resource that will enable the innovations required to meet the challenges of tomorrow.

OUR VISION FOR THE FUTURE

By 2020, we hope to be witnessing the emergence of a vibrant "global data ecosystem" to support the monitoring and implementation of the SDGs and in which:

This Is the Revolution

Integration of different data sources can reduce costs, increase coverage and drive faster data collection. The MY World survey, run jointly by the UNDP, UN Millennium Campaign and the Overseas Development Institute, has gathered over 5 million responses worldwide to a question about people's priorities for themselves and their families. Data has been collected through face to face interviews, via mobile phones and online. Standardisation of the question has meant that all the data has been aggregated into a single database, open to all, and the data can be disaggregated by country, gender, age and level of education. People have used it to identify country priorities, to identify patterns of concern about specific issues, and to illustrate differences and similarities in concerns by age and gender. MY World has shown how international organisations, together with civil society groups, can use data to feed people's perceptions and priorities into the heart of political processes.

Source: UN Millennium Campaign (http://vote.myworld2015.org/)

The Value of Better and More Open Data

Collecting data, processing data and turning them into information, using data and making them open for others to use and re-use all have costs. Deciding how much money to spend on data, as opposed to other priorities, is an economic and a political decision, and spending more money on data will not always be the right choice. Although research in this area is still limited, there is some evidence that more open data and new methods of data collection and use, can save money and create economic, social and environmental value:

- A report produced by accountancy firm Deloitte for the UK's Department for Business, Innovation and Skills estimates the economic value of the data held by the public sector in the UK and released for use and re-use to be around £5 billion per year. This includes £400 million per year as the value of lives saved from reduced death rates among cardiac patients, and time savings worth between £15–58 million from the use of real-time transport data and consequent adjustments in behaviour.[12]

- A report from McKinsey Global Institute puts the global value of better and more open data at $3 trillion per year (with most of this benefit accruing to the USA and Europe).[13]

- The U-report social monitoring platform established by UNI-CEF in Uganda has more than 240,000 young people reporting on issues that affect their communities. Early reporting of an infectious disease in banana production contributed to halting the spread of the disease, which could have cost the country $360 million per year if left unchecked.[14]

- Using mobile phone records to track the link between employee interactions and productivity, a small change in the schedule of coffee breaks at a Bank of America call centre, so that employees took their breaks together to encourage more interactions was found to increase productivity by $15 million a year.[15]

- **Governments** empower public institutions, including statistical offices, protecting their independence, to take on the needed changes to respond to the data revolution and put in place regulatory frameworks that ensure robust data privacy and data protection, and promote the release of data as open data by all data producers, and build capacity for continuous data innovation

- **Governments, international and regional institutions and donors** invest in data, providing resources to countries and regions where statistical or technical capacity is weak; develop infrastructures and implement standards to continuously improve and maintain data quality and usability; keep data open and usable by all. They also finance analytical research in forward-looking and experimental subjects.

- **International and regional organisations** work with other stakeholders to set and enforce common standards for data collection, production, anonymisation, sharing and use to ensure that new data flows are safely and ethically transformed into global public goods, and maintain a system of quality control and audit for all systems and all data producers and users. They also support countries in their capacity-building efforts.

- **Statistical systems** are empowered, resourced and independent, to quickly adapt to the new world of data to collect, process, disseminate and use high-quality, open, disaggregated and geo-coded data, both quantitative and qualitative. They may be less about producing data and more about managing and curating data and information created outside of their organisations.

- **All public, private and civil society data producers** share data and the methods used to process them, according to globally, regionally, or nationally brokered agreements and norms. They publish data, geospatial information and statistics in open formats and with open terms of use, following global common principles and technical standards, to maintain quality and openness and protect privacy.

- **Governments, civil society, academia and the philanthropic sector** work together to raise awareness of publicly available data, to strengthen the data and statistical literacy ("numeracy") of citizens, the media, and other "infomediaries," ensuring that all people have capacity to input into and evaluate the quality of data and use them for their own decisions, as well as to fully participate in initiatives to foster citizenship in the information age.

- **The private sector** reports on its activities using common global standards for integrating data on its economic, environmental and human-rights activities and impacts, building on and strengthening the collaboration already established among institutions that set standards for business reporting. Some companies also cooperate with the public sector, according to agreed and sustainable business models, in the production of statistical data for SDGs monitoring and other public purposes.

- **Civil society organisations and individuals** hold governments and companies accountable using evidence on the impact of their actions, provide feedback to data producers, develop data literacy and help communities and individuals to generate and use data, to ensure accountability and make better decisions for themselves.

- **The media** fairly report on the statistical and scientific evidence available on relevant dimensions of sustainable development and foster an evidence-based public discourse using advanced visualisation technologies to better communicate key data to people.

- **Academics and scientists** carry out analyses based on data coming from multiple sources providing long-term perspectives, knowledge and data resources to guide sustainable development at global, regional, national, and local scales. They make demographic and scientific data as open as possible for public and private use in sustainable development; provide feedback and independent advice and expertise to support accountability and more effective decision-making, and provide leadership in education, outreach, and capacity building efforts.

3. MOBILISING THE DATA REVOLUTION FOR SUSTAINABLE DEVELOPMENT: A CALL TO ACTION

A revolution is an idea—an inspiring vision of a world of fast-flowing data deployed for the public good, and of citizens and governments excited and empowered by the possibilities this creates. But it is also a practical proposition. Getting from here to there involves deliberate actions and choices.

This Is the Revolution

RapidFTR (Rapid Family Tracing and Reunification, http://www.rapidftr.com/) is an open source mobile application used to collect crucial information about children who have been separated from their families in disaster situations. Information is shared securely on a central database for family members looking for a missing child. RapidFTR uses the same type of security as mobile banking to ensure that family-tracing information, especially photos, is accessible only by authorised users, to protect these vulnerable children. In Nyakabande transit centre in Uganda, and Rwamwanja refugee settlement camp in South Sudan, RapidFTR reduced the time required for information to become available from more than six weeks to a matter of hours, speeding up the process of family reunification.

Source: UNICEF (http://www.unicef.org/infobycountry/uganda_70090.html)

Progress toward Universal Civil Registration and Vital Statistics (CRVS)

One of the most fundamental inequalities is between those who are counted and those who are not. Millions of people of all ages in low- and middle-income countries are denied basic services and protection of their rights because they are absent from official records. Lacking records of their birth and civil status, they are excluded from health coverage, schooling, social protection programs, and humanitarian response in emergencies and conflicts.

A well-functioning CRVS system is essential to overcome this injustice. It is also vital for policy making and for monitoring, generating statistics for policy formulation, planning and implementation, and monitoring of population dynamics and health indicators on a continuous basis at the national and local level. These data help to identify inequalities in access to services and differences in outcomes. They also improve the quality of other statistics, such as household surveys, that depend on accurate demographic benchmarks. One proven solution is through issuance of a digital identity, which gives government and business the ability to deliver citizen services electronically, boosting efficiency and driving innovation and serving people, often in isolated areas.

Despite progress in recent years, many countries still lack the capacity, infrastructure, and resources to implement well-functioning CRVS systems.

The good news is that international partners and countries have recently agreed on a CRVS scaling up investment plan.[16] The plan covers activities over a 10-year period from 2015 to 2024, with the goal of universal civil registration of births, deaths, marriages, and other vital events, including cause of death, and access to legal proof of registration for all individuals by 2030. Africa and Asia have already established regional programs to motivate political support, systematic national planning, and provision of technical assistance. And key donors[17] announced recently the establishment of a trust fund to support developing countries' plans to establish CRVS systems with the aim of accelerating progress toward the health-related Sustainable Development Goals.

Decisive action now, taking advantage of the current political opportunities, can set the scene and have a positive impact for years to come. Achieving the SDGs demands embracing the data revolution. We urge the *UN Member States and system organisations to dramatically speed up their work in this field* to support the global aspiration for sustainable development.

Data will be one of the fundamental elements of the accountability framework for the SDGs. Having high-quality data, and using it to create information that can track progress, monitor the use of resources, and evaluate the impacts of policy and programmes on different groups, is a key ingredient in creating more mutually accountable and participatory structures to monitor the new goals. However, we recognise that data is not the whole story. This report is about how data, and information, can be improved and made more accessible. The decisions on how those data and information will be used in any specific accountability framework for the SDGs belongs to the UN Member States and, as such, remains beyond the scope of this report.

Our recommendations for how to mobilise the data revolution for sustainable development suggest a comprehensive programme of action in four areas, illustrated to the right:

- principles and standards,
- technology, innovation and analysis,
- capacity and resources,
- leadership and governance.

At the heart of the recommendations in every area are people and the planet—our revolution is with them and for them.

PRINCIPLES AND STANDARDS

One of the key roles of the UN and other international or regional organisations is setting principles and standards to guide collective actions within a global community and according to common

© CIFOR

norms. We believe that mobilising the data revolution for achieving sustainable development urgently requires such a standard setting, building on existing initiatives in various domains.

We Recommend...
...that the UN develop a comprehensive strategy and a roadmap towards a new *'Global Consensus on Data'*, building upon existing efforts in other domains, setting principles and agreeing standards to build trust and enable cooperation, including:

- *Agree on and promote adoption of specific principles related to the data revolution*, drawing from and building upon those described in the next two pages, to be further developed by the appropriate UN bodies and agreed by their Member States;
- *Accelerate the development and adoption of legal, technical, geospatial and statistical standards*, in a range of areas including, but not limited to:

- ° Openness and exchange of data and metadata, including interoperability of data and information systems; demographic and geospatial information, including "geographic semantic" management and exchange; global exchange of information on illicit financial flows; open data and digital rights management and licensing;

- ° Protection of human rights, including: standards for anonymising data that is personally identifiable, and standards and enforcement mechanisms for data security, integrity, documentation, preservation, and access.

Basic Principles for the Data Revolution for Sustainable Development

The data revolution will need to be harnessed for sustainable and inclusive development through proactive measures and guided by the following key principles:

1. Data Quality and Integrity

Poor quality data can mislead. The entire process of data design, collection, analysis and dissemination needs to be demonstrably of high quality and integrity. Clear standards need to be developed to safeguard quality, drawing on the UN fundamental principles of official statistics and the work of independent third parties. A robust framework for quality assurance is required, particularly for official this includes internal systems as well as periodic audits by professional and independent third parties. Existing tools for improving the quality of statistical data should be used and strengthened, and data should be classified using commonly agreed criteria and quality benchmarks.

2. Data Disaggregation

No one should be invisible. To the extent possible and with due safeguards for individual privacy and data quality, data should be disaggregated across many dimensions, such as geography, wealth, disability, sex and age. Disaggregated data should be collected on other dimensions based on their relevance to the program, policy or other matter under consideration, for example, ethnicity, migrant status, marital status, HIV status, sexual orientation and gender identity, with due protections for privacy and human rights. Disaggregated data can provide a better comparative picture of what works, and help inform and promote evidence based policy making at every level.

3. Data Timeliness

Data delayed is data denied. Standards should be tightened and technology leveraged to reduce the time between the design of data collection and publication of data. The value of data produced can be enhanced by ensuring there is a steady flow of high-quality and timely data from national, international, private big data sources, and digital data generated by people. The data cycle must watch the decision cycle.

4. Data Transparency and Openness

Many publicly-funded datasets, as well as data on public spending and budgets, are not available to other ministries or to the general public. All data on public matters and/ or funded by public funds, including those data produced by private sector, should be made public and "open by default," with narrow exemptions for genuine security or privacy concerns. It needs to be both technically open (i.e., available in a machine-readable standard format so that it can be retrieved and meaningfully processed by a computer application) and legally open (i.e., explicitly licensed in a way that permits commercial and non-commercial use and re-use without restrictions). The underlying data design and sampling, methods, tools and datasets should be explained and published alongside findings to enable greater scrutiny, understanding and independent analysis.

5. Data Usability and Curation

Too often data is presented in ways that cannot be understood by most people. The data architecture should therefore place great emphasis on user-centred design and user friendly interfaces. Communities of "information intermediaries" should be fostered to develop new tools that can translate raw data into information for a broader constituency of non-technical potential users and enable citizens and other data users to provide feedback.

6. Data Protection and Privacy

As more data becomes available in disaggregated forms and data-silos become more integrated, privacy issues are increasingly a concern about what data is collected and how it is used. Further risk arises where collectors of big data do not have sufficient protection from demands from state bodies or interference from hackers. Clear international norms and robust national policy and legal frameworks need to be developed that regulate opt-in and opt-out, data mining, use, re-use for other purpose, transfer and dissemination. They should enable citizens to better understand and control their own data, and protect data producers from demands of governments and attacks by hackers, while still allowing for rich innovation in re-use of data for the public good. Within the agreed privacy constraints, people's rights to freedom of expression using data should be protected. People who correctly provide, collect, curate and analyse data need freedom to operate and protection from recrimination.

7. Data Governance and Independence

Many national statistical offices lack sufficient capacity and funding, and remain vulnerable to political and interest group influence (including by donors). Data quality should be protected and improved by strengthening NSOs, and ensuring they are functionally autonomous, independent of sector ministries and political influence. Their transparency and accountability should be improved, including their direct communication with the public they serve. This can include independent monitoring of the same public services, for example, or monitoring of related indicators such as public satisfaction with services.

8. Data Resources and Capacity

There is a global responsibility to ensure that all countries have an effective national statistical system, capable of producing high-quality statistics in line with global standards and expectations. This requires investments in human capital, new technology, infrastructure, geospatial data and management systems in both governmental and independent systems, as well as information intermediaries. At the same time, national capacity for data science must be developed to leverage opportunities in big data, to complement high-quality official statistics. Increased domestic resources and international support for developing countries are needed to have the data revolution contribute to sustainable development. Applications of big data for the public good must be developed and scaled up transparently, demonstrating full compliance with applicable laws.

All public data should be 'open by default'

9. Data Rights

Human rights cut across many issues related to the data revolution. These rights include but are not limited to the right to be counted, the right to an identity, the right to privacy and to ownership of personal data, the right to due process (for example when data is used as evidence in proceedings, or in administrative decisions), freedom of expression, the right to participation, the right to non-discrimination and equality, and principles of consent. Any legal or regulatory mechanisms, or networks or partnerships, set up to mobilise the data revolution for sustainable development should have the protection of human rights as a core part of their activities, specify who is responsible for upholding those rights, and should support the protection, respect and fulfilment of human rights.

Strengthening national capacities will be the essential test of any data revolution

TECHNOLOGY, INNOVATION AND ANALYSIS

Technology has been and will continue to be a fundamental driver of the data revolution. To harness the benefits of new technology, large and continuing investments in innovation are required at all levels, but especially in those institutions which are currently lagging behind. In addition, but beyond the scope of this report, an urgent effort needs to be made to increase access to information technologies by, among other things, increasing access to broadband, increasing literacy, including adult literacy, and increasing the use of ICT in schools worldwide, to ensure that all people, including the poorest, have access to the technologies that can improve their lives.

We Recommend...
...that the UN foster the establishment of a *"Network of Data Innovation Networks"* for sustainable development bringing together a range of partners and existing networks to generate knowledge and solve common problems. Some specific areas of activity could be:

- *Urgently leverage emerging data sources for SDG monitoring, through an 'SDG data lab'*: The lab should mobilise key public, private and civil society data providers, academics and stakeholders to identify available and missing data and indicators, as well as opportunities for benefitting from new methods, analytical tools and technologies to improve the coverage, timeliness and availability of indicators in each of the SDG areas. Drawing on the existing MDG monitoring architecture, and working with other networks such as the Sustainable Development Solutions Network, it would develop new methodologies for monitoring new goals from January 2016

- *Develop systems for global data sharing*: Identify areas where the development of common infrastructures to exploit the data revolution for sustainable development could solve capacity problems, produce efficiencies and encourage collaborations. One such suggestion would be a "world statistics cloud," to store metadata produced by different institutions but according to common standards, rules and specifications.

- *Fill research gaps*: Identify critical research gaps, such as the relationships between data, incentives and behaviour. Engage research centres, innovators and governments in the development of publicly available data analytics tools and algorithms to better capture and evaluate long-term trends affecting sustainable development.

- *Create incentives*: Engage social entrepreneurs, private sector, academia, media, civil society and other individuals and institutions in this global effort through initiatives such as prizes and data challenges.

CAPACITY AND RESOURCE

Strengthening national capacities in all areas from data production to use will be the essential test of any data revolution, in particular in developing countries where the basic infrastructure is often lacking. Monitoring a new and expanded set of Sustainable Development Goals will not be possible in many countries without new and sustained investment, so urgent mobilisation of new funds is needed.

We Recommend...

... that a proposal be developed for a *new funding stream* and innovative financing mechanisms to support the data revolution for sustainable development, for discussion at the "Third International Conference on Financing for Development," which will take place in Addis Ababa in July 2015. The proposal should be built on the following five pillars:

- *Investment needs*: An analysis of the scale of investments needed for the establishment of a modern system to monitor progress towards SDGs, especially in developing countries. This analysis, building on various attempts currently ongoing, should highlight the costs as well as opportunities for efficiency gains associated with different production systems. Particular attention should be paid to the need for investment in data to analyse the challenges facing the very poorest people and communities, and to involve them as users of data.

- *Managing funds*: A proposal on how to manage and monitor new funding for the data revolution for sustainable development, taking stock of existing sources and forms of funding. This should look at how funding from a range of sources could be used most effectively, and managed and disbursed in line with national priorities to incentivise innovation, collaboration and whole systems approaches, while also encouraging creativity and experimentation and accepting that not all initiatives will succeed.

- *Private sector participation*: A proposal on how to leverage the resources and creativity of the private sector, including an examination of suggestions for creating incentives for the private sector to invest given companies' expectations of time horizon and returns.

- *Capacity development*: A proposal to improve existing arrangements for fostering the necessary capacity development and technology transfer. This should include upgrading the "National Strategies for the Development of Statistics" (NSDS) to do better at coordinated and long-term planning, and in identifying sound investments and engaging non-official data producers in a cooperative effort to speed up the production, dissemination and use of data, strengthening civil society's capacity and resources to produce, use and disseminate data.

- *Global data literacy*: A proposal for a special investment to increase global data literacy. To close the gap between people able to benefit from data and those who cannot, in 2015 the UN should work with other organisations to develop an education program and promote new learning approaches to improve people's, infomediaries' and public servants' data literacy. Special efforts should be made to reach people living in poverty through dedicated programmes.

GOVERNANCE AND LEADERSHIP

Strong leadership by the UN is vital to make the data revolution serve sustainable development. Such leadership should be made very concrete through various actions and activities, and the continuous engagement of all relevant partners, maintaining a very open and transparent approach with governments, the private sector, NGOs, the media, and academic researchers. The primary aim would be to add value to existing institutional set-ups, accelerating the delivery of their outputs and building new partnerships. Short- and medium-term results should be clearly spelled out, and periodic reviews should be undertaken to ensure that global cooperation in this area is on the right track.

We Recommend …

…the establishment of a *"Global Partnership for Sustainable Development Data"* (GPSDD) to mobilise and coordinate as many initiatives and institutions as possible to achieve the vision sketched above. The GPSDD could promote several initiatives, such as:

- *World Forum*: The establishment of a biennial "World Forum on Sustainable Development Data," and associated regional and country level events and ongoing engagements. These would maintain momentum on data improvements, foster regular engagement between private, public and community level data collectors and users, showcase ongoing activities and initiatives, create a network of 'data champions' around the world, and provide practical spaces for innovation, knowledge sharing, advocacy and technology transfer. The first Forum should be organised by the end of 2015, once the SDGs are agreed.

- *Users forum*: Establish a "Global Forum of SDG-Data Users," to ensure feedback loops between data producers, processors and users to improve the usefulness of data and information produced. It would also help the international community to set priorities and assess results achieved, and could encourage replication and experimentation with user forums at country and agency level, increasing demand for and use of data.

Particular attention should be paid to how to involve poor and marginalised people and communities in the forum.

- *Partnerships and coordination*: Work in partnership with international and regional organisations, and with other initiatives looking at best practices related to public data such as the Open Government Partnership (OGP) and the G8 Open Data Charter. The aim would be to enhance coordination of work in various areas, share knowledge on SDG monitoring, and encourage good practice such as open data and harmonization. Also, to work together on developing common legal frameworks around rights to data and information and redress from abuses of data, to work together to implement new standards once agreed, and to streamline capacity building initiatives and reduce duplicated effort, mobilising new resources.

- *Data sharing*: Broker some key global public-private partnerships with private companies and civil society organisations for data sharing. Drawing on existing efforts already underway, these would provide models for best practice, useful for national and regional bodies trying to negotiate similar arrangements, would identify incentives and constraints specific to various industries, would allow for economies of scale, and would demonstrate the value and the possibility of sharing data and collaborating between public and private sectors.

We Recommend...

...some "quick wins" on SDG data to demonstrate the feasibility of different approaches, experiment and innovate with partnerships and methods as a first step to setting up longer term initiatives. In addition to the proposed "SDG Data Lab," these could include:

- *SDGs analysis and visualisation platform*: To be launched in September 2015, using the most advanced tools and features for exploring and analysing and re-using data, and demonstrating best practices in the engagement with data users through the provision of guidance and educational resources for data re-use, building on and coordinating with other platforms in other sectors. The development of the website would also represent a laboratory for fostering private-public partnerships and community-led peer-production efforts for data collection, dissemination and visualisation. It would be continuously updated during the lifetime of the SDGs, remaining a showcase for new ideas and innovations and a source of high quality and up to date information on progress.

• *A dashboard on "the state of the world":* This would harness the richness of traditional and new data, maintain the excitement and openness of the whole SDG process, engage think-tanks, academics and NGOs as well as the whole UN family in analysing, producing, verifying and auditing data, provide a place for experimentation with methods for integrating different data sources, including qualitative data, perceptions data and citizen-generated data, and eventually produce a 'people's baseline' for new goals.

Taken together, we believe that these recommendations could move the world onto a path of information equality, where all citizens, organisations and governments have the right information, at the right time, to build accountability, make good decisions, and ultimately improve people's lives. **This is the world we want…A World that Counts**

ENDNOTES

This report is the work of the UN Secretary-General's Independent Expert Advisory Group on the Data Revolution for Sustainable Development:

Enrico Giovannini (Co-Chair, Italy) Robin Li (Co-Chair, China), TCA Anant (India), Shaida Badiee (Iran), Carmen Barroso (Brazil), Robert Chen (United States), Choi Soon-hong (Republic of Korea), Nicolas de

Cordes (Belgium), Fu Haishan (China), Johannes Jütting (Germany), Pali Lehohla (South Africa), Tim O'Reilly (United States), Sandy Pentland (United States), Rakesh Rajani (Tanzania), Juliana Rotich (Kenya), Wayne Smith (Canada), Eduardo Sojo GarzaAldape (Mexico), Gabriella Vukovich (Hungary), Alicia Barcena (ECLAC), Robert Kirkpatrick (Global Pulse), Eva Jespersen (UNDP), Edilberto Loaiza (UNFPA), Katell Le Goulven (UNICEF), Thomas Gass (ex officio) and Amina J. Mohammed (ex officio).

NOTES

1. See, e.g., http://www-01.ibm.com/software/data/bigdata/what-is-big-data.html

2. ECLAC (2014). "Latin American Economic Outlook 2013: SME Policies for Structural Change," p. 124 (http://www.cepal.org/publicaciones/xml/5/48385/leo2013_ing.pdf)

3. McKinsey Global Institute (November 2013). "Lions go digital: The Internet's transformative potential in Africa." (http://www.mckinsey.com/insights/high_tech_telecoms_internet/lions_go_digital_the_internets_transformative_potential_in_africa)

4. See Ugandan Ministry of Health (www.mtrac.ug)

5. Enns, E.A and Amuasi, J.H. (2013). "Human mobility and communication patterns in Côte d'Ivoire: A network perspective for malaria control," published in *Mobile Phone Data for Development: Analysis of mobile phone datasets for the development of Ivory Coast. Selected Contributions to the D4D challenge sponsored by Orange.* (http://perso.uclouvain.be/vincent.blondel/netmob/2013/D4D-book.pdf)

6. The coding of the nature of the data in the MDG database (http://mdgs.un.org/unsd/mdg/Data.aspx) is as follows:
   - *Country data*: Produced and disseminated by the country (including data adjusted by the country to meet international standards).
   - *Country data adjusted*: Produced and provided by the country, but adjusted by the international agency for international comparability to comply with internationally agreed standards, definitions and classifications.

- *Estimated*: Estimated are based on national data, such as surveys or administrative records, or other sources but on the same variable being estimated, produced by the international agency when country data for some year(s) is not available, when multiple sources exist, or when there are data quality issues.
- *Modelled*: Modelled by the agency on the basis of other covariates when there is a complete lack of data on the variable being estimated.
- *Global monitoring data*: Produced on a regular basis by the designated agency for global monitoring, based on country data. There is no corresponding figure at the country level.

7. UNICEF (2013). Every Child's Birth Right: Inequities and trends in birth registration. (http://www.unicef.org/mena/MENA-Birth_Registration _report_low_res-01.pdf)

8. A UN Women's compilation of country surveys on violence against Woman is available from http://www.endvawnow.org/uploads/browser /files/vawprevalence_matrix_june2013.pdf

9. UNHCR (June 2014). "UNHCR Global Trends 2013: War's Human Cost." (http://unhcr.org/trends2013/)

10. This is also the aim of the initiatives launched around the world to go 'Beyond GDP'. For a review of these initiatives see www.wikiprogress.org

11. UN Global Pulse (June 2013). *Big Data for Development:* A Primer, p.4 (http://www.unglobalpulse.org/bigdataprimer)

12. UK Department for Business, Innovation & Skills and Cabinet Office (May 2013). "Market assessment of public sector information." (https:// www.gov.uk/government/publications/public-sector-information -market-assessment)

13. Chui, M. Farrell, D. and Jackson, K. (April 2014). "How government can promote open data." McKinsey&Company. (http://www.mckinsey .com/insights/public_sector/how_government_can_promote_open _data)

14. Kumar, R. (2014) "How Youth Saved Bananas in Uganda" (http:// blogs.worldbank.org/youthink/how-youth-saved-bananas-uganda)

15. Pentland, A. (October 2013). "The Data Driven Society," *Scientific American*, pp. 78–83

16. World Bank and WHO (May 2014). Global Civil Registration and Vital Statistics Scaling Up Investment Plan 2015–2024. Working Paper 88351. (http://www.worldbank.org/en/topic/health/publication/global -civil-registration-vital-statistics-scaling-up-investment)

17. The World Bank Group and the governments of Canada, Norway, and the United States

CONTRIBUTOR BIOGRAPHIES

Thomas Hardjono is the CTO of MIT Connection Science and Engineering. He leads technical projects and initiatives around identity, security and data privacy, and engages industry partners and sponsors on these fronts. Thomas is also the technical director for the Internet Trust Consortium under MIT Connection Science that implements open source software based on cutting edge research at MIT. Previous to this Thomas was the Director of the MIT Kerberos Consortium, developing the famous MIT Kerberos authentication software currently used by millions of users around the world. He has been active in the areas of security, applied cryptography and identity management for nearly two decades now, starting from the mid-1990s working in the emerging PKI industry as Principal Scientist at VeriSign, which became the largest PKI provider in the world. His work included devices certificates for DOCSIS cable modems, WiFi devices and the Trusted Platform Module (TPM) security hardware. He has chaired a number of key technical groups, including in the IETF, OASIS, Trusted Computing Group, Kantara and other organizations. At MIT Thomas has also been instrumental in the development of advanced identity management systems, including the first open-source implementation of Open Identity Connect protocol (now used by major social media platforms). Over the years he has published three books and over seventy technical papers in journals and at conferences. Thomas has a BSc degree in Computer Science with Honors from the University of Sydney, and PhD degree in Computer Science from the University of New South Wales in Australia.

David L. Shrier is a globally recognized authority on financial innovation. In his thought leadership efforts through his dual appointment at MIT Media Lab and Saïd Business School, University of Oxford, he advocates on ethics of data science and the uses of artificial intelligence for humanitarian good. His online fintech programs have engaged more than 10,000 students in over 120 countries, and he has published multiple books on fintech, blockchain and cybersecurity. David is a member of the FinTech Industry Committee for FINRA, the U.S. securities industry's self-regulatory body; is on the Fintech Trade & Investment Steering Board for the UK government's Department of International Trade; and has served in a policy advisory capacity for the 53 countries in the Commonwealth of Nations. He also informally engages with the European Parliament, European Commission, OECD, Bank of England, FCA, SEC, US Treasury, and FDIC on innovation, cybersecurity, digital identity, blockchain, and AI. In his private sector work, David helps corporations and governments to drive innovation ecosystems. He has developed $8.5 billion of growth opportunities with C-suite executives for Dun & Bradstreet, Wolters Kluwer, Ernst & Young, the Massachusetts Institute of Technology, GE/NBC, the Walt Disney Company, AOL Verizon, and Starwood, as well as private equity and VC funds. He has led a number of private equity and venture capital-backed companies as CEO, CFO or COO, in either interim or full-time capacities. Find more at VisionaryFuture.com.

Professor Alex "Sandy" Pentland holds a triple appointment at the Massachusetts Institute of Technology in the Media Lab (SA+P), School of Engineering and School of Management. He also directs MIT's Connect Science initiative, the Human

Dynamics Laboratory and the MIT Media Lab Entrepreneurship Program, and has been a member of the Advisory Boards for Google, Nissan, Telefonica, Tencent, and a variety of start-up firms. For several years he co-led the World Economic Forum Big Data and Personal Data initiatives. He has pioneered the fields of wearable computing and computational social science, generating several successful startups and technology spinoffs. Sandy was recently named by the Secretary-General of the United Nations to the Independent Expert Advisory Group on the Data Revolution for Sustainable Development. His article, "The New Science of Building Great Teams," won paper of the year in 2012 from Harvard Business Review. Sandy has previously helped create and direct MIT's Media Laboratory, the Media Lab Asia laboratories at the Indian Institutes of Technology, and Strong Hospital's Center for Future Health. He recently led a task force on big data & healthcare for the World Innovation Summit in Healthcare, held in Doha, Qatar. In 2012 Forbes named Sandy one of the "seven most powerful data scientists in the world," along with the founders of Google and the CTO of the United States, and in 2013 he won the McKinsey Award from Harvard Business Review. Prof. Pentland's books include Honest Signals, Social Physics, and Frontiers of Financial Technology. He was named to the National Academy of Engineering in 2014. Sandy holds a BGS from the University of Michigan and a Ph.D. from MIT.

Michiel Bakker is an MIT Computer Science PhD student and a research assistant in the Human Dynamics group at the MIT Media Lab, where he is supervised by Alex 'Sandy' Pentland. His research lies at the intersection of machine learning and computational social science, while focusing on a broad range of topics ranging from algorithmic fairness and privacy to human-computer interaction and deep learning. He is a native of Amsterdam and holds a bachelor's and master's degree in physics from TU Delft, where he worked and published on quantum computing at QuTech and IBM Q. Prior to continuing his education at MIT, he co-founded an e-commerce startup in London. At MIT, Michiel is supported by a Jacobs Presidential Fellowship.

Bernardo Garcia-Bulle received his MSc in Computer Science from ITAM (Mexico) and is doing his PhD at the Institute for Data, Systems, and Society at MIT. In the Human Dynamics group at the MIT Media Lab, he researched and participated in the application of AI to decision-making algorithms on social programs. At MIT, he seeks to apply statistics and computer science to the benefit of society.

Daniel "Dazza" Greenwood is an entrepreneur, innovator and national thought on design and deployment of scalable, distributed Trust Network and other digital systems. Dazza heads the digital business systems design and architecture firm CIVICS .com, which he founded in 1996. At MIT Media Lab and MIT Connection Science, Dazza lecturers and conducts R&D on big data, digital identity federation, personal data sharing and is developing the field of computational law and jurimetrics through law.MIT.edu events and projects. Privately, Dazza provides professional consultancy services to industry, government and civic organizations, including fortune 50 companies, national governments, and marketplaces through CIVICS.com. Dazza has catalyzed or led numerous industry, governmental and public-private initiatives aimed at developing innovative legal solutions, technical standards and business models.

Jake Kendall is the Director of the Digital Financial Services Innovation Lab (DFS Lab) housed at Caribou Digital. Formerly Jake was Deputy Director of Research and Emerging Technologies within the Financial Services for the Poor Team at the Gates Foundation where his team helped create the global data architecture for tracking financial inclusion and invested to create high potential emerging technologies. Jake is a published researcher and author and holds a PhD in Economics from UC

Santa Cruz and a BS in Physics from MIT. Prior to joining the Gates foundation, he spent time as an Economist with the Consultative Group to Assist the Poor (CGAP) within the World Bank and in two fintech start-ups in the field of public key cryptography. Jake also spent two years in Zambia as a fisheries extension agent with the US Peace Corps and worked, throughout his youth, a salmon fisherman in Alaska.

Cameron Kerry is a Visiting Scholar at the MIT Media Lab, a Distinguished Visiting Fellow at the Brookings Institution, and Senior Counsel at Sidley Austin, LLP in Boston and Washington, DC. His practice at Sidley Austin involves privacy, security, and international trade issues. Kerry served as General Counsel and Acting Secretary of the United States Department of Commerce, where he was a leader on a wide of range of issues laying a new foundation for U.S. economic growth in a global marketplace. He continues to speak and write on these issues, particularly privacy and data security, intellectual property, and international trade. While Acting Secretary, Cameron Kerry served as chief executive of this Cabinet agency and its 43,000 employees around the world, as well as an adviser to the President. His tenure marked the first time in U.S. history two siblings have served in the President's Cabinet at the same time.

Bruno Lepri leads the Mobile and Social Computing Lab (MobS) and is vice-responsible of the Complex Data Analytics research line at Bruno Kessler Foundation (Trento, Italy). Bruno is also research affiliate at the MIT Media Lab working with the Human Dynamics group and the MIT Connection Science initiative and he recently launched an alliance between MIT and FBK on Human Dynamics Observatories. He is also a senior research affiliate of Data-Pop Alliance, the first think-tank on Big Data and Development co-created by the Harvard Humanitarian Initiative, MIT Media Lab, Overseas Development Institute, and Flowminder to promote a people-centered big data revolution.

In 2010 he won a Marie Curie Cofund post-doc fellow and he has held post-doc positions at FBK and at MIT Media Lab. He holds a Ph.D. in Computer Science from the University of Trento. He also serves as consultant of several companies and international organizations. His research interests include computational social science, big data and personal data, pervasive and ubiquitous computing, and human behavior understanding. His research has received attention from several press outlets and obtained the best paper award at ACM Ubicomp 2014.

Alexander Lipton is Co-Founder and Chief Technical Officer of Sila, Co-Founder of Distilled Analytics, Partner at Numeraire Financial, Connection Science Fellow at MIT, and Visiting Professor of Financial Engineering at EPFL. He is a Board Member of Zilliqa, and sits on Advisory Boards of numerous FinTech Companies worldwide. In 2016 he left Bank of America Merrill Lynch, where he served for ten years in various senior managerial roles including Quantitative Solutions Executive and Co-Head of the Global Quantitative Group. Earlier, he held senior managerial positions at Citadel Investment Group, Credit Suisse, Deutsche Bank, and Bankers Trust. In parallel, Alex held academic appointments at NYU, Oxford, Imperial College, and the University of Illinois. Previously, Alex was a Full Professor at the University of Illinois and a Consultant at Los Alamos. In 2000 Alex was awarded the first ever Quant of the Year Award. He published eight books, including, most recently, "Financial Engineering—Selected Works of Alexander Lipton," and more than a hundred scientific papers.

Yves-Alexandre de Montjoye is a lecturer at Imperial College London and a research scientist at the MIT Media Lab. He recently received his Ph.D. in computational privacy from MIT. His research aims at understanding how the unicity of human behavior impacts the privacy of individuals—through re-identification or inference—in large-scale metadata datasets such as mobile phone, credit cards, or browsing data. Yves-Alexandre was recently named an Innovator under 35 for Belgium (TR35). His research has been published in Science and Nature SRep. and covered by the BBC, CNN, New York Times, Wall Street Journal, Harvard Business Review, Le Monde, Die Spiegel, Die Zeit, El Pais as well as in his TEDx talks. His work on the shortcomings of anonymization has appeared in reports of the World Economic Forum, United Nations, OECD, FTC, and the European Commission. Before coming to MIT, he was a researcher at the Santa Fe Institute in New Mexico. Yves-Alexandre worked for the Boston Consulting Group and acted as an expert for both the Bill and Melinda Gates Foundation and the United Nations. He is a member of the OECD Advisory Group on Health Data Governance. Over a period of 6 years, he obtained an M.Sc. from Louvain in Applied Mathematics, a M.Sc. (Centralien) from Ecole Centrale Paris, a M.Sc. from KU Leuven in Mathematical Engineering as well as his B.Sc. in engineering at Louvain.

Takeo Nishikata is a visiting scientist of MIT Media Lab, a researcher of Nomura Research Institute, and a member of the Council on Extended Intelligence which was established by IEEE and MIT Media Lab. His primary research interest lies in envisioning and building a novel financial infrastructure that better sustains our lives while ensuring individual privacy and security. He also involves standardization efforts. Most recently, he has led the use case group of ISO/TC 307 Blockchain and distributed ledger technologies as a convener.

Alejandro Noriega-Campero is a PhD candidate at the MIT Media Lab, whose research focuses on the use of human and artificial intelligence in social decision systems. He is also a master of science in Technology and Policy from the MIT Institute for Data, Systems, and Society (IDSS). His research lies at the intersection of decision sciences, artificial intelligence, causal inference, policy, ethics, and economics. The vision driving Alejandro's career is to bridge academic breakthroughs in AI with their sensible application for the public good. In the past few years he has conducted applied research projects with the United Nations' Big Data initiative (Global Pulse), the national governments of Mexico, Colombia, Costa Rica, Andorra, and Saudi Arabia, as well as several partners in industry. He currently leads a research collaboration between MIT and the Inter-American Development Bank (IDB) focused on developing "AI Systems for the Fair and Efficient Targeting of Social Programs"—such as Conditional Cash Transfers—across the globe. Alejandro is native of Mexico City, an alumnus of ITAM, and a Fulbright Fellow since 2013.

Nuria Oliver is a computer scientist with a PhD from MIT on perceptual intelligence. She has over 20 years of research experience, first at MIT, then at Microsoft Research (Redmond, WA) and finally as the first female Scientific Director at Telefonica R&D (Barcelona, Spain). Her work on computational human behavior modeling, human-computer interaction, Mobile computing and Big Data analysis, particularly applied for Social Good, is internationally known with over 100 scientific articles in international conferences and journals, cited over 10000 times and with several best paper awards and nominations. She is co-inventor of 40 filed patents and a frequent keynote speaker in international conferences. She is the first Spanish female computer scientist named a Distinguished Scientist by the ACM and a Fellow of the European Association of Artificial Intelligence. Her work has received many international awards, such as the MIT TR100 (today TR35) Young Innovator Award (2004), and the Gaudí Gresol award to Excellence in Science and Technology (2016). She has been selected as one of the "top 9 female technology directors" in Spain by EL PAIS (2012), one of the "100 leaders for the future" by Capital (2009), a Rising Talent by the Women's Forum for the Economy and Society (2009) and one of "40 youngsters with great potential in Spain" by EL PAIS (1999), among others. Her passion is to improve the quality of life of people, both individually and collectively, through technology. She also has great interest for scientific outreach and to inspire new generations–and particularly girls—to pursue careers in technology. Therefore, she is a frequent collaborator with the media and she gives talks both to the general public and especially to thousands of teenagers.

Jacopo Staiano is Research & Data Scientist at Fortia Financial Solutions Lab, and a research affiliate at the Harvard-ODI-MIT Data-Pop Alliance. Previously, he held post-doctoral positions at LIP6, UPMC—Sorbonne Universités and at the Mobile and Social Computing Lab, Fondazione Bruno Kessler (TN, Italy). He received his B.Eng. degree in Computer Engineering from the University of Pisa, before obtaining a MA in Sonic Arts from the Queen's University of Belfast, and a M.Sc. in Human Language Technology and Interfaces from the University of Trento. He holds a Ph.D. in Information and Communication Technology from the University of Trento. He has been visiting researcher at the Ambient Intelligence Research Lab, Stanford University, the Human Dynamics Lab, MIT Media Lab, and Telefonica I+D. His research interests include Computational Social Science, Affective and Pervasive Computing, Machine Learning and Natural Language Processing. His research has received attention from several press outlets, and obtained the Honorable Mention at ACM DIS 2012 and the Best Paper Award at ACM UbiComp 2014.

Arkadiusz Stopczynski received his PhD from Technical University of Denmark. He studied human interactions, social dynamics, and high-resolution networks in MIT Media Lab's Human Dynamics group. As part of his research, he worked on the Copenhagen Networks Study, a large-scale high-resolution social data collection and analysis, and developed the Smartphone Brain Scanner, a low-cost portable EEG system. Dr. Stopczynski currently works at Google, building systems aimed at augmenting complex team work.

Brian Sweatt is a transformational technologist who brings theory to life through advanced engineering systems. He has held engineering leadership roles in various tech startups including, most recently, Py (acquired by Hired, Inc). In the Human Dynamics group at the MIT Media Lab, his research centered on personal data stores and privacy-preserving computation. Brian holds an MS and BS, both in Computer Science, from the Massachusetts Institute of Technology.

Irving Wladawsky-Berger is a Research Affiliate at MIT's Sloan School of Management, and a Fellow of the MIT Initiative on the Digital Economy and of MIT Connection Science. In addition, he writes a weekly column for the *Wall Street Journal*'s *CIO Journal*. He retired from IBM in May of 2007 after a 37-year career with the company, where his primary focus was on innovation and technical strategy. He's been a Strategic Adviser on Digital Strategy and Innovation at Citigroup, HBO, and MasterCard. Dr. Wladawsky-Berger received an MS and a PhD in physics from the University of Chicago.

Guy Zyskind is the Founder and CEO of Enigma, a company that enables computing over encrypted data through a mix of secure Multi-party Computation (MPC) and Blockchain technologies. Enigma is the culmination of Guy's graduate thesis at MIT, where he also taught the first blockchain engineering class. Guy has authored several academic papers, most recently on privacy and the blockchain, including the Enigma whitepaper (downloaded over 100K times) and "Decentralizing Privacy: Using Blockchain to Protect Personal Data" that appeared in IEEE SPW 15'. Previously, Guy led the development of several start-up companies. Most notably, he was the Chief Technology Officer at Athena Wisdom (now Endor), an MIT Media Lab spin-off company involving Big Data Analytics and Network Science. Guy holds an M.S. from MIT and a B.S. in Electrical Engineering and Computer Science from Tel-Aviv University.

INDEX

Page numbers in italic refer to figures.